the time of Thomas Hob present day, and gives attention to the contemporary debate which Sir David Ross and the late Professor H. A. Prichard initiated and in which they have played a prominent part. He holds that this modern work in ethics has issued in a remarkable clarification of the ethical problem. This problem is to set in their proper relation one to another the three different moral notions of ' goodness,' ' virtue ' and ' duty.' Dr. Robinson maintains, however, that the solution of this problem requires as a preliminary a careful consideration of the nature of the situation in which moral distinctions arise and of action to which these distinctions are applied. In chapters on ' Act and Motive ' and ' The Moral Situation ' he carries to its conclusion this preparatory investigation; and in the remainder of the book he outlines an idealist solution which yet takes into account the insights of intuitionism.

This is a book of the first importance in its own particular field. It will immensely enhance the reputation of the author, whose *Faith and Duty* has already won recognition and praise, and has recently been named by the American Library Selection Committee as one of the fifty outstanding religious books of the year in which it was published. Here are extracts from the press reviews of that book:—

" Learned and stimulating . . . An important book which will be gratefully and widely studied "—*Theology*

THE CLAIM OF MORALITY

THE CLAIM OF MORALITY

by

N. H. G. ROBINSON, B.D., D.Litt.

With an Introduction

by

JOHN MACMURRAY

Professor of Moral Philosophy in the University
of Edinburgh

LONDON

VICTOR GOLLANCZ LTD

1952

PRINTED IN GREAT BRITAIN BY PURNELL AND SONS, LTD. (T.U.)
PAULTON (SOMERSET) AND LONDON

To
MY FATHER AND MOTHER
In grateful affection
I dedicate this book

CONTENTS

INTRODUCTION

It is a pleasure to commend to the general public a book
of the character and the quality of Dr. Robinson's *The Claim of
Morality*. It is not an easy book. If it were, it would deserve
neither commendation nor perusal. It is not difficult to write
lightly and excitingly about morality; but then the result must
be both cheap and dangerous. This book is neither. It measures
up to the importance of its subject. The competence of its
analysis and the thoroughness of its scholarship have already
been recognised by the academic authorities. But it is no mere
academic exercise. It well deserves the attention of all intelligent and serious-minded people. For it provides an unusually
clear statement of the outcome of more than two centuries of
British ethical thought; it reveals a steady progress in understanding and agreement running through the seemingly irre-
concilable divergencies of rival schools; and the difficulties it
may present to the reader belong to the subject it treats of, and
arise neither from any technicalities of philosophical usage, nor
from the style of the writing. What the book has to say can be
understood by any intelligent reader who is prepared to bring to
a serious discussion the seriousness of attention which it requires
and deserves. That there is still a large public in this country
ready to consider serious subjects seriously there is no reason
to doubt. If it were not so, our situation would indeed be serious.
The difficulty we face is rather one of choice. So many books
are written on more or less serious topics that no one can read
them all; nor is it easy to decide which among them has a prior
claim on our time and energy. I believe that this book should
be assigned a high priority.

The two peoples who have contributed most to the development of moral theory are the Chinese and the British. They are
also the peoples who have achieved, in different ways and
different circumstances, an outstanding record of social
stability. This is not to overlook the Greeks or the Hebrews,
because in both cases their interest in morality and the contribution they have made has been subordinate to a more
absorbing preoccupation; in the one case to general philosophy,

9

and in the other to religion. This connection of moral interest with social stability is no accident. Morality can provide, and where it is taken seriously it does provide, a solid basis of social cohesion which is independent both of the State and of the self-interest of the economic system. In our own history, it has provided the foundation for the life of freedom and for our own type of democracy. Freedom and democracy, as we understand them, are inseparable from an effective and lively sense of moral principle operative in all spheres of human relationship. What has made the British way of life possible; what has kept it in being through the stress of centuries, is a quick sensitiveness to moral issues pervading all classes of the people, and the will to act upon it. For morality is the only judge of law, and the only effective check upon the power of governments. So long as a people habitually regulate their relations with one another by a common moral code, they can set practical limits to political authority, and keep any government in its place. But where large numbers cease to live by moral principles or lose the capacity to recognise moral issues when they arise—and the second condition follows hard upon the first—a nation has no choice but to do as it is told by those who have the power to enforce obedience.

There are many who recognise that the present crisis of our civilisation is a moral crisis. But what help is to be had, they will ask, from poring over the writings of professional moralists, who busy themselves so much with generalities far removed from the actual problems of living experience, and spend their energy so frequently upon debates about subtleties of verbal usage? They provide no practical guidance for the plain man. They even make it clear that no such guidance is to be expected from them. Their business, they tell us, is to understand morality, not to inculcate, nor even to defend it. How different the scientists are! In science truth is guaranteed by results. There we really get somewhere; and every new discovery lays a solid basis for further achievement. There is sound reason for the study of science; for it helps us directly in our difficulties, and enables us to do what men have long wished to do, and have been unable to do for lack of knowledge. But to study the moralists is only to achieve bewilderment, or else to arrive through intricate and teasing argument at a conclusion which we knew well enough before we started. We "come out by the same door as in we went". The same old arguments go round and round for ever. The same theories appear and are refuted, only to reappear, as plausible as ever, as soon as the refutation has been forgotten. Granted that in our perplexity we need all the help that we can get to tell us what to do. The scientist tells us. The moral theorist doesn't even pretend to.

This frame of mind, which is now very prevalent though not so commonly put into words, is itself an expression of the moral crisis of our time. No one whose moral sense is keen and vigorous will be guilty of such a confusion of issues. Science does not tell us, in any moral sense, what to do. Rather it tells us how to do what we want. With equal equanimity it will instruct us how to avoid smallpox, how to crack a safe and how to kill our enemies. Science serves our interests, whatever they may be. Morality, however, is not concerned to serve our interests, but to help us decide when we may pursue and when we must sacrifice them. If in this sense we want to be told what to do, we should be better employed in voting or plotting for a totalitarian government. For then we should have an authority which would not only tell us what to do, but would see that we did it. On the other hand, if what we want is to serve our own interests with the help of the scientists, we shall get a totalitarian government however little we may want it. We cannot all have what we want; and if we all try, the victory will go to the strongest; and in our day the strongest are those who control effectively the power that science has let loose upon the world.

To expect the moralist, then, to tell us what to do is to seek to dodge the claim of morality. A moral decision is one which we take for ourselves, on our own responsibility, and for which we are prepared to answer. The study of morality cannot be "scientific". It is not an attempt to discover new facts about the world, nor to invent techniques for success in living. It is an effort to discipline the mind in view of the responsibilities of life. The athlete disciplines his body in order to "keep fit". He does not complain that his physical exercises are the same as those of the ancients, or that rival schools of physical training argue heatedly in favour of their own systems and against all the others. Nor does he give up in despair because he can see no relation between Swedish drill and climbing Mount Everest. If he did we should conclude that he was not really in earnest.

Moral discipline, of course, does not consist in reading the productions of moral philosophers. It is primarily a practical discipline. Only by a steady effort in action can the will be strengthened in its struggle with impulse. That morality is a matter of will rather than of knowledge is the characteristic modern standpoint. No doubt this is part of the truth; but it is not the whole truth. We assume too easily that we know what we ought to do, and that our difficulty lies in the all too human weakness which keeps us from doing it. Without enlightenment the will degenerates into mere obstinacy and fanaticism. In a stable society, where the pattern of life is fixed and clear to everyone, it may well be true that for the most part moral failure is due to weakness of will in the face of temptation. In the simple situations of direct human relationship it is perhaps nearly always so. But in a time like the present, when change is radical and incessant, and when issues grow more and more complicated, this belief becomes less obvious. We grow familiar with situations where the old rules provide no clear guidance and which are so complicated that it is hard to discern wherein the moral issue lies. We meet men of tried courage, who have proved their readiness to sacrifice their private interests to the welfare of their fellows, who find themselves frustrated and reduced to a despairing impotence because they cannot find the thing to do. In such ways we rediscover the need for a moral discipline of the mind, and realise that there is an important truth, complementary to our own, in the Socratic doctrine that virtue is knowledge.

In every age, men who have taken seriously their moral responsibility have known that good will is not enough. Too often it is merely a synonym for laziness and complacency. They have disciplined themselves, not merely by trying harder to live by the light they possess, but by seeking more light to live by. They have sought it by constant self-examination and self-criticism; by a searching analysis of their motives and by careful attention to the consequences of their behaviour. What they have sought by these exercises has been an increase in the range and accuracy of moral judgment and a cultivation and refinement of moral discrimination. It is difficult to imagine any other means to these ends.

It is with such thoughts in mind that I commend this book to the attention of serious readers. Quite apart from the theoretical interest of the subject, the study of its contents has, I believe—and even if the author were to disclaim the intention—an immediate, if indirect, practical importance. For whoever reflects with any seriousness upon the moral issues of his own experience will soon find himself at grips with the questions which are debated by the schools, and will know that he needs the answers for himself.

JOHN MACMURRAY

PREFACE

THE ARGUMENT OF the following pages divides naturally into two parts. The first of these traces the gradual clarification of the ethical problem from the time of Hobbes to the present day, and concludes that the task of the moralist is to set in their proper relation one to another the three different types of moral judgment ("Act A is right or wrong", "Motive or character B is morally good or morally bad, virtuous or vicious", and "State of affairs C is good or bad"), and so to reveal the field of morality as a single self-coherent system. It may not be possible to do this completely, morality may have ragged edges; but, so far as it goes, it should appear as a self-consistent whole. Then, in the second part, in the light of this formulation of the problem, an idealist solution is adumbrated which seeks to take account of the important analytic work of other contemporary schools of ethical thought. Part of the argument has already appeared in print in two articles in *Philosophy* ("Act and Attitude", November 1943, and "The Moral Situation", October 1949), and to the Editor of that journal I am indebted for permission to use again what was there published; while the whole work has been approved by the University of Glasgow as qualifying for the degree of Doctor of Letters.

The footnotes reveal my debt to those who have taken a prominent part in the ethical discussion; but in making my own small contribution to a great theme I would acknowledge my good fortune in having had as my teachers in the various philosophical disciplines the late Professor A. A. Bowman, Professor H. J. Paton, Sir Oliver Franks, and the Very Rev. Professor John Baillie. In the Dedication I have tried to pay a tribute of a more intimate nature, and although my mother has not lived to see it in print I have chosen to leave it in the form in which it was first penned. Finally, my warm thanks are due to the publishers for their unfailing kindness and courtesy, to the Carnegie Trust for the Universities of Scotland who have generously guaranteed the production of this book, and to Professor John Macmurray for his very kind Introduction,

N. H. G. ROBINSON

INTRODUCTION: THE PROBLEM

ETHICS IS THE study of human conduct and character; but it studies its object from a special point of view. Human conduct constitutes a large body of facts, the causes of which, for example, can be discovered or at least investigated; but ethics is not primarily concerned with that investigation. It is not interested in this body of facts or their causes except in so far as they have a bearing upon the special object of ethics. The special object of ethics is not the particular facts which together make up the realm of conduct, but rather that realm as a whole and as having one peculiar characteristic, namely, that the facts which comprise it might have been other than they are and in many cases ought to have been. Ethics is concerned with human conduct and character as the subjects of praise and blame. Its subject-matter is the world of values and the realm of conduct in so far as the former can be realised in the latter.

So defined, ethics clearly excludes any study of human action, such as psychology, which is not interested in conduct as the bearer of values. On the other hand, it also excludes any examination of values which are not realisable in conduct. It excludes, for example, an examination of aesthetic values, which may indeed be realisable by means of human conduct but do not attach themselves to the conduct itself. An artist may succeed in painting a picture which is beautiful, but it is the result of his labours, not the labour itself, which earns the epithet.

Here, however, a question may well be raised, for we do in fact speak of beautiful actions. Such a usage is not without its ambiguity. Sometimes we are speaking metaphorically and really mean that the action is good and worthy to be praised. Then, of course, although our language is loose, the fact described by it falls within the scope of ethics. On other occasions, however, we speak quite literally of actions as beautiful; we speak, for instance, of someone's singing or of the acting of an actor as well and beautifully done. Yet, even so, it does not follow that the suggested definition of the scope of ethics is too wide, for although the usage in question is literal and exact it may still be doubted whether it is really an act which is the subject of these predicates. Certainly when a particular piece of singing is described as beautiful it is not the song as a particular collection of words and a certain musical setting that is intended. Nor is it the singing of it by a particular singer, but rather the actual rendering of the song by that singer on a given occasion. Consequently, if it is not the act which is properly said to be beautiful, it is something conditioned by it and connected with it. Indeed it would seem that the subject of the aesthetic attribute in all such cases is not the act itself but an entity mentally and imaginatively constructed which is conditioned by the act.

Ethics, then, is the study of the world of values so far as they are realisable in the realm of conduct. More than that, however, ethics is the *systematic* study of its object. It came into being when Socrates laid it down that the proper study of man is man, and when, passing beyond inspired moral intuition and pragmatic counsel alike, he sought behind the great variety of moral ideas for a single unifying principle. Certainly when we inquire whether Socrates ever did find such a principle we are at first impressed by the negative nature of his results. One after another of his ethical discussions seems to have ended inconclusively; but commenting on this fact A. E. Taylor says: "We are to understand that the attempt to define one virtue ends in something which is no more a definition of that virtue than of another, for the reason that in principle *all* virtue is one."[1] That in itself is a solid achievement, and the beginning of ethics.

The starting-point of the ethical inquiry is a large body of moral judgments, judgments of the ordinary moral consciousness, not necessarily consistent one with another, and certainly not displaying at first glance the working of any one comprehensive principle. And the aim of the inquiry is to apprehend these various judgments as forming together a single self-coherent system.

It does not follow, however, that ethics is the *scientific* study of its object; in other words, that ethics is a science. It may be so, but for long it has been regarded rather as a branch of philosophy. Of course, on the other hand, it may well be that the time has come for ethics, as for psychology, to separate off

[1] *Socrates*, p. 146.

from philosophy and to stand upon its own feet as a distinct science. The question, however, is not simply a question about names, nor is it a question of degree, whether, for example, there is now enough of ethics to deserve the label of a distinct study. Indeed for long it has been looked upon as a roughly distinguishable branch of philosophy deserving to be regarded as a separate department. The question whether ethics is a science is one, not of degree, but of principle. And the principle is this, that a science in dealing with its special problems can for the purpose of their examination treat them in isolation from all other problems without thereby ruling out the possibility of their solution.

For ethics this means in effect two things.

In the first place, if ethics is a science then it does not fall within the domain of ethics to raise a question concerning the possibility of morality in general; the question, that is to say, whether or not the will is free. That is a problem which cannot be solved apart from considerations which belong to epistemology and philosophy, and to the thinking required for its solution the science of ethics is a stranger. It is not concerned with this problem, but accepts as its starting-point the reality of a realm of conduct which might have been other than it is. A similar point is made by Professor John Baillie with regard to the science of theology. "The business of theology," he says, "regarded as a science, is rather to bring to light the hidden grounds of our belief in the love and providence of God and in the immortality of the soul than to tell us *whether* we are to believe in these things."[2] In the same way, ethics as a science may bring to light the relation between the belief in a free will and the other beliefs of the ordinary moral consciousness; but it is not at all for the science of ethics to question the possibility of morality itself.

In the second place, if ethics is a science it will, in examining the content of morality, confine itself to the witness of the ordinary moral consciousness. It is possible that philosophy, like religion, might seek to instruct the moral consciousness of men, and might therefore give expression to propositions of the form, "X ought to be morally approved". With this pretension itself, on the part either of religion or of philosophy, the science of ethics has no quarrel; but it does not accept such judgments except as they commend themselves to the ordinary

[2] *The Interpretation of Religion*, p. 21.

moral consciousness. It is with the world of values that the science of ethics is concerned, but only so far as that world is recognised by the practical consciousness of humankind. Or, as Seth has put it in his *Ethical Principles*, "the task of the ethical thinker is not to construct a system of rules for the conduct of life, but to lay bare the nerve of the moral life".[3]

Subject to these two limitations, then, there can in theory be a science of ethics; and the question next arises whether there is anything left to be a science, whether in fact by ruling out certain questions as beyond the scope of scientific ethics we have not ruled out the main questions of interest in the history of ethical discussion. But although it is true that in the case of ethics, as indeed in the case of other sciences, the discussion of its peculiar problems has been conducted historically in close association with the discussion of other problems of a more general and philosophical nature, it is also true that when abstraction has been made from the latter there still remains a fairly clearly defined group of problems requiring investigation.

For example, although it is incompetent for ethics to question the possibility of morality in general, it has none the less an intrinsic interest in the particular form of free-will which morality requires. Further, although it is not at liberty to impose rules upon the ordinary moral consciousness, it has a duty to discover, or to try to discover, order and unity of principle in the judgments to which that consciousness gives expression. Consequently, there is in fact as well as in theory a science of ethics.

Now this classification of ethics as a science has an important bearing upon the method by which the study seeks to arrive at its conclusions. A science, we have seen, can deal with its problems in isolation from other problems. That is to say, in order to be adequate a scientific theory must, firstly, answer the questions raised by the science, and, secondly, it must do so in accordance with the facts which give rise to these questions. A science therefore can, and must, test itself by reference to the facts which fall within its proper section of reality. In the case of ethics these facts are the judgments of the ordinary moral consciousness. No ethical theory can be regarded as satisfactory if it flies in the face of these moral affirmations;

---

[3] *Ethical Principles* (5th ed.), p. 13.

and, on the other side, a theory is entirely adequate if it answers
the ethical questions in complete harmony with the facts from
which it starts. Consequently, ethical thinking must make constant reference to the facts with which it deals. It will propound
a theory, discover what is involved in it, and test its adequacy
against the touchstone of the ordinary moral judgment.

This in fact was the method employed by Socrates. Time and
again, in seeking a satisfactory definition of some virtue, he
would develop a theory, then work out its implications, and
finally test it. If it involved regarding as virtuous an act which
was not commonly so regarded then the theory was immediately
rejected, whereas if the act in question was generally admitted
to be virtuous the theory was considered as so far satisfactory.
It is also the method adopted in as recent a book as that which
contains the Gifford Lectures of Sir David Ross. At the beginning of these he describes his method as one of examining,
comparing, criticising and clarifying the various dicta of the
moral consciousness;[4] and then, in quoting Kant with approval,
he says: "Kant's method was the same. 'I have adopted in
this work', he says in the Preface to the *Grundlegung*, 'the method
which I think most suitable, proceeding analytically from
common knowledge to the determination of its ultimate
principle'; and to this 'common knowledge' he again and
again returns, as to that on which his own theory is based and
by comparison with which it must from time to time be
tested."[5]

Clearly, there is a certain resemblance between this method
and the hypothetico-deductive method of experimentation
known to the physical sciences, although the element of precision and measurability is absent from the former. There is
indeed a further difference to which Sir David Ross draws
attention. In the physical sciences, he says, "we have a more
direct avenue to truth; the appeal must always be from
opinions to the facts of sense-perception".[6] The point is that
in ethics, on the other hand, the "facts" are judgments not
all of which are true. But this difference must not be pressed
too far. Certainly, it is the case that here and there amongst
the affirmations of the moral consciousness there are judgments
which are no doubt false; but it is also the case that for ethics
the moral consciousness is a source of truth and its affirmations
are regarded as for the most part true. If it were not so, if its

---

[4] *Foundations of Ethics*, p. 1.   [5] *Ibid.*, p. 2.   [6] *Ibid.*, p. 3.

dicta were the subject of radical doubt, then ethics as a science would cease to exist.

Moreover, when the moral consciousness does give expression to a proposition, X, which is in fact untrue, its falsity is not apparent to ethics until the moral consciousness itself rejects it. It is not as if ethics had no facts to which an appeal could, and must, be made, but rather as if its "facts" could be altered, or rather clarified, by repeated appeals and experimentation. Its facts are complex. They are judgments of the moral consciousness, and they may require a great deal of clarification; but they are none the less the final court of appeal, and the science of ethics can never supersede the moral consciousness, to which it owes its origin. The matter has been put with clarity, with regard to the sister science of theology, by Professor Baillie when he says that the method of theological science is "the interrogation of the religious consciousness with a view to discovering what religion really is";[7] and that principle also applies, *mutatis mutandis*, to ethics and the moral consciousness.

We have seen that ethics, both as the systematic study of its object and as practising a certain method, came into being in ancient Greece with the work of Socrates. The contribution of Greek thought, however, was greater even than that, for it has also provided the type of one prevailing answer to the ethical question. The fundamental position of Greek thought on this matter was clearly stated by Aristotle at the beginning of the *Nicomachean Ethics* when he said: "Every art, and every science reduced to a teachable form, and in like manner every action and moral choice, aims, it is thought, at some good."[8] It is not, it is to be noticed, that every action and every moral choice ought to aim at some good, but rather that in fact they inevitably do. The only variation possible is in the degree of knowledge with which men do pursue their good, knowledge not only of the appropriate means to a given end but also of the ends in which the good of man most truly resides. All men in every act aim at some good, but not all of them do so "according to knowledge".[9] Thus, as it has been said, "Socrates agrees on one point with Hedonism, that wrong doing is due to miscalculation; but the miscalculation is not one of 'amounts of pleasure', but of values of good".[10]

[7] *The Interpretation of Religion*, p. 14.   [9] Cf. St. Paul, *Epistle to the Romans*, x. 2.
[8] *Nicomachean Ethics*, 1094a.   [10] A. E. Taylor, *Socrates*, p. 144.

It is from this general starting-point that there naturally arises Socrates' doctrine that virtue is knowledge.[11] This means, of course, that virtue can be produced by means of education, and that wrong-doing is due to ignorance. Now this position undoubtedly has an appearance of paradox, and seems to imperil any real belief in moral responsibility. Yet even in Socrates there are mitigating points. The knowledge of which he speaks is not to be identified with true opinion. "True virtue", as A. E. Taylor puts it, "is an affair of intense conviction, personal *knowledge* of the true moral 'values'."[12] Moreover, in Greek philosophy generally there is the recognition that the education required to produce virtue must include discipline. It is seen that uncontrolled passion may prevent a man from knowing where his true good lies. Thus Aristotle excludes from the study of Moral Philosophy, not only young men, but also the man of youthful temper, on the ground that "since he is apt to follow the impulses of his passions, he will hear as though he heard not, and to no profit, the end in view being practice and not mere knowledge".[13]

If now we seek to advance beyond this position and inquire what that object is the knowledge of which is to be identified with virtue, we do not receive from Greek thought any clear and unequivocal reply. It is, of course, the Good; but what then is the Good? In Plato's *Protagoras*[14] it would seem to be pleasure, but in the *Republic*[15] such a suggestion is regarded as blasphemous. For Aristotle it is thought to consist of certain activities performed in the way of excellence, that is, in accordance with the principle of the mean,[16] and is regarded as including also happiness[17] and the possession of such external things as friends, wealth, and political influence.[18]

Now, in the first place, it is clear from all this that ancient Greek thought did not entirely succeed in marking off and isolating the proper object of ethical study. For it is commonly supposed that friends, influence and possessions are not indispensable elements of the moral life. That is not to say that they do not have moral significance. On the contrary, it is plain

---

[11] Cf. Sidgwick, *History of Ethics*, p. 24.
[12] *Socrates*, p. 145. Cf. Burnet, *Socrates*, para. 9, in E.R.E., vol. II.
[13] *Nicomachean Ethics*, 1095a.
[14] 351A.
[15] 509A.
[16] *Nicomachean Ethics*, 1097b–1098a, 1104a–1107a.
[17] *Ibid.*, 1095b–1096a.
[18] *Ibid.*, 1098b–1099b.

that they have; but the part they play in the moral life is rather that of an occasion of virtue than a component of it.

In the second place, however, even if the object of ethical thought had been thus more strictly delimited, it could hardly be said that Greek philosophy has provided a completely satisfactory solution to the ethical problem. In particular, its account of virtue is not sufficiently definite, and its account of vice seems, on the face of it, false.

When Aristotle tried to set out a theory of virtue he started from the position, common to the ethical thought of his time, that all things aim at some end or good, and he then proceeded to distinguish two different kinds of end. "There plainly is", he says, "a difference in the Ends proposed: for in some cases they are acts of working, and in others certain works or tangible results beyond and beside the acts of working."[19] In some cases the activity itself is an end in itself, whereas in others the end is something beyond the activity to which the latter is no more than a means. Now once this distinction has been drawn, the reader of Aristotle is inclined to ask to which kind of end an adequate theory of virtue must refer. Is virtuous activity to be identified with an activity which is its own justification, or is it to be identified with an activity justified by an end to which the activity itself is only the means? Yet, although the question is natural enough and almost inevitable, Greek philosophy does not answer it. At any rate it does not answer it decisively. So far as Greek philosophy has a complete and final theory of virtue, it is a theory which in different parts has reference to both kinds of end. It is indeed true that over a wide area the theory proceeds in terms of those ends which are identical with the activities themselves; yet the theory does not finally rule out the inclusion of the other kind of end as well. Thus, in the *Philebus*, although Plato denies that pleasure and the highest good are identical, he holds none the less that a life without pleasure is not to be chosen;[20] and with that Aristotle also would agree.

If then this is accepted as the final position of the theory, it follows that virtuous action consists sometimes of an activity which inevitably realises its end, since the end and the activity are the same, and, at other times, of an activity which is in essence the hitting of a mark which may well be missed, even when the agent has taken all the steps he can take in order to

[19] *Ibid.*, 1094a.   [20] 21D, 63E.

hit the mark.[21] That is to say, virtue sometimes depends on the agent alone, and sometimes on the agent together with certain conditions in the external world. But as against this, the ordinary moral consciousness would demand that the theory should go on to favour the one possibility to the exclusion of the other, for to that consciousness the distinction between the two possibilities appears, not just as an interesting distinction within the limits of a single principle, but as no less than a difference between two principles. It would seem, therefore, that although Greek ethical thought rightly insisted that all virtue is one, it failed to exhibit that unity by bringing the variety of moral phenomena under the rule of a single principle.

It is commonly supposed, however, that Greek ethical thought errs more in its theory of vice than in its theory of virtue; and here too the charge of indefiniteness may be made. Once more the starting-point is that all things aim at some end or good. Now, so far as virtuous action is regarded as an activity which is an end in itself, vicious action must be an activity wrongly regarded as good. In other words, the fundamental error consists of a false judgment of value. On the other hand, where the end is thought of as lying beyond the action itself, there is a double possibility of error. The root of vice may then be either a false judgment of value, for example, that end B is good, or a false judgment of fact, for example, that act A will have B as its result.

Yet this charge of indefiniteness does not exhaust the difficulties with which the ordinary moral consciousness is confronted as it seeks to understand the Greek view of vice. That view, it has been seen, wavers between the proposition that the root of vice is a false judgment of value and the proposition that it is a false judgment of fact. To that, however, the moral consciousness objects, not only that it is a fluctuation between two very different principles, but also that neither seems to be true. Both accounts have this in common, that vice essentially consists of making a false judgment and acting upon it; and that means that it is possible to act viciously while acting conscientiously. With that contention, however, the moral consciousness hesitates to agree, for it cannot help believing that if a man acts according to his lights he has done

[21] On the Greek view, it is to be noticed, mere *aiming* at the mark, without *hitting* the mark, is not sufficient to constitute virtue.

all that is required of him. On the other hand, it must be admitted that the Greek view offers a plausible explanation of how men come to act contrary to their true good, for it asserts that they follow such a course under the appearance of its being better than it is. The moral consciousness, therefore, does not flatly rule out the Greek position as rank error, but it does insist that it be subjected to a rigorously critical examination.

Greek thought then succeeded, not only in propounding the ethical question, but also in providing one of the main types of answer to it, and that in a manner promising for the further development of the subject.

With the spread of Christianity some four or five hundred years later, the moral life began to be widely regarded under quite a different ruling idea than that of the good. The new religion undoubtedly transcended the old Hebrew faith and philosophy of life, but it did so in the way of fulfilling the latter. There was a great deal of common ground between them; and as a result Christianity not only transcended the older religion but also served to transfuse throughout the Gentile world ideas which had been present to the minds of Israel for several hundred years before the birth of Socrates.

One such idea was the conception of the moral life, not as a pursuit of the good, but as obedience to the law of God. To the mind of Israel, of course, this was not a contribution to ethical theory. The interests even of the spiritual leaders of Israel were very far removed from ethical problems, her religion was an eminently practical affair, and the faith she developed was wrought out in the context of historic and dramatic events. But when Christianity carried over this central idea, it carried it into a world for which ethics had already become a branch of systematic study, and it was natural that in the course of time the theoretical implications of this practical outlook should be investigated.

Indeed one would have expected a consideration of these implications much sooner than it actually took place. As it happened, however, the intellectual interest in Christianity gravitated toward other problems, and even when an approach was made in this way to the practical life the questions raised were not concerned with the general form of morality, but rather with its detailed content and the ability of man to realise it. Thus we find in St. Ambrose and St. Augustine an

attempt to give a systematic account of Christian morality
in the form of a list of Christian virtues; and later, Moral
Theology makes its appearance as that study of particular
cases in morality which was to become the developed system of
casuistry for which the Middle Ages are notorious.

All this falls short of being a theory of the formal aspect
of morality, and in fact it was not until the period of Scholas-
ticism that this side of the matter received attention, and we
have to look to the leading figure of the time, St. Thomas
Aquinas, for a considerable treatment of the subject. Even
here, however, we do not find a clear consciousness that the
ideas of law and end are two quite different ruling principles
in the field of ethics. On the contrary, they are to be found in
St. Thomas side by side, and, as Sidgwick has put it, St. Thomas
is "scarcely aware . . . of the difficulty of reconciling the
position, that will or purpose is a rational desire always
directed towards at least apparent good, with the freedom of
choice between good and evil that the jural view of morality
seems to require".[22] For the great Scholastic there was no
such thing as the modern problem of the relationship between
rule and end in morals, and no doubt one reason was that the
interest of Aquinas was not specifically ethical. His aim was
much more comprehensive, no less than to join together
revelation and reason (by which was chiefly meant the work
of Aristotle), and his great achievement was the medieval
synthesis.

None the less, by his systematic treatment of law he unwittingly compelled ethics to take account also of this ruling
concept in its attempt to provide a coherent theory of morality.

The point from which St. Thomas starts is the eternal law
of God which covers the entire created world, irrational
as well as rational. Now much of this law does not apply, and
may well be unknown, to men; but that part which does apply
and is discerned by natural reason is called by St. Thomas
natural law. "The natural law", he says, "is nothing else than
the rational creature's participation of the eternal law."[23]
The point is that natural law consists of that part of the eternal
law which a rational creature can discover by the use of its
own reason as applicable to rational beings. It does not,
however, exhaust the law by which rational creatures are

[22] *History of Ethics*, p. 144.
[23] *Summa Theologica*, 2, 1, Q xci (*Selected Writings* (Everyman), p. 85).

bound. Besides this there is what Aquinas calls divine law, which applies to men but cannot be discerned by the natural reason. It can be communicated, not by reason, but by special revelation; and it is therefore something external to man.

Thus alongside his account of morality as a number of virtues, St. Thomas Aquinas brings the whole field under the rule of another principle, that of the law of God; and within this he distinguishes natural and divine law as being respectively that part which a man can discover for himself and that part which only God can communicate to him.

It was upon this distinction within the realm of law that later thinkers saw fit to seize; and in particular, two of them, Duns Scotus and William of Occam, argued that the whole law was of the type distinguished by Aquinas as divine law. For them the entire law of God was quite external to man, it commanded his will without convincing his intellect. The law was bound to appear arbitrary, but it was not for man to reason why. Indeed it was even held that for God too His law was arbitrary, His will was unbound by reason; but that was a point which belonged to theology and not to ethics.

More than that, however, if these thinkers were right in regarding the law of God as arbitrary to man, then ethics as a branch of systematic study would cease to exist. For the purpose of the investigation is to bring the variety of moral duties and values under the rule of a single principle, while the doctrine in question implies that there is in fact no such principle. It cannot be denied that in reducing all morality to the law of God Duns Scotus has unified the field of moral conduct, but the unity he introduces is not a unity amid differences, but a unity which denies the differences. He has not brought the many duties under the rule of a single principle; rather he has reduced them to one solitary duty, namely, to obey God. There is nothing in the actual content of the command to render it obligatory, no reason that we should obey it nor beauty that we should desire it. The details of the command are entirely irrelevant, and the only significant factor is He who issues the command. We have only one duty, and that is obedience to God.

In all this, however, Duns Scotus insists on a greater degree of unity than the case will allow, for although the moral consciousness is prepared to find that its various duties are all the same kind of thing, it does not believe that they are pre-

cisely the same thing over and over again, nor that the differences are entirely irrelevant. It does not believe, for example,
that when it refrains from theft or adultery the nature of the
things avoided has nothing at all to do with the case and might
equally well have been quite opposite from what they are. It
is ready enough to discover a unity in the plurality, but it
will not believe that the variety can be reduced to mere
repetition of precisely the same thing. It recognises that there
may well be a duty to obey God, but it is not the one and only
duty that men have. Rather it is either one duty amongst
many, or else a general duty present in every other duty
without being the only source of their obligatoriness, providing
an extra motive to obey but not the only one.

Moreover, it is a presupposition of this view that God and
His law are recognisable quite independently of any general
knowledge of right and wrong. Our knowledge that God is
and that men ought to obey Him is logically prior to our
knowledge of detailed moral distinctions such as our recognition that it is right for a man to keep a promise that he has
made. It is assumed that we have some means, other than a
knowledge of detailed moral distinctions, by which we can
judge whether a law purporting to be the law of God is
genuinely so or not.

Now the Reformation was partly a protest against this
position. According to Herrmann, for example,[24] Protestantism has this belief in common with the Roman form of
Christianity, that the command of morality is the command of
God, but this tenet is interpreted by the two sides in different
ways. In particular, there are two points of divergence. In
the first place, for Protestantism the moral law is internal to
man and not external, he sees it from the inside, as it were,
and appreciates the special urgency peculiar to each of its
demands. Secondly, the moral law so understood is the clue
men have by which they can recognise God as God.

The issues involved in this are in the main theological;
but one result of the reinterpretation of Christian teaching was
that the moral law came to be regarded as at the same time a
law and a standard internal to man, and consequently the
ethical implication was avoided that men have in reality only
one duty, viz., to obey God. This implication, as we have seen,
is not acceptable to the ordinary moral consciousness, for it

[24] *The Moral Law*, paras. 10-12.

reduces the moral distinctions of the latter to merely amoral differences.[25] The moral consciousness demands of every ethical theory the recognition that an agent has different duties to perform in the course of the moral life, and not simply the same duty in different contexts which have no inherent connection with the duty itself; and this demand is met by the reinterpretation of Christian morality which came with the Reformation.

Thus there arises a second main type of ethical theory. According to it, men are guided, not only by their desires, but also by the light of an inner law; and the moral life is conceived, not as a pursuit of the good, but as a life of obedience to the dictates of that law. Moreover, in doing wrong a man is regarded as rejecting the claims of morality and rebelling against the commands of the law, rather than as acting under a mistaken apprehension of what is good.

It has already been stated that ethics arises as an attempt to discover a unifying principle beneath the various moral judgments and ideas of the ordinary consciousness; and the difference between the two theories with which we have been dealing lies in the different principles they respectively uphold as revealing unity amid this variety. The one brings the moral field under the ruling principle of "good", while the other brings it under that of "right", "lawful" or "obligatory". It would then seem that the task of subsequent ethical discussion is either to decide between these two rival principles or else to indicate a third principle more fundamental than either.

The problem, however, is not quite so simple as that, for neither of these two principles is a hypothesis which may serve its turn in the history of the science and then be cast aside to make room for a better. On the contrary, they are themselves ideas of the moral consciousness; and consequently, if either is taken as the ruling principle, the ethical task is not completed until it is also shown how the other fits into the framework which its rival provides. Whereas, if there is reason for adopting a third principle, a place must be found for those other two within the framework of which the former is the corner-stone.

---

[25] The theory suffers from the further defect that it leaves to reason merely the task of applying the external law; but reason cannot even apply a completely arbitrary law.

Within this scheme of ethical discussion there are, in principle, several possible developments of ethical theory; but in practice there have been two main lines of thought. On the one hand, the theory of the moral life which has represented it as a pursuit of the good has always been able to recognise the existence of moral laws by regarding them as the outcome of moral experience, more or less rough generalisations indicating the directions in which the good is most probably to be found. On the other hand, the theory which has refrained from thus regarding "right" as derivative and subordinate, and has instead insisted upon it as a fundamental concept, has usually either ignored the concept of "good" or left it standing unrelated.

The ethical problem, then, is to unfold the systematic nature of our moral judgments by bringing them under the rule of a moral principle, and, in particular, by setting the two obvious moral principles, the right and the good, in their proper relation one to another.

PART ONE

THE SOLUTION IN HISTORY

CHAPTER I

THE ETHICS OF THE EIGHTEENTH CENTURY

(A) SENTIMENTALISM

IT WAS IN the late seventeenth and in the eighteenth centuries that British ethical theory began to take form; and it is a curious fact that it started as a reaction against what was virtually a denial of any systematic morality. It was provoked by the cynicism of Thomas Hobbes; and that may account for the fact that it leaves an impression of incompleteness, proceeding as it does along two quite different lines of thought which seem nowhere in the period to come to definite grips the one with the other. The main consideration was to discredit any wholesale attack upon morality and to justify our ordinary moral judgments as on the whole well-founded, rather than to reveal them as forming together a single system. The discussion was a lengthy one and valuable, and there was no doubt a good deal of truth in both lines of critical reaction to Hobbes; but the resultant ethical theories suffer from the fact that for the most part the one is quite ignorant of the other.

Hobbes was a materialist. That is to say, he was prepared to give an account of everything, including spirit, in terms of matter and motion; but it was not upon his materialism that his critics chiefly fastened. The structure which he erected upon this foundation had itself distinctive features upon which later thinkers were quick to seize.

Thus, having described man's mental activities, such as desiring, in terms chiefly of motion, Hobbes went on to lay down that all our desires are self-regarding, that there is no such thing in man's nature as an altruistic desire. In making this point Hobbes was talking, not about what ought to be, but simply about what actually is; and his doctrine on this matter is a psychological one, although if it is true it is entirely relevant to the discussion of ethics. It is not, however, to be identified with the doctrine known as psychological hedonism. In fact Hobbes does not appear to have held that the single object of all desire is pleasure. He speaks persistently of a variety of objects of desire, it is his plain intention to define "good" as "that which is desired", and, he says, "these words of Good, Evill and Contemptible, are ever used with relation to the person that useth them, there being *nothing* simply and absolutely so".[1]

Yet, if Hobbes was not a psychological hedonist, he was none the less a psychological egoist and in the most thorough-going fashion. Although men did not simply desire pleasure but rather a great variety of different things, each and every desire, he held, was entirely self-regarding. Even those desires in which men seemed to be concerned with the welfare of others had only an appearance of benevolence, and in reality they were just as self-centred as any other. Thus, the pity which a man feels when he beholds the calamity of someone else arises "from the imagination that the like calamity may befall himselfe".[2]

All desires then were self-regarding; but besides these particular desires Hobbes recognised a general inclination of all mankind, "a perpetuall and restlesse desire of Power after power, that ceaseth onely in Death".[3] Man was not only moved by various particular self-regarding desires, but was also the subject of an endeavour to have at his disposal the means to satisfy as many of these desires as often as possible; and this means was precisely what the author of the *Leviathan* meant by power.[4]

Now in all this our author was describing human nature as it actually is and not as it ought to be, and indeed in describing it as he did he seems to have left no room whatsoever for moral obligation. He did not hesitate, however, to use the language of morality, and in two principal respects. In the first place, he spoke[5] of a right of nature which each man had to use his power for his own preservation, and he frankly recognised that this amounted to a natural right "of every man to every thing". That is, of course, a strange right to confer upon men, and one might well ask what kind of right it is that has chaos and not order as its necessary effect upon the social relationships of men. But the explanation is quite simple, for although Hobbes allowed the language of morality he did not

---

[1] *Leviathan*, pt. i, ch. 6 (italics mine).   [3] *Ibid.*, pt. i, ch. 11.
[2] *Ibid.*, pt. i, ch. 6.   [4] *Ibid.*, pt. i, ch. 10.
                    [5] *Ibid.*, pt. i, ch. 14.

allow the reality of it. A right, in his eyes, was something entirely negative, the mere absence, as he himself confesses, of "externall Impediments", that is, not a moral right at all.

The other place in his system where Hobbes found room for at least the language of morality is that in which he spoke of the laws of nature. Now does the system of Hobbes as so far expounded leave any room at all for laws of nature? Can men, having the general nature which Hobbes has accorded them, be the subjects of a natural law, that is, of a law to the transgression of which no immediate penalty is plainly attached? To these questions the answer is that just as for Hobbes there is no absolute good, a thing is good simply because someone desires it, and there is nothing desired because it is first of all good, so there is no such thing as a categorical and moral imperative, a law which commands us to do something whether we want to or not, for the only forces by which men are moved to act are self-regarding desires and aversions. Consequently, every law must command the means to an end and not any particular end itself. In that case there can be laws of a categorical though amoral nature only if there is some desire which all men have in common. Failing that condition any law there is will not only govern the means and not the end, but will also govern the means in a merely hypothetical fashion, under the supposition that a particular end is in fact desired. The condition is, however, fulfilled in the *Leviathan*, for its author allows one universal desire, the general inclination to have the power to satisfy one's particular desires. Given this common desire, at least one condition is fulfilled of the reality of a categorical law which commands the means and not the end.

There would seem, however, to be a further condition, for if a natural law is to command the means to a given end it can do so only if that end is such that the means to it is so perfectly plain and certain that it may be said to be commanded by a law of nature, and a different opinion can only be regarded as quite unreasonable and a rebellion against this law. Yet the realm of means to ends, generally speaking, is a realm of something less than complete certainty. The objects we pursue lie in the future, and we cannot be sure of the future beyond all shadow of reasonable doubt. Otherwise mortal life would be a much more simple and less exciting experience than it actually is. To this, if one may be allowed to speak for Hobbes, the answer is that while all that has been said may be true in general of the means to ends under the conditions of a settled society enjoying the institutions of law and government, it does not hold in a state of unregulated nature in which each man strives by every means in his power to ensure the continued satisfaction of all his desires, with complete indifference to the fortunes of others except in so far as they affect his own. And Hobbes did believe that in the state of nature without government the life of man was "solitary, poore, nasty, brutish, and short".[6] It must then be supposed that Hobbes not only held that all men have one object of desire in common, power and as much of it as possible, but also regarded the means to this end as abundantly clear, so clear indeed that to doubt it was wholly unreasonable and nothing short of flying in the face of a plain law of nature. This must be supposed unless one is prepared to allow that introducing laws of nature Hobbes was really modifying his account of human nature and was now admitting that men are sometimes moved to act in obedience to a moral law which they are obliged to obey whether they want to or not. But it is the former supposition which is in closer harmony with the general point of view which Hobbes adopted.

Now in dealing with the laws of nature Hobbes enunciated no fewer than fifteen, but he was prepared to sum them all up in the dictum, "Do not that to another, which thou wouldest not have done to thyselfe".[7] Thus, the laws of nature come in the end to this, that in order to have as much power as they can to satisfy their desires men ought to consider one another, ought to agree to give up some of the power which they possess or to which they have a natural right. In this matter, however, Hobbes held no brief for the policy of unilateral disarmament, but insisted that a man must do no more than desire conditions of peace until others are ready to act along with him. This means that the fifteen laws of nature can be reduced to one which commands the formation of a settled society under law and government duly instituted.

The settled society thus formed was called by Hobbes the Commonwealth, and the laws of the Commonwealth are the source of all particular distinctions between what is right and what is wrong.[8] Law is not founded upon morality, but morality upon law; the sovereign has entire right and power to alter the

---

[6] *Leviathan*, pt. i, ch. 13.   [7] *Ibid.*, pt. i, ch. 15.
[8] *Ibid.*, pt. ii, ch. 18.

law as he sees fit, and there is no independent and more fundamental distinction between right and wrong to which the sovereign can be referred in an appeal by his subjects—the most they can do in extreme cases is to show a preference for a return to that state of nature where every man has a right to everything. The only moral distinctions there are are determined by the will of the sovereign.

Thus, just as the theologians of the Middle Ages reduced the variety of moral experience to a mere repetition of the one duty to obey God, so here in the system of Hobbes in all our duties we have really and essentially one simple obligation, to obey the will of our political sovereign. The analogy between the two positions is for the most part close and exact; but there is one important point of divergence, for to the mind of Thomas Hobbes the one duty we have was not really a duty at all. It was not a command of any moral law, but a dictum of plain common sense, and to disobey was not really wrong but absurd.

Now in all this there were three main positions open to criticism by anyone who believed in the authenticity of moral experience.

In the first place, the doctrine of psychological egoism offered an obvious target for attack, because on the face of it moral experience does seem to presuppose that men can be moved to action by something other than self-centred desires. Secondly, the critic might also be concerned to insist that to the ordinary moral agent moral distinctions are not completely arbitrary and non-rational, depending either on the will of God or on that of a political sovereign. He might well be concerned to maintain, on the contrary, that the moral agent does himself appreciate the rightness of certain actions and the wrongness of others. And thirdly, although Hobbes did leave room in his system for a categorical imperative, it is really only the appearance of morality that he allows, for the imperative he admits does not command something despite our desires, but relates itself instead to one particular desire which all men have in common and the means to which is so obvious that it cannot reasonably be the subject either of discussion or of doubt; and this subversion of morality provides the moralist with a more general, and perhaps more fundamental, line of attack.

In English ethics, however, it was along the first two lines that the reaction proceeded. On the one hand, the sentimental school set themselves to show by an examination of human nature that the doctrine of psychological egoism was quite untenable; while, on the other hand, the intellectual school maintained at some length that moral distinctions are not determined by an arbitrary will, but that reason itself is able to distinguish between certain things as right and others as wrong. Along these two lines almost exclusively the English reaction proceeded; and it was not until Kant that the third position was set aside. For although, on the face of it, the natural law of Hobbes resembles the categorical rather than the hypothetical imperative of Kant, it is actually the latter which shares with it an essential reference to desire.

The first exponent of the sentimental school was Anthony Ashley Cooper, Earl of Shaftesbury, whose *Enquiry Concerning Virtue* was first published at the very end of the seventeenth century, was re-issued on various occasions, and was translated into German in 1768.

At an early stage in the *Enquiry* Shaftesbury set aside the doctrine of psychological egoism which Hobbes had enunciated and the state of nature he had bluntly described. Instead of holding that the only motive to action is a self-centred desire he insisted that there are no fewer than three different kinds of affection which may lead to action.[9] There are, first of all, what Shaftesbury called the natural affections, by which he meant those affections which aim directly at public good. Then there are the self-affections the object of which is private good. In the last place there are unnatural affections which tend neither to public nor to private good, but are, it would seem, perversions of human nature of one kind or another. And if this division represents a tolerably adequate analysis it means that a quite fundamental position in Hobbes has gone by the board.

Further, and in accordance with this sounder psychological doctrine, Shaftesbury rejects the idea of a state of nature in which the life of man is "solitary, poore, nasty, brutish and short"; and in its place he puts the idea of a system or of a whole consisting of parts. This conception he regards as applicable to a much wider field than that of human and moral relationships. It is applicable even to the insensible world, and there it means that although by a process of abstraction a part may be described as good if it fulfils the end of its nature, yet, strictly speaking, no part can be really good except in so far as it promotes the end of

[9] *Enquiry*, bk. ii, pt. i, sect. iii.

the whole to which it belongs. Similarly, in the sensible world a part can be accurately regarded as good on one condition only, not just if it happens to promote the good of the whole system or species, but that it is moved by an affection which normally does promote the good of the whole. Thus, even if a part is on a particular occasion moved by an affection which on this occasion does in fact promote the good of the whole, yet if this promotion is accidental and if as a rule the affection in question has a contrary effect, then the part is not properly judged good at all.

This is quite a reasonable point for Shaftesbury to have made. In the case of insensible creatures we can only judge them good or bad according to their actual movements and effects, for there is no other criterion. But sensible creatures have a character of their own, the character of the affections by which they are moved, which may on occasion be belied by the quality of their actions and their effects. A savage beast, for example, may act in anything but a savage manner, not through any change in its natural temper, but simply through fear of its keeper; and in that case the beast is just as savage as before. In such cases, Shaftesbury held, where character and actions may fall apart, it is the tendency of its affections which determines the goodness or badness of the creature, and not the nature of its accidental results.

This did not mean that a sensible creature could be judged good only when moved by affections which aimed directly at the good of the whole. It was not the object of the affection but it's customary effect upon the whole which provided the criterion of goodness; and when Shaftesbury came to speak of rational beings he freely allowed that the self-affections in a certain degree were necessary to promote the good of the whole and that public affections might be either too strong or too weak ordinarily to promote that good.

Yet Shaftesbury did not just say that rational beings were good if moved by affections which usually promoted the good of the whole or species, in this case public good. The nature of men was more complicated than that of other sensible beings. Not only were they moved by affections, but they were capable of making these affections objects and of experiencing an affection for an affection. Consequently, in order that a man should be good (or virtuous, as this human goodness was called), it was necessary not only that he should be moved by an affection ordinarily working in the public interest, but also that he should be aware of that and be moved by a sense of the worthiness of such conduct.[10] Indeed Shaftesbury was almost inclined to say that virtue was at its highest when there was very little else moving in that direction except the "affection for an affection"; but his final verdict was that in such cases, where virtue is greatly assailed and yet prevails, the virtue is not really any greater but is certainly more easily discerned.

Now whatever advantages this theory has over the system of Hobbes it is certainly not so simple and straightforward; and indeed it appears to contain an element of ambiguity. The criterion of goodness in man seems to be a double one. In order that an action should be virtuous it must proceed from an affection which ordinarily promotes the public interest, and there must be a consciousness of the affection as doing so. Besides that, however, there must be an *affection* for the affection, a sense of its worth and nobility. Yet it is possible to imagine a man acting from an affection for which he has an affection and which he regards as noble, but an affection which normally has an *adverse* effect on the public good. In such a case it would seem that so far as he is acting from a sense of worth his action is virtuous, and so far as he is acting from an affection which normally hinders the public good it is vicious. It cannot, however, be both, and Shaftesbury can fairly be asked to choose between his two standards. And in fact he made an attempt to do so. He asserted that a mistake in right, that is, a wrong sense of worth, "must of necessity be the Cause of vitious Action, in every intelligent or rational being".[11] Yet he was not altogether happy with this solution, and was quick to add that it must be a gross mistake of this kind if vice is to be produced in the manner indicated; the mistake, for example, of regarding reverence for monkeys and cats as far nobler than mere filial love. In lesser matters, it would seem, the sense of worth determined what was virtuous notwithstanding an adverse effect on public good.

This, of course, was unsatisfactory, and Shaftesbury's theory contained the seed of ethical dissension. At first, however, this seed remained inactive. For there was a plant of somewhat wilder growth which found a place in Shaftesbury's thought in this way.

According to Hobbes every action proceeded from a self-centred desire, and was therefore immediately justifiable to the agent. Shaftesbury, on the other hand, was saying something

[10] *Enquiry*, bk. i, pt. ii, sect. iii.   [11] *Ibid.*, bk. i, pt. ii, sect. iii.

else. As we have seen, what precisely he was saying is not perfectly clear. It may have been, You ought to act with a regard to the public interest, or it may have been, You ought to act in such a way that your action will commend itself to your sense of worth; but, in either case, the question "Why?" was almost bound to arise, a question with which Hobbes had no need to concern himself. For Shaftesbury, however, it was not an easy question, and in trying to answer it he proceeded to a lengthy and detailed argument the aim of which was to prove that in doing only what was in the public interest a man was promoting also his own interest.[12]

The implication was that if this elaborate proof failed to convince, Shaftesbury's imperatives were deprived of their persuasiveness. For this section of his inquiry sought to discover, not the *de facto* effects of virtue, but a convincing reason for practising it. In other words, Shaftesbury has reverted to something which closely resembles the psychological egoism of Hobbes. He does not indeed hold that every desire is self-centred, nor does he try to reduce all apparently benevolent desires to self-regarding ones; but he does imply that although men have public affections there is no convincing reason for giving rein to them or for moderating self-affection unless it can be shown that such a policy is in a man's own interest.

This point was taken up by Francis Hutcheson, who was Professor of Moral Philosophy at Glasgow from 1729 until 1746.

Hutcheson agreed with much of what Shaftesbury had said. He agreed, for example, that Hobbes was quite wrong in attempting to reduce all principles of action to self-regarding desires, and that on the contrary men were frequently moved by public affections. Further, he was in complete sympathy with Shaftesbury in his belief in the existence of a moral sense whereby men were able to review the desires by which they were moved, approving of some and disapproving of others. He shared also the view that by this "superior sense", which he called a moral one, "we perceive Pleasure in the Contemplation of virtuous actions in others, and are determin'd to love the Agent (and much more do we perceive Pleasure in being conscious of having done such Actions our selves) without any view of further natural Advantage from them".[13]

So far Hutcheson was at one with Shaftesbury; but he went on to insist upon two points with one of which Shaftesbury would

[12] *Enquiry*, bk. ii, pt. i, sect. i.   [13] *Inquiry*, Introduction.

have been loath to disagree, while to the second he would have been able to give his assent only by modifying the intention of his long argument to the effect that public and private interest coincide.

In the first place, Hutcheson argued that the sense of moral worth is not at all a sense of prospective natural advantage. For one thing, moral goodness and natural good are easily distinguished. The former attaches to actions, while the latter belongs to objects which excite pleasure; and, whereas we may well envy the man who is in secure possession of many natural goods, we love him whose wealth is measured in terms of moral quality and character. Moreover, the *senses* of the two things can also be seen to fall apart. If it were not so, how, for example, could we approve of the good actions of long ago which could not possibly affect our private interest one way or the other? How also could we approve of the good actions of others since *ex hypothesi* they are to their advantage and not ours? Certainly, when I am considering a particular course of action which commends itself to my sense of mortal worth, I may persuade myself to pursue some other course on the ground that it, rather than the other, is to my own interest. But, in such a case, I have not decided that the second action is morally better than the first. I have simply persuaded myself to perform it whether it is so or not. As Hutcheson put it, "this moral Sense has this in common with our other Senses, that however our Desire of Virtue may be counter-ballanc'd by Interest, our Sentiment or Perception of its Beauty cannot".[14] Consequently, Hutcheson declared, a sense of moral worth is essentially distinct from a prospect of advantage.

With this argument and proof Shaftesbury would doubtless have agreed; but he could not so easily have accepted the second point which Hutcheson proceeded to make, namely, that our motive in performing a truly virtuous action is never a desire for the pleasure we shall have in knowing that we have done it, nor is it any other self-regarding affection.[15] The true spring of really virtuous action is, he maintained, "some Determination of our Nature to study the Good of others".[16] It is, he held, "some Instinct, antecedent to all Reason from Interest, which influences us to the Love of others; even as the moral Sense determines us to approve the Actions which flow from this Love in our selves or others".[17] "This disinterested affection", he

---

[14] *Inquiry*, sect. i, para. v.
[15] *Ibid.*, Introduction and sect. ii *passim*.
[16] *Ibid.*, sect. ii, para. ix.
[17] *Ibid.*, sect. ii, para. ix.

added, "may appear strange to Men impress'd with Notions of Self-Love as the sole Motive of Action, from the Pulpit, the Schools, the Systems, and Conversations regulated by them"; but there it is, and if men would only examine the most simple instances they would no longer doubt of its existence.

With much of this Shaftesbury would have sympathised. Indeed the central point is a reaffirmation of his own doctrine that there are public affections. It conflicts, however, with the intention of his proof that public and private interest coincide, for the importance of that proof lies in the fact that for Shaftesbury it supplies the one convincing reason there is for practising virtue. If this does not mean that Shaftesbury has abandoned his earlier belief in public affections and reverted to the system of Hobbes, it does at least imply that alongside every public affection there is a principle of self-love (whether it be the "moral" sense or some more plainly self-regarding affection[18]) which must be aroused before the public affection can issue in action. Yet, against even this, Hutcheson was anxious to insist that since human nature is as he and Shaftesbury had described it in opposition to Hobbes, a sufficient reason for performing an action is that it has in view the interest of others.

Indeed Hutcheson was prepared to restrict the use of the word "virtuous" to such intentionally benevolent action. "If we examine", he said, "all the Actions which are counted amiable any where, and enquire into the Grounds upon which they are approv'd, we shall find, that in the Opinion of the Person who approves them, they always appear as Benevolent, or flowing from Love of others."[19]

There are two points here. The first, with which Shaftesbury agreed, is that it is the intention and not the actual outcome which determines the morality of an action. Thus Hutcheson is to be found declaring that "an unsuccessful attempt of Kindness, or of promoting publick Good, shall appear as amiable as the most successful, if it flow'd from as strong Benevolence".[20] The second point is that innocent examples of Self-Love in action, which are in fact necessary for the good of the whole, were regarded by Hutcheson as morally indifferent. They could be virtuous only if there was also an "Intention to concur with that Constitution

<hr />

[18] If moral sense (for example, as a principle of self-respect), then Hutcheson's criticism that the moral sense and a prospect of advantage are distinct is relevant. If self-love, then his assertion that virtue proceeds from a non-self-regarding determination of our nature has considerable force.
[19] *Inquiry*, sect. iii, para. i.   [20] *Ibid.*, sect. iii, para. i.

which tends to the Good of the Whole ", or a "direct View" on
the part of the agent "of making himself more capable of serving
God, or doing good to Mankind ". [21] Shaftesbury, on the other
hand, did not speak with a single voice on this matter. Where he
was thinking of the moral sense as a sense of worth in actions, he
spoke as if private affections could be virtuous without the presence of an intention having respect to the good of the whole;
whereas, where he regarded the moral sense as a sense of what is
and what is not in the public interest, he easily slipped into a position similar to that which has just been set forth in Hutcheson's
name, for there the moral sense itself provided the consciousness
of public good.

On this subject of the criterion of virtue, as on the egoistical
issue with Hobbes, Hutcheson spoke more clearly and more
consistently than Shaftesbury. Like the latter he recognised a
sense by which we perceive an immediate goodness [22] or beauty
in actions, and he held fast to it, refusing for the most part to
confound it with a sense of what is and what is not in the
public interest. He inquired into the ground of this immediate
approval, raising the question, in effect, what quality an action
must have in order that the moral sense should approve of it as
good, and he came to the conclusion that the one qualification
required is benevolence.

So far, indeed, Hutcheson held consistently to the single
principle that the morality of an action is determined by the
quality of the affection or motive leading the agent to act.
When, however, he passed from the consideration of moral
actions in general to a discrimination on moral grounds between
actions all of which are virtuous, he began to use expressions
which suggest a somewhat different moral principle.

Here are his own words on the matter. "In comparing the
moral Qualitys of Actions, in order to regulate our Election
among various Actions propos'd, or to find which of them has
the greatest moral Excellency, we are led by our moral Sense of
Virtue to judge thus; that in equal Degrees of Happiness,
expected to proceed from the Action, the Virtue is in proportion
to the Number of Persons to whom the Happiness shall extend

[21] *Inquiry*, sect. iii, para. v.

This means that, whereas Shaftesbury put a principle of self-love alongside
every public affection in order that there should be action at all, Hutcheson put
a principle of public affection alongside every private affection in order that
there should be virtue in these parts.

[22] *Ibid.*, Introduction.

(and here the dignity, or moral Importance of Persons, may compensate Numbers); and in equal Numbers, the Virtue is as the Quantity of the Happiness, or natural Good; or that the Virtue is in a compound Ratio of the Quantity of Good, and Number of Enjoyers."[23] That is to say, he continued, "that Action is best, which procures the greatest Happiness for the greatest Numbers".[24]

Now the question raised by such a statement is this. Can it be interpreted in terms only of the principle that it is the quality of the motive which determines the morality of the action, or must it be regarded as introducing a second criterion of virtue? On the face of it, Hutcheson does appear to have passed from the quality of the motive to the social effect of the action, and he has even anticipated the very formula of utilitarianism. Is it not possible, however, that the reality of the matter belies the appearance, and that in this section of his argument, as in the rest of it, Hutcheson has faithfully confined himself to the principle of the sentimental school? There is one fact about Hutcheson's discussion which would suggest an affirmative answer to this question, the fact, namely, that time and again he spoke, not of the actual social effects of an action, but of those expected or intended. From the fact that Hutcheson did draw this distinction it may well be argued that to his mind, although one affection could be distinguished from another without reference to its content or object—love and hate, for example, are different in themselves—yet the quality of either affection, and therefore its moral worth, could not be completely determined without such reference. This means that when Hutcheson speaks of the virtue being greater the greater the numbers intended to be affected and the greater the happiness expected to be produced, he has not gone over to the utilitarian principle but has regard to numbers and the amount of happiness because these are indications of the purity of the benevolent affection from which the action proceeds. Thus, filial affection, which by the nature of the case can have it in view to affect only a small number of people, may therefore, and with some justice, be regarded as benevolence restricted and restrained, that is to say, as impure benevolence.

"The moral Beauty, or Deformity of Actions", Hutcheson declared, "is not alter'd by the moral Qualitys of the Objects, any further than the Qualitys of the Objects increase or

---

[23] *Inquiry*, sect. iii, para. viii.   [24] *Ibid.*, sect. iii, para. viii.

diminish the Benevolence of the Action.''[25] What he meant was that the morality of an action is not altered by the moral character of the people affected by it except in so far as that may indicate a special degree of benevolence. Benevolence toward bad characters may be more virtuous than benevolence toward good, "since it argues such a strong Degree of Benevolence as can surmount the greatest Obstacle, the moral Evil in the Object".[26] Moreoever, if Hutcheson, true to the sentimental principle, was thinking along these lines in connection with the moral character of the people affected, it may well be held that he was thinking along the same lines in connection with their numbers and the amount of happiness they were expected to enjoy.

There is, however, one admission in his argument which seems to point in a different direction. It is the allowance that when the principle of "the greatest happiness of the greatest number" is being applied, "the Dignity, or moral Importance of Persons, may compensate Numbers". At first glance this means that a restricted benevolence is regarded as more virtuous than something purer and more universal. But, when the point is examined, it is found that by the "dignity and moral importance of persons" Hutcheson intended to denote those people who have in a special degree the ability and the will to promote the happiness of all, and he was therefore simply allowing that in more humble people a pure benevolence, in order not to be dissipated, may choose on certain occasions to study the special interests of a special few so that the good of the whole may be the more advanced. "All strict Attachments to Partys", he said, "Sects, Factions, have but an imperfect Species of Beauty, unless when the Good of the Whole requires a stricter Attachment to a Part, as in natural Affection, and virtuous Friendships; or when some Parts are so eminently useful to the Whole, that even universal Benevolence would determine us with special Care and Affection to study their interests."[27] In other words, a pure benevolence need not be short-sighted.

Now in all this there are really three main questions at issue: (i) What place has self-love in the moral life? (ii) What is the criterion of moral action? and (iii) If the criterion is to be found in the verdict of a moral sense, what quality or qualities must an

---

[25] *Inquiry*, sect. iii, para. vii.   [26] *Ibid.*, sect. iii, para. vii.
[27] *Ibid.*, sect. iii, para. x.

action or affection have in order to commend itself to this moral sense?

On the first of these questions, the starting-point was the psychological egoism of Thomas Hobbes. That was one possible answer to the question, namely, that self-love is the whole of the moral life, that there is no principle of action other than that, and that in spite of appearances there is no such thing as altruism.

This answer, we have seen, did not satisfy Shaftesbury, who preferred to admit the existence of public affections, desires which were not self-centred but had regard rather to the interests of others. This doctrine Shaftesbury consistently held so long as he was investigating the nature of virtue; but this investigation was only one part of his total inquiry, and no more important in his eyes than the other part which propounded the question, What obligation is there to virtue, what reason to embrace it? His answer on this point proceeded entirely in terms of self-interest by proving the coincidence of public and private good. In other words, as Hutcheson paraphrased it, "that which excites us to these Actions which we call Virtuous is an Intention to obtain the sensible Pleasure" which arises from the gratification of our moral sense.[28] If, however, this is what Shaftesbury intended to defend, or if it is the position towards which he was at least working, then his teaching is simply a reversion to the theory of Hobbes without the incredible kind of natural state which the latter depicted. According to this revision of the *Leviathan*, the natural state is a social one, because men are naturally determined to study the interests of others,[29] and yet in every action, even in the most benevolent of actions, the agent's reason for doing it is to have the pleasure of having done it. There is, that is to say, a self-regarding element in every public affection. And that is the second answer to the first main question.

It is not, however, an entirely satisfactory answer, because for one thing a desire which by means of benevolence aims at an effect on the agent's mind is just as self-regarding as one which by similar means aims at some effect on his fortune. Moreover, although it is certainly possible to act in an altruistic fashion while having in view one's own interest, such action is essentially parasitical and is insufficient of itself to support a social order of

[28] Cf. Hutcheson, *Inquiry*, Introduction.
[29] Cf. Shaftesbury, *Enquiry*, bk. ii, pt. i, sect. i.

things. On the contrary, the latter presupposes as its real foundation genuinely benevolent conduct. Finally, it may be argued that the possibility of pleasure on the occasion of a virtuous action presupposes an independent reason for performing the action. And so it does. Yet up to a point Shaftesbury may have been right. If it is possible, as presumably it is, to perform a certain action to avoid the pain of an evil conscience —"I should have a bad conscience over it," we hear it said— then surely it is possible to perform the action to enjoy the positive pleasure involved. But once again this way of acting is parasitical and presupposes the possibility of performing the action from an entirely different motive. If an agent persistently performs virtuous actions with a view to the pleasure he derives from them, he must ultimately act entirely for the pleasure, so altering the nature of the act and destroying the foundation of the pleasure, namely, the independent recognition of a way of acting as virtuous. The truth is that we cannot hold apart, as Shaftesbury tried to do, the nature of an act and the reason we have for doing it. [30]

It seems then that Shaftesbury can offer us no final resting-place in this matter. We must either return to the psychological egoism of Hobbes, or else advance to some more altruistic position such as that of Hutcheson.

The best known advance, however, is that associated with the name of Joseph Butler, the greatest name, according to Newman, in the Anglican Church. Butler, who was Bishop of Bristol from 1738 to 1750, and of Durham thereafter for the last two years of his life, was a typical member of the sentimental school. "We have a capacity", he said, "of reflecting upon actions and characters, and making them an object to our thought. . . . acting, conduct, behaviour, abstracted from all regard to what is, in fact and event, the consequence of it, is itself the natural object of the moral discernment, as speculative truth and falsehood is of speculative reason. Intention of such and such consequences, indeed, is always included; for it is part of the action itself: but though the intended good or bad consequences do not follow, we have exactly the same sense of the action as if they did." [31] Thus Butler gave expression to the central tenet of sentimentalism; and the distinctive characteristic of

[30] " We have consider'd *what* Virtue *is*, and to whom the Character belongs. It remains to inquire *What Obligation* there is *to* Virtue; or *what Reason* to embrace it." *Enquiry*, bk. ii, pt. i, sect. i.

[31] *Dissertation ii.*

his position was the fullness with which he described human nature as a system, a hierarchy of practical principles, consisting of particular affections and passions overruled by benevolence and self-love, and these themselves governed by conscience.

So far indeed Butler's system was clear and consistent; but his views on the place of self-love in the moral life were not without ambiguity. On the one hand, he did not make Shaftesbury's mistake of separating the question of the nature of virtue and that of the obligation or reason to embrace it, and so he did not allow that the answer to the latter question must proceed entirely in terms of self-interest. "Your obligation to obey this law [of conscience]", he said, "is its being the law of your nature. That your conscience approves of and attests to such a course of action, is itself alone an obligation. Conscience does not only offer itself to shew us the way we should walk in, but it likewise carries its own authority with it, that it is our natural guide." [32] All this was indeed involved in Butler's view of human nature as a system or hierarchy of practical principles which differed not only in quality but also in authority. It is indeed the plain implication of all that went before. Yet it was not Butler's last word on the subject.

On the contrary, one of his best known ethical affirmations was this. "Let it be allowed," he said, "though virtue or moral rectitude does indeed consist in affection to and pursuit of what is right and good, as such; yet, that when we sit down in a cool hour, we can neither justify to ourselves this or any other pursuit, till we are convinced that it will be for our happiness, or at least not contrary to it." [33] And that of course raises the question at once of Butler's consistency. In the first analysis, however, it can hardly be supposed that Butler was simply contradicting his earlier position, for his statement of that position was particularly clear and definite. There is therefore an initial presumption in favour of any hypothesis which can reconcile his later regard for happiness with his earlier system.

Indeed, Butler is not alone in presenting his readers with this problem of interpretation, for there is a remarkable similarity between the course of his own argument and that of Hutcheson's. Both were anxious to rebut Hobbes, and to do so in a more self-consistent manner than Shaftesbury had done. Both made the attempt in terms of other than self-regarding affections; and both were concerned to point out that not only was virtue of

<hr />

[32] *Sermon iii.*   [33] *Sermon xi.*

that nature, but also there was an obligation to practise it apart altogether from self-interest. Yet in the end both found themselves under the necessity of making some concession to the principle of self-love.

Butler's concession has already been quoted, and Hutcheson's was in these terms. "The principal Business", he said, "of the moral Philosopher is to shew, from solid Reasons, 'That universal Benevolence tends to the Happiness of the Benevolent . . .' that so no apparent Views of Interest may counteract this natural Inclination; but not to attempt proving 'That Prospects of our own Advantage of any kind, can raise in us real Love to others'. Let the Obstacles from Self-Love be only remov'd, and Nature it self will incline us to Benevolence."[34]

This is a carefully guarded statement, and Hutcheson does not consider himself to be contradicting his earlier discussion. He is himself convinced, and thinks it a principal task of moral philosophy to prove, that the virtuous life is the most happy one; but that conviction has nothing to do either with the essential nature of virtue or with the obligation to practise it. If indeed the conviction is of more than merely academic interest its sole practical function is the negative one of allaying strong selfish passions which would interfere with the easy exercise of virtue. Such a concession to self-interest appears a perfectly consistent one.

Now Butler also believes that the virtuous life is the truly happy one, and he gives that conviction the same practical relevance as Hutcheson did. In fact the eleventh *Sermon* explicitly deals with a situation in which virtue has gone out of favour because men are so taken up with their own self-interest, and it deals with that situation in the very manner in which we should have expected Hutcheson to deal with it, by seeking to show "that there is no peculiar rivalship or competition between self-love and benevolence . . . and that in one respect benevolence contributes more to private interest, i.e. enjoyment or satisfaction, than any other of the particular common affections, as it is in a degree its own gratification".[35] So far Butler and Hutcheson are in agreement; and the point which they both make affords a third answer to our question, namely, that although self-love may often seem a rival to virtue, it is in fact no such thing, but either has no connection with virtue (Hutcheson) or plays a subordinate part in virtue, supplying a mere portion of its content (Butler).

[34] *Inquiry*, sect. vii, para. ii.   [35] *Sermon xi.*

Yet, it must be admitted, in setting out this point Butler made statements which seem to go considerably further. Allowing the nature of, and the obligation to, Virtue to be as he had described them, he yet could not justify to himself "in a cool hour" virtuous or any other conduct unless he could see that it was for his own happiness, "or at least not contrary to it". He even declared that "every particular affection, benevolence among the rest, is subservient to self-love by being the instrument of private enjoyment".[36]

That is a serious admission. Yet, if we are to trust Butler's language, he was while making it both fully conscious of his earlier statements and unaware of any inconsistency. To his mind, they can all stand together; and that fact presents a problem of interpretation. Yet, his affirmations on this matter are hardly full enough to justify any confident reconstruction of his intention. Moreover, the question suggests itself what kind of motive this self-love is, if for the moment it may be called a motive at all. For, in the first place, it arises, not when we are faced by the possibility of acting, but rather when we sit down in a cool hour to reflect; and, secondly, it can favour action, not always because there is any necessary connection between it and the action in question, but sometimes on the negative ground that they are not contrary.[37] With these peculiarities in mind, one is driven to suppose that what Butler had in view was not a motive at all, able to favour one action rather than another, but something much more indeterminate, like a feeling of incompleteness, for example, or a vague desire to move forward to some other state of oneself, the condition of action in general perhaps, able merely to decide between action on the one hand and mere passivity on the other, but nothing so determinate as a motive which would decide between one possible course of conduct and another.

The evidence, however, is too scanty to permit of any positive statement of Butler's meaning; and the most that can be fairly said is that perhaps here we have in embryonic form a fourth answer to our question.

The second main question was a much simpler one. It was, What is the criterion of moral action? And to this the answer of the sentimental school was for the most part unequivocal. The criterion, it said, is the verdict of the moral sense or conscience. Now one might well expect to find differences of

[36] *Sermon xi.*   [37] Cf. Butler, *Sermon xi.*

opinion, even within the school, if one were to press the question somewhat further and inquire regarding the exact nature of this sense. For the word is not used with precisely the same meaning as when we speak of the five bodily senses; and in fact variations are to be found on this point as we pass from one author to another. To Shaftesbury, for example, the moral sense was essentially an affection for an affection; yet even for him it was more than that, it was also a sense of worth. Hutcheson, in his turn, used the phrase a "Sentiment of Action";[38] and Butler spoke of "the principle of reflection", the "reflex approbation or disapprobation",[39] "a moral faculty, whether called conscience, moral reason, moral sense, or divine reason; whether considered as a sentiment of the understanding, or as a perception of the heart; or, which seems the truth, as including both".[40]

There are not a few variations possible in the exact determination of the nature of conscience or the moral sense. Yet, although the moral sense may certainly be regarded either as in some way a sense, or as an emotion, or as some combination of these, it is more to the point in the present connection to note that underlying these differences there is a more fundamental ethical doctrine which the authors have in common. It is the doctrine that the fundamental moral judgment is the reflective or self-conscious one which deals with agents and their affections or motives.

There are moral judgments of other kinds, judgments about ends, about consequences, and about acts; and these, along with judgments which deal with motives, are important elements, on the intellectual side, of moral experience. The characteristic peculiar to the sentimental school is that of these different moral judgments it chooses the reflective or self-conscious judgment as basic, or at least as no less fundamental than the others.[41]

There now remains the third question, What quality must an action or affection have in order to commend itself to the moral sense? Now the discussion of the positions occupied by Shaftesbury and Hutcheson revealed two different answers to this question. On the one hand, Shaftesbury tended to regard

[38] *Inquiry*, sect. i, para. ii.
[39] *Preface to Sermons*.
[40] *Dissertation ii.*
[41] Butler, indeed, in the first paragraph of the *Preface*, speaks as if these and one other type were equally basic; but he does not develop this idea.

as good those affections from which proceeded actions having a beneficial effect on society as a whole; whereas, on the other hand, Hutcheson's teaching was that affections are morally better the more purely benevolent they are.

Indeed, there are in principle three distinct opinions on this matter. In the first place, it may be held that a motive is good or bad according to the nature of the actual effects upon society of the action to which it leads. Whether this be a true or a false account of the matter is not at the moment in question. What is to be noted is quite a different point, namely, that in either case this position is not in harmony with the essential doctrine of sentimentalism. For one of its implications is that the reflective type of moral judgment is subordinate to an unreflective type which deals, not with motives, but with the consequences of acts. In other words, the decisive quality is a quality of the actual results and not of the affection which has some part in producing them.

In the second place, in order to avoid this difficulty, it might be argued that the quality upon which the goodness or badness of the motive depends is the quality, not of the actual results, but of the probable results. In so far, however, as there is a divergence between actual and probable results, it is clear that the quality of the latter is not the quality of any existing thing, and is certainly no more the quality of the motive than it is of the actual consequences. This theory too is no more sentimentalism than was its predecessor.

The third possibility is that the quality of the motive is determined by the intention of the agent, that is to say, neither by the actual, nor by the probable, results as such, but by those which the agent intends. Now it is clear that the character of a man's intention has a much closer connection with the quality of his motive than has the character of the actual results he brings about or the character of the probable results. Indeed, the motive, if we can separate it at all from the act which it suggests, has no moral quality apart from that act. Love and hate, for example, must be regarded as morally neutral until we are told something of the object which is loved or hated. A motive as a factor in morality is a determination of our nature to do acts of a certain kind, and in this way benevolence is a determination to do good to others. Moreover, the purity of the benevolence depends on those towards whom we are moved to act benevolently. If they are confined within a narrow circle of kinship, then Hutcheson would say that the benevolence is less pure, has less moral value, than otherwise would be the case. And this is good sentimentalism.

Yet the position is not without its difficulties. For if the reflective type of moral judgment is to avoid the suspicion of involving a subjective and relative preference for one type of conduct rather than another, a preference, that is to say, which may vary from one individual to the next, then it must be a judgment made on some principle, and an important task of ethics will be to discover that principle. Hutcheson, as we have seen, finds it in benevolence, and certainly the principle of benevolence meets the needs of theory. But it does not accord well with the facts of the case. If at the same time we are to hold (i) that the reflective type of moral judgment is the fundamental type, and (ii) that a motive can be judged morally good only in so far as it is benevolent, then benevolence is the whole of morality; and that is simply contrary to fact.

On examination, then, eighteenth-century ethical sentimentalism has been found wanting. The question still remains, however, whether the fault lies with the general and essential approach of sentimentalism or merely with the particular theories formulated at that time; but the answer to that question must be left to emerge at a later stage in the discussion.

CHAPTER II

THE ETHICS OF THE EIGHTEENTH CENTURY

(B) INTELLECTUALISM

SENTIMENTALISM WAS A reaction against the theory of Thomas Hobbes which sought to establish itself by attacking the very foundation of Hobbism and holding instead that man's affections are not at all entirely self-regarding. Hobbes, however, offered a target to independent thought, not only in the foundation of his system, but also in its implications, and especially in one particular implication. He had held that all man's actions and affections are selfishly conceived, and it followed from that that in the system of Hobbes there was no place at all for a law which men must obey whether they wanted to or not. Man, as Hobbes described him, was unable to recognise a law as law, that is, as binding upon himself, unless it were artificially buttressed by rewards and punishments; and from that position it was an easy step to suppose that the law itself was of artificial origin, for the obligatoriness of the law and the law itself are barely separable, and if the one depends upon the arbitrary fiat of someone's will it is difficult to avoid the conclusion that the other does so as well. Hobbes was therefore compelled to insist that moral distinctions arise through the command of some legislator, and that apart from that command they are nothing. But it was possible to argue that reason recognises these distinctions independently of any commandment; and it was this line which the ethical school of intellectualism followed.

One of the first in the field was Ralph Cudworth whose work properly belongs to the seventeenth century, since he died in 1688, but his treatise was not published till long after his death, in the year 1731. Moreover, his general approach to the subject was in complete harmony with the position of the eighteenth-century intellectualists, and the title of his book admirably suggests the main tenet of the school, *Eternal and Immutable Morality*.

Cudworth's principal point was that moral distinctions are not artificial and arbitrary, that, on the contrary, as his title indicates, they are eternal and immutable, belonging to the very nature of things. Honesty and rightness, for example, go as surely and as necessarily together as triangularity is conjoined with the property of having the three angles equal to two right angles. Honesty, that is to say, is right independently of any commandment and all legislators. There are, of course, certain things, as Cudworth was quite prepared to admit, which are in themselves not right, which are morally neutral, and which are yet made right by the express commandment of someone having legislative authority. But, Cudworth insisted, two things must be noticed. In the first place, such artificial duties presuppose as their foundation an obligation which is naturally an obligation and is not just made so by an act of someone's will, namely, the obligation to obey the legislative authority in question. But more than that, in the second place, if we are to speak quite accurately, we must allow that in such cases these indifferent acts have not really been made right, that what is right is the obedience, and not the performance of this particular action which has been commanded.[1]

Now the ostensible ground of Cudworth's belief that moral distinctions are natural is the proposition that will can be the efficient cause but not the formal cause of something other than itself.[2] Whether that be true or not, it is clear that it belongs to ontology rather than ethics; and the question arises as to what legitimate place such a proposition can have in ethical theory. In answer to that, it may reasonably be doubted whether it is sound procedure to ground a position in ethics upon a metaphysical theory which can only, by the nature of the case, be less confidently asserted. In this particular instance, the truth is that Cudworth has pitched his case higher than was required by ethical theory, and that in doing so he has gone beyond ethics altogether. Not content to hold simply that so far as our knowledge of them is concerned moral distinctions are quite independent of anyone's volition, he insisted that that is true so far as ultimate reality is concerned as well. He held, not only that *we* recognise honesty to be right and binding apart completely from its being commanded by some

---

[1] *Eternal and Immutable Morality*, bk. i, ch. ii, para. 5.
[2] *Ibid.*, bk. i, ch. ii, para. 1.

authority, but also that even God's will is determined by His
wisdom and intellect rather than vice versa.[3] In the present
connection, however, it is sufficient to note that the higher
position includes the lower, and that Cudworth did hold that
for us there is some necessary connection between honesty
and rightness, for example, independently of its being commanded. This necessary connection is for Cudworth exactly
comparable to that which we admittedly recognise between
triangularity and the property of having three angles equal to
two right angles; and this position is defensible even if Cudworth's views of God and the ultimate reality are regarded
as untenable. For the principal ethical point is this, that moral
distinctions are for us prior to, and independent of, arbitrary
will.

This point was strongly reaffirmed by Samuel Clarke in
his Boyle Lectures, published in 1706 under the title *A Discourse
on the Unchangeable Obligations of Natural Religion*. Towards
certain given persons and in a given set of circumstances, he
held, certain actions are clearly and naturally fitting, while
certain others are unfitting, some are right and others are
wrong. Between the character of any such action and its
rightness or wrongness there is a necessary, unalterable and
reasonable connection, comparable to the necessary connections of mathematics. Indeed, Clarke did not regard his mathematical instances as mere illustrations which in a general way
resembled his moral cases. Rather he thought of them as more
clearly understood examples of precisely the same principle.
Speaking of moral distinctions he declared, "For a Man
endued with Reason, to deny the Truth of these Things, is the
very same thing . . . as if a Man that understands Geometry
or Arithmetick, should deny the most obvious and known
Proportions of Lines or Numbers, and perversely contend that
the Whole is not equal to all its parts."[4]

The connection, then, is a natural and reasonable one, it is
perceived by the understanding, and the cause of bad conduct
in any particular case is either negligent misunderstanding or
absurd passions which overrule right reason.[5] In either case,
wrong-doing is practical absurdity and inconsistency. Moreover, if, as against all this, it is argued that people do sincerely
differ on moral matters, Clarke has two replies: the first, that

---

[3] *Eternal and Immutable Morality*, bk. i, ch. iii, paras. 4–7.   [4] *Discourse*, i, 1.
[5] *Ibid.*, i, 3.

such cases are not so frequent as may be supposed, and the second, that in any case they prove, not that there is no natural connection between certain kinds of action and rightness and between certain other kinds of action and wrongness, but that in some cases these two kinds of action may be exemplified in one and the same action. [6] Further, even if there were a whole nation entirely ignorant of moral distinctions, the position, Clarke holds, would still be unaffected. Ignorance of a truth does not prove that there is no truth there to be discovered. What would be a real embarrassment is a people accepting a quite contrary set of moral distinctions to that which we ourselves recognise; but Clarke does not suppose that there is or can be anyone who, understanding the terms, believes that dishonesty and injustice are right and their opposites wrong.

For Clarke, then, moral distinctions are natural and not artificial, discovered by the understanding and not imposed by arbitrary will. But if, as he supposes, there is a necessary connection between certain kinds of action and rightness, is there not some common quality of all these actions in virtue of which they are necessarily right? Here and there in the *Discourse*, no doubt, there are suggestions of an affirmative answer to this question, namely, that conduciveness to the public advantage is the sole criterion of rightness in actions; but when Clarke is given time to expound and expand his theory it quickly appears that this is not his considered view of the matter. For one thing, he recognises duties to God and duties to self which are not easily brought under such a rubric. In the second place, he explicitly rejects the idea. "Others have contended", he says, "that all Differences of Good and Evil, and all Obligations of Morality, ought to be founded originally upon Considerations of Publick Utility . . . But . . . what is for the Good of the whole Creation, in very many Cases, none but an infinite Understanding can possibly judge . . . But Truth and Right (whether Publick or Private) founded in the eternal and necessary Reason of Things, is what every Man can judge of, when laid before him." [7]

Now that is a most significant statement. In it Clarke admits that in the last analysis, that is, to the mind of God, all right

---

[6] He gives a non-moral example of this, but derives it from the realm of sense (Selby-Bigge, *British Moralists*, ii, p. 10). It is clear, however, that similar cases occur with the understanding, as when, for instance, there are differences of rational opinion regarding the answer to a conundrum.

[7] *Discourse*, i, 7.

conduct may be justifiable by reference to the good of the whole. But he also clearly insists that although moral distinctions are rational distinctions to us and not arbitrary ones, they cannot be justified to us in terms of public utility. In other words, he rejects the most likely common quality of all right actions, and in rejecting it he does not replace it by another. That is to say, so far as Clarke's theory goes, there is no one property which all right actions have and in virtue of which they are right. And that is intuitionism as well as intellectualism.

The fact is that as an ethical theory intellectualism is capable of being developed along two quite different lines. In the first place, it may insist that there is a reasonable and necessary connection between a certain kind of behaviour and the moral agent as such. This means that there is a law discoverable by reason independently of any consideration of practical situations, and it is a law which the agent is morally obliged to impose upon these situations as they occur. In the second place, however, intellectualism may hold, not that there is such an *a priori* law, but that reason can elicit from practical situations, as they turn up, a rule of conduct which is reasonable and not arbitrary, and which may yet vary with the character of the situation. In this case the necessary connection is not between a certain kind of behaviour and the moral agent as such, but is a reasonable connection between a certain kind of act and a certain set of circumstances with which a particular agent is faced. Further, it was this latter type of reasonable connection which Clarke had in mind when he said that "from the different relations of different Persons one to another, there necessarily arises a fitness or unfitness of certain manners of Behaviour of some persons towards others", and, *exempli gratia*, declared, "'tis without dispute more Fit and reasonable in itself, that I should preserve the Life of an innocent Man, that happens at any time to be in my Power, or deliver him from any imminent danger, tho' I have never made any promise so to do, than that I should suffer him to perish, or take away his Life, without any reason or provocation at all."[8]

In this sense, then, moral distinctions are reasonable; and because they are reasonable they are logically antecedent to

---

[8] *Discourse*, i, i.
Cf. " The Conformity of such Actions to Reason, or the Rectitude of them, is their Agreeableness to the Nature and Circumstances of the Agents and the Objects" (Balguy, *Foundation of Moral Goodness*, Selby-Bigge, ii, p. 75).

all positive commandment and to every promise of rewards
and punishments. Virtue is not just enlightened self-interest,
it is worthy to be chosen for its own sake, and if virtue and vice
were equally balanced in regard to their effects on the agent's
interest a man would be base indeed who would choose the
latter. Yet in fact and in this life, in spite of the reasonableness
of virtue, virtue is not self-sufficient, for whereas vice is often
profitable virtue frequently entails suffering, and sometimes
even death itself. Rewards and punishments, or rather the
prospect of them, is required as a support to virtue under
present conditions, and it is a moral and reasonable demand
of our nature that virtue should be rewarded and the balance
thus restored.

Such, then, is Clarke's ethical theory; and in its main pro-
visions it is closely followed by John Balguy, whose contribution to the discussion appeared in 1728 when the first part
of his *Foundation of Moral Goodness* was published. Indeed,
Balguy refers to the *Discourse* as "that excellent, that inestimable
Book, Dr. S. Clarke's Boyle's Lectures"; and, in fact, his own
chief merit derives, not from his exposition of the positive
theory, but from his careful comparison of it with the rival
position of sentimentalism.

Thus Balguy's contribution to this discussion can be conveniently considered under three heads, namely, first, negatively, the faults he has to find with sentimentalism; secondly,
and positively, the advantages which, on his view, lie with
intellectualism over sentimentalism; and thirdly, the place he
allows to affection and sentiment in the moral life.

(1) Now his first objection to sentimentalism is that it founds
the moral life upon something which is either a sentiment
or a sense, something which is merely *given* to us and which, so
far as we can see, might have been entirely different, or even
contrary, had the Maker of all things chosen differently. As it
happens we approve benevolent actions, but had we been
made differently we might equally well have approved selfish
actions. This means that on the sentimentalist theory there is
no necessary connection between the nature of an act and the
rightness or wrongness of the act. What renders an act right
or wrong is not its own character but its effect upon us, and it
is our contribution to that effect, the contribution of our make-
up, which is decisive. If we had been made differently we might
well have regarded as right the very actions we now regard as

wrong. And certainly, if this is what sentimentalism implies, it spells the end of an absolute moral standard; it is in fact ethical relativism.

Moreover, it can hardly be denied that Balguy's criticism carries weight against much of what was written by the sentimentalist school. Yet it is important for the present argument to delimit precisely the effect of this criticism. Eighteenth-century sentimentalism consisted essentially, or at least for the most part, of two propositions held in conjunction, namely, (i) that the fundamental moral judgments are those reflective or self-conscious moral judgments, the subjects of whose predicates are the *motives* of agents, and for that reason the theory merits the title of sentimentalism since a man's motives may be described as sentiments; and (ii) that these judgments are merely the report of the effect of these motives upon a sentiment or a sense, and for this too the theory merits the title of sentimentalism. [9] Between these two propositions there is, however, no necessary connection; and which of them is to be chiefly borne in mind depends on which affection is emphasised when we speak of an "affection for an affection".

Now it is clear that Balguy's criticisms hold against the second of these positions, but are irrelevant so far as the first of them is concerned. It may be, of course, that at the eighteenth-century stage of ethical discussion the second was the more important, although, as we have already seen, sentimentalism was, in Butler at least, on the verge of transcending that position. But, at any rate, the peculiar relevance of sentimentalism to modern ethical theory lies in the first of its two propositions, and that position has not so far been imperilled by Balguy's offensive.

Having delivered himself, however, of these preliminary shafts, our author proceeded to come to closer grips with his opponent. He picked on what appears to be an implication of sentimentalism, namely, that virtue is greater the stronger the benevolent affection and less the weaker it is; and he challenged both sides of this conclusion. Virtue, he said, may be great in spite of, perhaps even because of, a weakly benevolent affection; whereas there may be little or no virtue in the presence of much benevolence. Now there is something in what Balguy had to say, for, on the one hand, there is a

[9] Cf. p. 54 above.

sentimentalism which arises from very strong affection and which is yet morally misleading, while, on the other hand, a virtuous performance which triumphs over contrary natural predispositions is on that very account greatly to be admired. Yet in the latter case it may be held that there must be a motive strong enough to perform the act whatever that motive may be, and in the other that the motive in question may in reality be neither benevolent nor good. But, at any rate, Balguy has shown that the position is not so clear and simple as might at first be supposed.

(2) Further, behind this criticism there lurks another, that surely, contrary to the apparent implication of sentimentalism, the measure of a man's virtue is not his natural endowment. Virtue, Balguy would have said, is an achievement and not a gift; and this leads naturally to the enunciation of one of the advantages which he considered intellectualism to possess, namely, its consistency with the notion that virtue can be taught and acquired.

Another advantage which he claimed for his own theory was that it could allow duties towards the agent himself, which could yet hardly be classified as benevolent actions; and this indeed points to one of the weaknesses of eighteenth-century sentimentalism for that theory implied that benevolence is the whole of morality, an implication which is contrary to the facts.

(3) In spite of his objections, however, and his complete rejection of the rival theory, Balguy could not escape the question whether sentimentalism was a total error, whether it was not only false itself but also based on falsehood, whether there were no benevolent affections at all, and, if there were, what place, if any, they had in the moral life. In the same way, there was a question concerning the reality and the importance for morality of the "affection for an affection". In reply Balguy admitted the existence of these affections, but held that to found morality upon them is to find the foundation of moral goodness in the lower part of man's nature, and to subject reason, the higher part, to what is inferior. "I grant", he said, "the Reality of such Affections, and the Usefulness of them, in respect of human Nature, yet I can by no means look upon them as essential to Virtue; nor can I think that any Instinct has a Place in its Constitution. To speak properly, Reason was not given us to regulate natural Affection, but natural Affection

was given us to reinforce Reason, and make it more pre-valent."[10] These affections were at the most "Auxiliaries, aiding us in our Duty, and supporting and seconding our Reason and Reflection".[11]

Thus what Shaftesbury and his school regarded as the very foundation of morality was for Balguy simply a support to duty and virtue which was not at all essential to their nature and had no place in their "constitution". It was, that is to say, an external support which tended to move men on a line parallel to the path of duty but not coincident, not identical with it. Presumably this verdict was applicable both to affections and to Shaftesbury's "affection for an affection". If that is so, then Balguy did not question the supposition that reflective moral judgments are merely the reports of the effect upon our senti-ments of different kinds of action; and, in consequence, he simply dismissed those self-conscious moral judgments as in fact not moral judgments at all.

In 1758 there was published a book entitled *A Review of the Principal Questions in Morals*. Its author was Richard Price, and its title was well chosen, for in it Price did bring under review the main issues of the day in ethical theory. Traditionally, he has been classed as an intellectualist, along with Cudworth, Clarke and the others, but he did not blindly take over the tenets of his predecessors in the school and revealed instead a quite independent judgment, making a determined and solid effort to gather truth together from every direction.

He was in complete agreement, however, with the rejection by intellectualism of what we have called the second proposition of sentimentalism, the proposition, namely, that reflective moral judgments are simply reports of the effect of motives and affec-tions upon a sentiment or a sense. If these judgments were merely reports of such a kind, then, were our nature different from what it is, they might well have to affirm a quite different, or even contrary, connection, for example, that benevolent actions are vicious and not to be approved. But Price did not believe that these connections were just contingent connections of fact mediated by what happened to be our nature. He believed that moral judgments were not merely factual reports but represented insights or intuitions of the understanding and affirmed a quite necessary connection. A right act was not one

---

[10] *Foundation of Moral Goodness*, pt. i (Selby-Bigge, para. 554).
[11] *Ibid.*, pt. i (Selby-Bigge, para. 527).

which happened to commend itself to some sentiment or sense with which we happened to be endowed; it was rather an act which was necessarily fitting to the agent in certain circumstances and could be seen to be so by the understanding.

So far Price was in line perfectly with the earlier writers of his school; and in fact this harmony was even more extensive. For Price agreed with Balguy that although morality had thus its real foundation in reason, it had an external support in the instinctively benevolent nature with which men happened to be endowed, and in their instinctive sentiments which found pleasure in the consideration of their virtuous actions. This support, it must be emphasised, was external, it had no necessary connection with virtue, and unlike morality it derived, not from reason, but from the instinctive nature with which men were endowed. It was quite impossible to conceive of moral distinctions as contrary to what they were, but it was easy to imagine the instinctive nature of men as supplying to morality, not a help, but a hindrance.

At this stage, however, Price introduced a novel point. Besides this external aid, he said, virtue has also a support which derives from reason itself. The understanding, by which we recognise moral distinctions, itself gives rise to desires and affections which favour virtuous conduct, and to a sentiment which approves of these affections. It is through this reflective sentiment that we regard certain actions as amiable as well as right, and it is through it also that we have the ideas of beauty and deformity of actions.

Now at the beginning of his *Review* Price was careful to distinguish the beauty and deformity of actions from their rightness and wrongness; and when he now turns to the discussion of the former pair the importance of the distinction soon becomes apparent. The beauty and deformity, we find, do not belong in the least to the actions themselves. "Every one must see", he says, "that these epithets denote the delight; or, on the contrary, the horror and detestation felt by ourselves; and, consequently, signify not any real quality or characters of actions, but the effects in us, or the particular pleasure and pain, attending the consideration of them."[12] It is, we may say, a necessary pleasure, a rational pleasure, a moral pleasure, but it is still our pleasure, and not a quality of the actions.

Thus, while, so far as instinctive sentiments are concerned,

---

[12] *Review*, ch. ii (Selby-Bigge, para. 628).

Price agrees with Balguy that reflective moral judgments are (i) mere reports of effects in us, and (ii) not *moral* judgments at all, yet, on the other hand, Price does allow that there are some such judgments which, although they are mere reports of effects in us, are in a sense moral judgments none the less, since our contribution to these effects depends, not on the instinctive nature which we happen to possess, but upon our essential moral nature.

In all this, of course, Price, like Balguy, fails to take account of the possibility that sentimentalism might be reformulated as holding (i) that the reflective moral judgment is the fundamental moral judgment, and (ii) that it is not at all a mere report of effects in us, but affirms instead a necessary and reasonable connection, for example, that certain motives are morally good. Indeed, at one point it appears that Price ruled out this possibility entirely by treating "morally good" as synonymous with "right", and therefore, on the face of it, as applicable to what is done from motives rather than to the motives themselves. "Morally good and evil," he says, "reasonable and unreasonable, are epithets also commonly applied to actions, evidently meaning the same with right and wrong, fit and unfit."[13]

It cannot, however, be assumed that Price's usage of the word "right" is identical with the common modern usage;[14] and in fact we find him defining quite otherwise the subject of which "right" (and, therefore, for him, "morally good") is the proper predicate. By an action he means "not the bare external effect produced, but the ultimate principle of conduct, or the determination of a reasonable being, considered as arising from the perception of some motives and reasons and intended for some end. According to this sense of the word action, whenever the principle from which we act is different, the action is different, though the external effects produced may be the same".[15]

If this statement is to be taken seriously as a deliberate contention—and it obviously sets out to be taken in that way— then it raises a quite fundamental question regarding Price's ethical theory. All along, for Price, the fundamental moral

[13] *Review*, ch. vi (Selby-Bigge, para. 670).
[14] Cf. Ross, *The Right and the Good*, ch. i *passim*, and, especially, p. 3 (" It seems to me clear that ' right ' does not mean the same as ' morally good '; and we can test this by trying to substitute one for the other.").
[15] *Review*, ch. i, sect. iii (Selby-Bigge, para. 622).

judgment has been that of which "right" is the predicate, and all along the proper subject has been actions. It now appears that by actions Price has meant, not that which is done from some motive, but that together with the motive, and indeed the emphasis is to be laid on the motive. It is that which is right, morally good, fitting and reasonable. In consequence, it may well be doubted whether Price is an intellectualist after all. Certainly, he regards moral distinctions as reasonable and necessary distinctions; but does he consider as the fundamental type of moral judgment that of which the subject is a motive, or that of which the subject is something which is done from a motive? Is he not a sentimentalist of a new and refined type?

Now the answer to the latter question must be in the affirmative if Price's fundamental moral judgment has a motive as its subject, for in the course of our discussion it has been held that the difference between sentimentalism and intellectualism most relevant to modern ethics is not the difference between assigning moral distinctions to arbitrary sense or sentiment and assigning them to universal reason but rather the difference between taking a motive as the fundamental subject of moral propositions and taking the act which is done from some motive. If this interpretation of the two schools is allowed, Price's definition of an action seems to place him unreservedly amongst the sentimentalists. Yet, in the end, the matter appears decisively in quite a different light.

The settlement of this problem comes in answer to a further question; for example, What motive or motives must actions have in order to be judged right or morally good, that is, virtuous? The answer is, Price holds, "that an agent cannot be justly denominated virtuous, except he acts from a consciousness of rectitude, and with a regard to it as his rule and end. . . . This observation appears to me undoubtedly true, and of the greatest importance on this subject".[16] To reach this conclusion he lays down first "that the perception of right and wrong does excite to action, and is alone a sufficient principle of action";[17] and thereafter he proceeds to inquire whether this principle "be not further the only spring of action in a reasonable being, as far as he can be deemed morally good and worthy; whether it be not the only principle from which all actions flow which engage our esteem of the agents; or, in

[16] *Review*, ch. viii (Selby-Bigge, para. 704).
[17] *Ibid.*, ch. viii (Selby-Bigge, paras. 706–7; cf. para. 682).

other words, whether virtue be not itself the end of a virtuous agent as such".[18] His reply to this is that it is as he has suggested, since we must consider "that alone as most properly done by an agent, which he designs to do, and that what was no way an object of his design is not strictly imputable to him".[19]

The meaning of this is, of course, that the only virtuous, morally good or right motive is the sense of obligation, duty or rightness. That in turn implies that the moral judgment that a certain motive is virtuous, morally good or right, presupposes a more fundamental moral judgment to the effect that a certain act which can be done from some motive is right, morally good or virtuous. This statement reveals at once both a wealth and a poverty of moral terms; but Price avoids extreme ambiguity by describing the quality of acts as abstract or absolute virtue, and the quality of motives as practical or relative virtue, a distinction which is more clearly grasped in the modern form which distinguishes right acts from morally good motives.

In spite of his infelicitous terminology, however, Price has proved himself an able intellectualist, who, in a more adequate fashion than any of his predecessors, contrived to find room in his scheme for the reflective moral judgment, the bone of sentimentalism. There are, in fact, for Price, four different kinds of moral judgment. The two less important are both factual reports of the effect of actions on our sentiments, and one is in a sense moral, while the other is totally amoral. The third type, also a reflective judgment, affirms a necessary and reasonable connection between a certain kind of motive and virtue, and presupposes the fundamental moral judgment that a certain kind of act is right, necessarily and by the light of reason.

To this Price has one more point to add. He has already said that a sense of obligation is a necessary motive for virtuous action, he has also said that a sense of obligation is a sufficient motive to produce actions, and he now adds that it is sufficient to produce virtuous action. The agent may be mistaken in his estimation of the situation with which he is faced, but if he acts sincerely he has achieved virtue. It is right for a man to do what he thinks right. "There is a sense in which it may be

[18] *Review*, ch. viii (Selby-Bigge, para. 708).
[19] *Ibid.*, ch. viii (Selby-Bigge, para. 709).

said, that what any being, in the sincerity of his heart, thinks he ought to do, he indeed ought to do, and would be justly blameable if he omitted to do."[20]

No account of eighteenth-century intellectualist or rationalist ethics would be complete without some reference to the work of Immanuel Kant, who died in 1804 in his eightieth year. To omit his contribution to the subject would be to ignore a line of thought which has had a strong influence on the subsequent discussion. On the other hand, it must be confessed, Kant's moral philosophy takes its place, not only in the developing line of ethical thinking, but also as one and only one part of Kant's own comprehensive philosophy. His ethics is not separate from his epistemology. His work on morals is a sequel to, and is dependent upon, his earlier *Critique of Pure Reason*. Yet a consideration of the principles of the Critical Philosophy would be out of place in the present connection, since the aim of this section is not the historical one of discovering precisely what Kant, for example, said and why precisely he said it, but rather the aim of comprehending the development of ethical thought, so that the modern ethical problem may be seen in its proper perspective. Indeed it is remarkable that Kant should have a considerable place in that development, since his system of thought is both intricate and closely knit, and appears therefore to present an "all or nothing" choice. It is a tribute to the power of Kant's thought that in different ways he has left his mark on epistemology, on theology, and, not least, on moral philosophy.

Thus the task which confronts us at the moment is that of extracting from the system of Kant those features which are salient from the point of view of later discussion. Fortunately, Kant has unwittingly lent his aid in this project, for he has undertaken two distinguishable ethical inquiries, and he himself has drawn a clear line between them. His starting-point is the claim of morality of which we are aware in moral experience and which we variously express in the judgments of the ordinary moral consciousness. Now, plainly, two questions arise regarding this claim, the first referring to its nature, and the second to its reality. The latter turns largely upon the question of freedom, for "I ought" implies "I can", and therefore unless I can the obligation is simply unreal. Kant has, however, a more technical way of expressing the matter,

[20] *Review*, ch. viii (Selby-Bigge, para. 699).

namely, by asking, Is there pure practical reason? [21] and, Is there any possibility of a synthetic use of pure practical reason? [22] These are questions which he can answer only by undertaking his critical examination of the Practical Reason. Prior to that inquiry, however, he can leave aside the question of the reality of the moral claim, and investigate its nature instead. Such an inquiry he calls an analytical one, and it is undertaken in the first two sections of the *Grundlegung*. [23]

The inquiry is an analytical one; that is to say, it is "nothing more than the investigation and establishment of *the supreme principle of morality*"; and, Kant adds immediately, "this alone constitutes a study complete in itself". [24] But if it is complete in itself, it is at any rate conducted under the shadow of the possibility that the claim, the nature of which is to be investigated, *may* after all be unreal and illusory. Whether the moral claim is so illusory or not can be determined only in consequence of a critical examination of practical reason. In the meantime, however, according to Kant, the analytical inquiry may proceed.

How then must it proceed? The answer is that the starting-point is to be found in the ordinary moral consciousness and the different moral judgments which it makes. These judgments are for the most part particular, and it is the task of the investigation to discover within them the supreme principle of morality. For Kant two things are necessary in this attempt; one, that we should rise from the particular to the universal, and the other, that of the apparently universal we should seize upon what is genuinely so, that is, the *a priori* as opposed to the merely empirical. Thus Kant himself divides the inquiry into two stages, the one the "Transition from the Common Rational Knowledge of Morality to the Philosophical", and the other the "Transition from Popular Moral Philosophy to the Metaphysic of Morals". We must, he holds, "not merely advance by the natural steps from the common moral judgment to the philosophical, but also from a popular philosophy, which goes no further than it can reach by groping with the

[21] *Critique of Practical Reason* (Abbott's E. T.), p. 87.

[22] *Grundlegung* (Abbott), p. 65.

[23] The third section makes the transition to the other inquiry, and is by Kant entitled "Transition from the Metaphysic of Morals to the Critique of Pure Practical Reason".

[24] *Grundlegung* (Abbott), p. 7.

help of examples, to metaphysic (which does not allow itself
to be checked by anything empirical . . .) ". [25]

Starting then with the judgments of the ordinary moral
consciousness, Kant finds at the outset that there is nothing
absolutely good except the good will. All intellectual talents,
temperamental endowments, and gifts of fortune, things which,
when speaking loosely, we might easily call good, are not so
without qualification. Used and directed by a bad will they
would not lessen, but would actually aggravate the badness.
Their value, in other words, depends upon the moral worth of
the will by which they are employed. It seems, therefore, that
there is nothing absolutely and unconditionally good except
the good will itself.

Moreover, the good will is good quite independently of any
results which it may achieve, or any effects upon the actual
situation which it may accomplish. So far from its goodness
being measured by its efficacy, it does not depend in the
slightest upon the latter. A perfectly good will, that is to say,
may be as impotent as it is perfect. "Even if it should happen
that, owing to special disfavour of fortune, or the niggardly
provision of a step-motherly nature, this will should wholly
lack power to accomplish its purpose, if with its greatest
efforts it should yet achieve nothing, and there should remain
only the good will (not, to be sure, a mere wish, but the
summoning of all means in our power), then, like a jewel, it
would still shine by its own light, as a thing which has its whole
value in itself." [26] Although to some the idea of a perfectly
good but ineffective will may seem absurd, it is a "notion
which exists already in the sound natural understanding,
requiring rather to be cleared up than to be taught". [27]

Thus from the judgments of the ordinary moral consciousness
we obtain the idea of a will which is the only thing absolutely
and unconditionally good, and which is so whether or not it has
any effect at all on the practical situation with which it is
faced; and the remaining purpose of the inquiry is to analyse
the nature of such a will. Proceeding to this, Kant immediately
introduces another notion, that of duty, and he seeks to relate it
to the idea of the good will. In fact a connection is not hard to
find, for a dutiful will is necessarily a good will, although a will
which is necessarily good is not a dutiful one. Duty is present

[25] *Grundlegung*, p. 29.   [26] *Ibid.*, p. 10.
[27] *Ibid.*, p. 13.

only where there is the possibility that the good will may not be realised. The notion of duty, in other words, "includes that of a good will, although implying certain subjective restrictions and hindrances".[28] Thus, whenever a human will is good, it is also dutiful, and vice versa; but it would be inaccurate to speak of duty in relation to God simply because there is no possibility of God's will being anything but good. The divine will, therefore, is to be called, not dutiful, but holy.

Does then the conditional identification of the good will with the dutiful will assist us in our analysis of the former? Clearly it does, for when we direct our attention to the dutiful will we are able at once to affirm that a volition is not dutiful unless the matter willed is willed because it is our duty. We do not describe as moral the merchant who, without any regard for honest dealing as such, yet contrives to keep his record perfectly clean because he knows that in the long run that is the more profitable course. He has acted, according to Kant, *as* duty requires, but not at all *because* it requires, and on that account his volition has no moral worth whatsoever. Kant would even hold that in the case of a man who acts benevolently, not because it is his duty so to act, but simply because he happens to be altruistically inclined, no more moral worth attaches to the volition than to that of the enlightened egoist. To be dutiful a volition must have regard to duty.

Further, if we consider an instance of the dutiful will, a case in which a volition is made having regard to duty, we are compelled to admit that its moral worth does not derive from any worth attaching to the actual effect of the volition upon the practical situation. For the designed effect may not ensue, and the alteration which does occur may have no value whatsoever, and yet this will not detract from the goodness of the dutiful will. It may be my duty, for example, to keep a certain promise, and the worth of my volition which has that duty in view does not derive from any worth attaching to the state of affairs in which my promise has been fulfilled, for with the best will in the world I may fail to fulfil it and yet the goodness of my will is unaffected.

This of course is merely a repetition of the earlier statement that a perfectly good will may be at the same time a perfectly impotent one, and it simply underlines the fact that in dealing with the dutiful will we have not left the good will behind. The

[28] *Grundlegung*, p. 13.

former is identical with the latter, now subject of course to certain hindrances.

Yet the point deserves to be underlined at this stage for it has an important bearing upon the further elucidation of the matter on hand. Consider, for example, a will which seeks dutifully to fulfil a promise. It is agreed that the moral worth of that will does not derive from any value attaching to its actual effect, which may in fact have no value whatsoever. Whence then is the moral worth of the volition? If it is not from the effect of the volition it must be from the reason for it, what Kant calls its maxim. What then is the maxim in this case? Presumably it is the law that men ought to fulfil their promises. But within this we may distinguish two things, the form of law and the particular content of this law, namely, promise-keeping. The latter, however, refers us again to the effect of the volition, so that the maxim which renders a will morally good is a law without content, admittedly a very odd kind of law indeed. "But what sort of law can that be", asks Kant, "the conception of which must determine the will, even without paying any regard to the effect expected from it, in order that this will may be called good absolutely and without qualification?"[29] It can only be "the universal conformity of its actions to law in general, which alone is to serve the will as a principle, i.e. I am never to act otherwise than so *that I could also will that my maxim should become a universal law*".[30] In other words, my will is good only if I can will without contradiction that its maxim should become a law applicable to all rational beings.

In all this we have been guided largely by an example, and it is possible to deal with the subject on a somewhat higher level. For, in the first place, we can consider it from the point of view of law in general. Now imperatives divide themselves into two main classes, the categorical and the hypothetical. The form of the latter is, "If you desire end X, perform act Y", and consequently any action done in obedience to such a law has no more than an instrumental value, instrumental to the end in question. But the end has in turn no more than a relative value, for, as we have seen, there is nothing unconditionally good except the good will. It follows, therefore, that an act cannot be dutiful if it is done in obedience merely to a hypothetical imperative. Thus the good will has respect only to a categorical imperative; and if we abstract from all empirical content we

<hr>

[29] *Grundlegung*, pp. 17-18.   [30] *Ibid.*, p. 18.

find that there is "but one categorical imperative: Act only on that Maxim whereby thou canst at the same time will that it should become a universal law".[31]

Now the trouble with the hypothetical imperative was two-fold. In the first place, an action done in accordance with it had simply an instrumental value, deriving entirely from the end it subserved. Secondly, the end itself had no more than a relative and conditional value—it was good for me *if* and only if I happened to desire it. There are therefore two reasons why the good will as such has no connection with hypothetical imperatives, the first that an action done in accordance with such an imperative depends for its value upon its effect, and the second that in any case the effect has only a relative value. Now these two obstacles would be avoided if there were an end, (i) which already exists and is therefore to be served by actions in some closer fashion than by being brought into existence as a result of them, and (ii) which is a rational and necessary end, having, that is to say, an absolute worth. Is there then any such end? Kant's answer is that there is. "Man", he says, "and generally any rational being *exists* as an end in himself, *not merely as a means* to be arbitrarily used by this or that will, but in all his actions, whether they concern himself or other rational beings, must be always regarded at the same time as an end."[32] From this there follows the second formulation of the practical imperative, namely, "So act as to treat humanity, whether in thine own person or in that of any other, in every case as an end withal, never as means only".[33]

Kant, however, is not content to leave the matter there, and he proceeds to make a third formulation, what he calls a "complete characterisation" which is obtained by combining the two earlier ones. The ruling concept is that of a kingdom of ends, which manifestly includes both law and end; and the formula is to the effect "that all maxims ought by their own legislation to harmonise with a possible kingdom of ends as with a kingdom of nature".[34]

Such, then, is the ethical theory of Immanuel Kant; and the line of criticism which it has provoked is fairly constant. On the one hand, it is held that Kant's first formulation of the categorical imperative, which after all he regards as the strict one,[35] points out a necessary characteristic of moral law,

[31] *Grundlegung*, p. 38.   [32] *Ibid.*, p. 46.   [33] *Ibid.*, p. 47.
[34] *Ibid.*, p. 55.   [35] *Ibid.*, p. 55.

namely, that other things being equal it is the same for every-one; while the second formulation succeeds very much in exhibiting the substance of morality. On the other hand, it is commonly insisted that Kant's theory cannot be accepted as the last word in ethics, and that in particular it contains two fundamental flaws, of which the one is denominated Kant's rigourism and refers to his tenet that wherever inclination is present as a help to the line of conduct which morality demands it detracts from the moral worth of the action, and the other is called his formalism and refers to the charge that although suitability to be a universal law is a necessary characteristic of moral demands it is not by itself sufficient to determine the nature of these demands, failing to yield any precise moral direction without the aid of some other suggested moral principle.

At the present stage of the discussion, however, it will be sufficient to note a more general point which distinguishes Kant's form of intellectualism from that favoured by the English moralists previously considered. According to the latter, as we have seen, reason discovers in the course of practical experience that in certain kinds of situation certain kinds of action are necessarily fitting and right. The resultant moral judgment is a necessary and not a contingent one. There is for reason a necessary connection between the situation and the right action; but reason is only the discoverer of this connection. For Kant, on the other hand, reason itself is the author of the moral law. It brings the demand with it to the world of practical situations. Thus both for Kant and for the English intellectualists reason is the moral faculty; but to the former reason is the author, to the latter the mere discoverer, of the moral law. In other words, while both assert that moral judgments affirm a necessary and rational connection, the one holds that the demands expressed in these judgments issue from within, and the other holds that they issue from without. In the one case, in the last resort it is my reason which makes the demand, and in the other it is fundamentally the situation which does so, and my reason simply discovers it.

Now this divergence of view raises an issue between Kant and the English intellectualists regarding the general nature of the moral life. On the one hand, the implication is that morality is a matter of meeting the moral demands as and when they occur in the course of the practical life, while, on the other side, the demand is rather to be regarded as there from the beginning and morality as a matter of bringing all practical situations under its rule. And the question raised is this, Does the pattern of the moral life as we ordinarily understand it belong to the one side or to the other?

Before, however, we can deal with questions such as this other formulations of the supreme principle of morality must be passed under review.

CHAPTER III

UTILITARIANISM

IT HAS ALREADY been laid down that there are three main types of ethical judgment, which distinguish themselves one from another according as they take as their subject motives, acts or consequences. Corresponding to this division of ethical judgments there is a similar classification of ethical theories according as they take as the fundamental type of moral judgment the first, second, or third of those three kinds. Thus sentimentalism, as we have already seen, was essentially an attempt to treat as the fundamental type of moral judgment that which has a motive as its subject; whereas intellectualism took as its basic judgment that which deals with actions.[1] We did see, however, that even in Shaftesbury there was a tendency to be unfaithful to the principle of sentimentalism. Sometimes he spoke quite consistently to the effect that in order to be virtuous an action must be done from a motive which is deemed worthy; but at other times he referred to good motives as those which were likely to have a beneficial effect upon the public interest. In this way, even in sentimentalism, there was a tendency for the centre of moral interest to move from motives

[1] But is Kant's theory of this kind? This question, however, cannot be answered with complete certainty, and that for two reasons. (i) Prior to Kant there was a strong ethical tradition that " right " was subordinate to " good ", and perhaps even that " right " meant " productive of good ". Be that as it may, Kant certainly insisted, not only that when we call an act right or dutiful we do not mean that it has good results, but even that *in fact* acts are right whether they have good results or not. So far Kant's position is tolerably clear, but after this point it becomes ambiguous; and to the end it remains uncertain whether Kant departed from the ethical tradition because he disagreed with its implicit belittlement of " right ", or, instead, because he differed from it with regard to " good ". For he did hold that the good ends at which right acts were traditionally held to aim were good only in a very suspect sense. In fact they were not unconditionally good, but only relatively so; and there was nothing unconditionally good save the good will, and a good will was one which spent itself in doing its duty. What then did Kant mean? Did he believe that acts are right, not because of good results, but because of what they are in themselves? Or was it rather his view that they are right if, and only if, they proceed from a good will? In other words, is moral obligation an ultimate fact, or is it derivative from the conception of the good will? (ii) Even if it is allowed that on the whole Kant adopted the former of these alternatives, and was therefore an intellectualist rather than a sentimentalist it is clear that he did not find the ground of rightness exactly in the character of an act. Rather, he looked beyond the act to a possible kingdom of ends; and that, as we shall see later (p. 329), is not strictly an intellectualist position.

to consequences, and therefore a tendency to introduce an altogether different type of ethical theory, one which regarded as
fundamental the moral judgment which deals with the effects
and consequences of actions.

The plainest examples of this type of ethical theory, however,
are provided by utilitarianism, which had its beginnings in the
eighteenth century, which continued in strength throughout the
nineteenth century, and which cannot be ignored in the
twentieth. For, as Sidgwick explains the term, "by Utilitarianism is meant the ethical theory that the conduct which, under
any given circumstances is objectively right, is that which will
produce the greatest amount of happiness on the whole".[2]

Although there were in other writers, such as Shaftesbury
and Hutcheson,[3] anticipations of the utilitarian point of view,
the earliest statement of the principle as the fundamental
principle of morality is to be found in a short treatise written by
John Gay, published anonymously in 1731, and prefixed to
Law's translation of King's *Origin of Evil*. It was entitled *Preliminary Dissertation: Concerning the Fundamental Principle of Virtue
or Morality*, and it laid down a definitely utilitarian position
which was closely followed by later writers; by John Brown,
whose *Essays on the Characteristics* was published in 1751; by
Abraham Tucker, who wrote *The Light of Nature Pursued*,
consisting of no fewer than seven volumes, which appeared
between 1768 and 1774; and by William Paley, who made his
contribution in *The Principles of Moral and Political Philosophy*,
a book which, published in 1785, went through no fewer than
twelve editions before the end of the eighteenth century.

These four writers indeed are to be regarded as the principal
spokesmen of a distinct school within the borders of utilitarianism, and they are commonly called the Theological Utilitarians.

According to Paley, who is the best known exponent of the
school's thought, virtue is to be defined as "the doing good to
mankind, in obedience to the will of God, and for the sake of
everlasting happiness".[4] At first sight, such a definition does not
seem to belong to any particular type of ethical theory, but
appears to draw equally and indiscriminately from three

---

[2] *Methods of Ethics*, iv, i, 1.
[3] Hutcheson anticipated even the formula of utilitarianism, "the greatest
happiness of the greatest number". Cf. *Inquiry*, sect. iii, para. viii (Selby-Bigge,
para. 121).
[4] *Principles*, bk. i, ch. vii (Selby-Bigge, para. 1013).

different types, holding as it does that in virtue the motive is of such a kind, the act is of such a kind, and the consequences are of such a kind. Nor is the matter helped by Paley's later contention that all rival theories in the field ultimately coincide,[5] a statement which suggests that in Paley's mind certain fit and proper distinctions have become blurred. None the less we are not on that account excused from asking whether in the end Paley did regard one of the three types of ethical judgment as more fundamental than the others.

In the first place, then, Paley holds that in order to be virtuous an act must be in accordance with the will of God, but it must also be such as to have a beneficial effect upon the happiness of the whole. But what are we to say of an action which has apparently no such effect and is yet in accordance with the will of God as we understand it? Paley's answer is that such an action is right, but that "right" is a relative term, denoting "no more than conformity to the rule we go by, whatever that rule be".[6] The suggestion is that different men go by different rules, and that actions done in accordance with these rules are therefore right, but not necessarily virtuous. Before we can say that they are virtuous and absolutely right, as we might say, we must know that the rule we "go by" reflects the will of God, that is, what *really* is the will of God. Now the criterion of that is the tendency of the rule to promote the happiness of all, and of this men apparently are judges. "Reason", says Paley, "is the principle, by which we discover or judge of the actual constitution of the world, by which some things, as such and such actions, for example, produce happiness and others misery."[7] It appears, therefore, that as between the character of acts and the nature of their consequences the criterion of virtue is to be found in the latter.

Having got so far, we might well expect Paley to hold that the obligation to virtue arises from the happiness which is to be produced by it, but this position he persistently avoids. Instead, he lays it down that "we can be obliged to nothing, but what we ourselves are to gain or lose something by"[8], for we can only act with a view to our own pleasure. Nothing else has the power to move us to action, and the motive to virtue arises from the fact that in the life after death God exactly

[5] *Principles*, bk. ii, ch. i (Selby-Bigge, para. 1015).
[6] *Ibid.*, bk. ii, ch. i (Selby-Bigge, para. 1015).
[7] *Ibid.*, bk. ii, ch. i (Selby-Bigge, para. 1015).
[8] *Ibid.*, bk. ii, ch. ii (Selby-Bigge, para. 1019).

adjusts our fortunes there to our conduct here. It is on this account (and not because of the earlier introduction of the will of God in the definition of virtue) that Paley and the other members of his school are described as Theological Utilitarians. "It is their emphasis on the supernatural sanction which constitutes Gay, Brown, Tucker and Paley theological utilitarians, and which, starting as they did with the selfish theory of the moral motive, renders their system of utilitarianism alone consistent." [9]

Consequently, theological utilitarianism carries with it two implications. The first is that the judgment about motives, although it has a prominent place in the exposition of the theory, is not at all the fundamental moral judgment. Indeed, it is not a moral judgment at all, for all actions, be they good or bad, are done from the same motive, a desire for personal pleasure. It follows, therefore, that of the three kinds of judgment which Paley combines in his famous definition of virtue, the judgment which deals with consequences is alone left as possibly the fundamental moral judgment and as indicating the necessary and sufficient condition of virtue. This indeed it must indicate, to Paley's mind, for while every act is presumably or potentially right, being in accordance with *some* rule, and every motive is as good as another since all are one, a beneficial effect upon the happiness of all does not belong to every act, and therefore this is the one variable factor which may be present or not and which may consequently serve to distinguish virtue from vice. But although Paley regards this type of judgment as the *fundamental* type in morals, he does not regard it as a *moral* judgment, for he does not say that the happiness of all is good and he explicitly denies that it is a source of moral obligation. For the agent the happiness of all is only a means to his own pleasure. On the other hand, he does not say that the agent's own pleasure is by itself a source of obligation, for there is no virtue where that pleasure is achieved directly as an immediate effect of the action. In short, in dealing with morality Paley has robbed it of every conceivable moral judgment and has reduced its unconditional worth to a merely instrumental value. The right act is reduced to an act done in accordance with some rule or another and not necessarily the right rule; the good motive loses its virtue in becoming the one possible motive of all men; and the best results are no better than any means which

[9] Hastings, *Utilitarianism*, in E.R.E., vol. 12, p. 559b.

effectively promotes its proper end. Paley is able to combine three quite different moral judgments within the limits of a single definition, because, unconsciously though no less surely, he empties each and all of their specifically moral content.

Moreover, this criticism of Paley is given additional substance by the second implication of theological utilitarianism, which takes the form of a peculiar theory of "moral" obligation. A man is obliged, according to Paley, "when he is urged by a violent motive resulting from the command of another".[10] Later he says that "all obligation is nothing more than an inducement of sufficient strength, and resulting, in some way, from the command of another".[11] And following upon that he explains the difference between prudence and duty as "this; that, in the one case, we consider what we shall gain or lose in the present world; in the other case, we consider also what we shall gain or lose in the world to come".[12] These statements, however, do not make the matter perfectly clear. For example, he emphasises the violence of the motive which leads to virtuous conduct, yet it can hardly be supposed that he means that this motive is always successful in competition with other motives; in other words, that virtue is inevitable. What he appears to have in mind is the rivalry in a man's mind between the prospect offered by a bird in the hand and that afforded by two in the bush. Both have their appeal, and the appeal of the latter is what we call moral obligation. It is, that is to say, the influence on the will of much prospective pleasure which can be achieved only in certain indirect and roundabout ways. It is the indirect means which makes conduct virtuous; it is the ultimate end which makes it worth-while to, or even possible for, any human agent. In other words, virtue is a means to an end, and moral obligation is just a special kind of natural attraction.

The school of thought, however, with which the title of Utilitarianism has been most commonly associated is that which owed its origin to Jeremy Bentham who, born in 1748, lived until the year of the great Reform Act of 1832. Bentham's interests were practical as well as theoretical; he was keenly concerned with matters relating to law and politics, and, whether for this reason or some other, he was not greatly anxious to publish his writings. Indeed, although his *Introduction*

---

[10] *Principles*, bk. ii, ch. ii (Selby-Bigge, para. 1017).
[11] *Ibid.*, bk. ii, ch. iii (Selby-Bigge, para. 1021).
[12] *Ibid.*, bk. ii, ch. iii (Selby-Bigge, para. 1022).

to the Principles of Morals and Legislation was ready and in print in 1780, it was not actually published until 1789, and then only in response to the repeated requests of his followers, while his *Deontology* was even longer delayed and did not appear until two years after his death.

His position has much in common with that of the Theological Utilitarians, and in particular he agrees that the ultimate criterion of right action is its effect upon the happiness of the whole. "An action", he holds, "may be said to be conformable to the principle of utility . . . when the tendency it has to augment the happiness of the community is greater than any it has to diminish it."[13] But he will not accept the will of God as a proximate criterion. For one thing, the revealed will of God is not acceptable as such a criterion because it requires interpretation and is not itself a sufficient guide; while, secondly, the presumptive will of God is in no better case since that phrase means merely "what is taken to be the will of God in the light of some other moral principle".[14]

Moreover, he will not allow even as a proximate criterion Shaftesbury's moral sense or the intuitive understanding of the English intellectualists, for ultimately, he holds, these two very different theories come to the same thing, namely, a denial that there is any moral principle.[15] In fact there is no royal road to the discovery of what is right. The only safe guide is the principle of utility, the principle which lays it down that we are to seek the greatest happiness of the greatest number. By happiness Bentham means pleasure and the avoidance of pain; and he insists that our application of this principle is similar to a rough mathematical calculation.

This point is indeed one of Bentham's main contributions to the utilitarian theory of ethics, and it involves what is known as the hedonistic calculus, that is, a method of discovering which act will produce the greatest happiness of the greatest number. The assumption is that pleasures are roughly measurable quantities, and Bentham enumerates seven circumstances which must be taken into account in trying to measure the likely resultant happiness of any action. They are the intensity of the resultant pleasure, its duration, its certainty or uncertainty, its propinquity or remoteness, its fecundity or the chance it has of

[13] *Principles*, ch. i (Selby-Bigge, para. 362).
[14] Cf. Bentham, *Principles*, ch. ii (Selby-Bigge, para. 376).
[15] Cf. Bentham, *Principles*, ch. ii (Selby-Bigge, para. 371–2).

being followed by other pleasures, its purity or the chance it has of not being followed by pain, and its extent, that is the number of persons to whom it extends.

Now that is a careful and plausible analysis, and plainly it does reveal something, but it does not obviously imply that pleasures are roughly measurable quantities. Consider, for example, two acts A and B, the extents of whose hedonistic effects are equal. Further, let it be supposed that so far as all but two of the other circumstances are concerned these provide no ground for choosing between the actions. So far neither can establish itself as against the other. But it may be that act A has the advantage in regard to intensity, act B in regard to duration. How then is the agent to decide between them? If the difference in intensity is small and the difference in duration great, he may be inclined to decide in favour of act B; and if the difference in duration is small and the difference in intensity great, he may well favour act A. And in either case it may be said with some plausibility that the decision is the necessary outcome of the application of the principle of utility as Bentham understood it.

Let us suppose, however, that in the case of act A the intensity is twice that following upon act B, whereas the duration in the case of act B is twice the duration of the pleasure resulting from act A. Are we then to say that on the principle of utility the two acts are equally right? It would seem so, for in one case the hedonistic value might be numerically expressed as 2×1, i.e., 2; and in the other, as 1×2, i.e., 2. Such an account of the matter, however, is accurate only if it is assumed that any change in one of the seven circumstances is to be given precisely the same weight as a proportionately equal change in any other. Thûs, in the case just given, the account is accurate only if it is assumed that if you start with a certain amount of pleasure you get double that amount by *doubling* it in respect of duration, or by *doubling* it in respect of intensity, or in fact by *doubling* it in respect of any one of the other five circumstances which, on Bentham's theory, govern the amount of pleasure.

That this assumption is true, however, cannot be taken for granted. What Bentham has unquestionably done is to provide by careful analysis a list, not necessarily an exhaustive list, of different respects in which different pleasures may be compared; but that does not prove that the different pleasures can be measured against each other. On the contrary, unless a common denominator is also to be provided, it indicates that they cannot. If the only relevant respect in which collections of eggs differ is their number then it is possible to measure one collection against another; but if their number, weight, colouring and shape are all relevant there is no possibility of comparative measurement whatsoever. How can we possibly tell what degree of certainty, fecundity, or purity in one action must be allowed the same weight as a given degree of intensity in another action?

Furthermore, it is plain that pleasures are more difficult to deal with even than collections of eggs which can be compared in several different respects, for the former do not have the advantage of being more or less the same thing to everyone who comes in touch with them. Pleasure is not something which can be divided up, handed over and possessed. Rather we take or find pleasure in something other than the pleasure itself, and different people find or take it in all sorts of different places. In other words, pleasure is a quality of an experience, and even if several people have the same experience there is nothing at all to guarantee that they will find the same pleasure in that experience. One person may thoroughly enjoy a concert while the man in the next seat is simply bored.

Now the critical exposition of utilitarianism so far given carries with it three general implications regarding that ethical theory. In the first place, it implies that when I consider what my duty is, I undertake a calculation and comparison of all the consequences of all the actions possible for me in the given situation. Secondly, it implies that when I decide that act A is my duty I may be in error, and my error may be due to one or more of three possible mistakes, for (a) I may be mistaken in my belief that act A will have consequences X,Y,Z, and similarly in regard to the other possible acts; (b) I may be mistaken in my belief that X,Y, and Z will give a certain pleasure to the people affected by them, and similarly in regard to the other consequences; and (c) lacking any common denominator of intensity, duration, etc., I can only *guess*, at the end of my long calculation, that the pleasure resulting from act A is *greater* than the pleasure resulting from any other possible action, and of course my guess may be mistaken, if indeed it is in any way significant.[16] And in the third place, utilitarianism, as we have

[16] We do, of course, say that " my pleasure was greater " but we mean by that that it was greater in intensity *or* in duration, and so on, *not* that it was greater in "intensity-duration-etc."

expounded it, implies that *if* there is such a thing as genuinely moral obligation it arises because certain people other than the agent have desires; it arises, that is to say, from the fact, neither of need nor of claim, but of desire.

The conditional form of this third implication is deliberate and significant, for it is possible that Bentham may yet follow the Theological Utilitarians in their egoistic interpretation of human conduct, an interpretation which, as we have seen, destroys moral obligation entirely. And in fact Bentham is in agreement with his predecessors on this issue. "It has been shown," he says, "that the happiness of the individuals of whom a community is composed . . . is . . . the sole standard, in conformity to which each individual ought, as far as depends upon the legislator, to be *made* to fashion his behaviour. But whether it be this or anything else that is to be *done*, there is nothing by which a man can ultimately be *made* to do it, but either pain or pleasure."[17] On this matter Bentham's views are in almost complete harmony with those of the earlier writers we have already considered, and the main difference is a subordinate one, that whereas Paley was disposed to lay the strongest emphasis upon the theological sanction, Bentham was inclined rather to despise it. "As to such of the pleasures and pains," he says, "belonging to the religious sanction, as regard a future life, of what kind these may be we cannot know."[18] Yet, wherever the emphasis may fall, the principle is plainly the same, and the implication also, that virtue is no more than a means to an end.

Whatever difficulties may be found, however, in the utilitarian theory, it cannot be doubted that through the work of Bentham and his followers its position as an ethical theory demanding at least careful consideration, if not definite assent, was well and firmly established. So much indeed was this the case that by the year 1861 one of these followers was able to publish a contribution to ethical discussion under the simple title *Utilitarianism*.

In this essay John Stuart Mill upholds the central doctrine of utilitarianism, insisting that the criterion of right action is "the greatest happiness of the greatest number". He deals also with critics of the theory, and in the main argues that their criticisms are based upon one misconception or another of Bentham's

---

[17] *Principles*, ch. iii (Selby-Bigge, para. 378).
[18] *Ibid.*, ch. iii (Selby-Bigge, para. 382).

principles. More than that, he is prepared even to hold that to utilitarianism, stealthily introduced, is due in large measure the plausibility of rival theories. Thus he regards Kant's system of of thought as "one of the landmarks in the history of philosophical speculation", he quotes also Kant's formulation of the categorical imperative, but he insists that in the light of this first principle we cannot discriminate between actions except in so far as we assume that a rational will cannot countenance an adverse effect upon the general happiness.

Mill's defence of the theory, however, was not a completely blind one; and in fact there are two important respects in which he himself was ready to modify the conclusions of his predecessor. Bentham had taught, as we saw, that the criterion of right action is "the greatest happiness of the greatest number", and he had laid down seven circumstances which must be taken into account in seeking to compare the effects of different actions in the light of this criterion. Mill, on the other hand, could not be content to leave the matter at that point. And the reason was this. He was well aware that of two possible courses of action one might have all the advantages, or at the least the balance of advantage, when the two courses were weighed by means of Bentham's seven circumstances; it might offer, for example, pleasure more intense, more lasting and much purer than the other,[19] and yet all who had any acquaintance with both courses were unanimous in their choice of the other.

Now there are two possible explanations of this embarrassing fact. The first is that the greatest happiness principle is after all not the criterion of right action, since in this particular instance it contradicts the verdict of the ordinary moral consciousness. But this is not an explanation which Mill is prepared to accept, and to the end he professes the utilitarian theory of ethics. The other explanation is that Bentham's list of relevant circumstances is not exhaustive and lacks indeed the most important of all, the circumstance of quality. In this way Mill must be thought to add an eighth circumstance which is relevant to the computation of the greatest happiness, and if he says little of the other seven it is because he believes that an advantage on this score must be given much more weight than a proportionately equal advantage in any one of the other seven. What Mill does not see is that by increasing the number of relevant circumstances he has made the utilitarian principle

[19] Cf. Mill, *Utilitarianism*, ch. ii.

still less a criterion of right action than it was in the hands of Bentham, and that by quietly paying more attention to one circumstance than he pays to another he silently confesses the bankruptcy of the hedonistic calculus.

The second qualification with which Mill accepts Bentham's position relates to the sanctions which are to be recognised. Like Bentham he accepts what he calls the external sanctions; but in addition to these he insists that there is an internal sanction which is closely associated with the social feelings of mankind. What then does Mill understand by this internal sanction? "The internal sanction of duty," he says, "whatever our standard of duty may be, is one and the same—a feeling in our mind; a pain more or less intense, attendant on violation of duty, which in properly cultivated moral natures rises, in the more serious cases, into shrinking from it as an impossibility."[20]

In all this Mill is probably trying to shake himself free of the heritage of psychological hedonism, and he is struggling towards a view of moral obligation which does not reduce it to a special case of natural attraction. It may well be doubted, however, whether he has achieved more than a very partial success. He lays all the emphasis upon feeling—the feeling of pain when duty is ignored, and possibly also the feeling of pleasure when it is obeyed; and it is not at all evident that he avoids a position which would in the end regard duty merely as a means to escape this pain and to enjoy this pleasure. Moreover, in seeking to prove that the *general* happiness is the moral end he bases his proof upon psychological egoism. Each man, he says, desires his own happiness, and "the general happiness therefore is a good to the aggregate of all persons".[21] The truth is that, beginning with psychological hedonism and passing from that by means of the principle of association to disinterested desire, Mill is never quite able to escape from the influence of his starting-point.

Indeed, it was left to Henry Sidgwick (1838–1900), whose *Methods of Ethics* was first published in 1874, to restate utilitarianism with the general happiness recognised as the moral end, with the effect of an act upon that happiness accepted as the criterion of its rightness or wrongness, but, for the first time, without the encumbrance of psychological hedonism. In fact this was the signal service which Sidgwick rendered to

[20] *Utilitarianism*, ch. iii.   [21] *Ibid.*, ch. iv.

utilitarian theory and to the development of specifically
utilitarian thought; and although he had also much of value
to say in the way of coming to terms with other and rival
theories, his importance for the present discussion lies in the
fact that he enabled utilitarianism to shake itself free of its
historical bonds and to advance thereafter as a genuinely
ethical doctrine.

At this stage in the inquiry, however, it may be well to refer
to another school of ethical thought which enjoyed a considerable vogue during the life-time of its chief exponents, but
which seems to fall outside the line of logical development in
moral theory. It is commonly known as evolutional utilitarianism, although by Herbert Spencer, its leading representative,
it was denominated rational utilitarianism as opposed to the
empirical utilitarianism of Bentham and Mill.

Herbert Spencer's was a long life connecting the first
quarter of the nineteenth century with the corresponding
quarter of the twentieth (1820–1903), and almost throughout
his main activity was philosophical. "The real life which he
lived," it has been said, "was the subjective life, which is best
recorded by a description of his philosophy."[22] At the age of
thirty-eight he set himself the ambitious task of propounding a
complete system of philosophy, of which the crowning-piece
was to be *The Principles of Ethics*. This was indeed to be the end
and justification of the whole endeavour, and in fact Spencer
broke what he regarded as the logical sequence of his work lest
he should be unable to complete his plan and so be compelled
to leave the main point of it unaffirmed. In 1879, therefore, he
published *The Data of Ethics*, and it was not until 1892–3 that
the remainder of *The Principles* was ready to appear.

In the Preface to the former he sets down the object which
underlies, not only the ethics, but the whole system of philosophy. "My ultimate purpose," he says, "lying behind all
proximate purposes, has been that of finding for the principles
of right and wrong in conduct at large, a scientific basis."[23]
The necessity for this endeavour arose from the fact that
religious faith was losing its grip upon men's minds and hearts;
and, says Spencer, "few things can happen more disastrous
than the decay and death of a regulative system no longer
fit, before another and fitter regulative system has grown up to

[22] Elliot, *Herbert Spencer*, in E.R.E., vol. 11, p. 764a.
[23] *Data of Ethics*, Preface, p. vii.

replace it".[24] It was not that Spencer regretted the decay of religious faith, but rather that he regarded as urgent the task of preparing to replace it a scientific faith likewise productive of rules of conduct.

Now, so far as we have yet seen, the typically theological type of ethics is virtually a denial of the science of ethics as we have defined it, for the implication is that moral distinctions are not self-authenticating to the ordinary moral conscious-ness, but are derived from, and are indeed manufactured by, the arbitrary will of God. In other words, ethics as a science is deprived of the court of appeal which it otherwise finds in the moral consciousness; and the same thing happens if that consciousness is ignored in the name of science instead of religion. It is at least likely, of course, that moral distinctions will not be derived from an arbitrary will but rather by the logical explication of a scientific theory; yet both positions have it in common that they deny these distinctions to be self-authenti-cating to the moral consciousness. Leslie Stephen, who shared the outlook of Spencer, did indeed entitle his contribution *The Science of Ethics*, but, if our anticipation is correct, the evolu-tionary approach denies that ethics *is* a science and makes it instead a mere appendix to non-ethical science.

How then does Spencer work out a regulative system based upon science? He starts with the proposition that a part cannot be adequately considered in isolation from the whole of which it is a part. The relevance of the point is that consequently moral conduct cannot be properly treated apart from conduct in general, and that that in turn cannot be properly treated apart from the evolution of conduct. Now, according to Spencer, a consideration of the evolution of conduct reveals in the higher stages an increasing quantity of life, and by quantity is meant breadth as well as length, that is, variety of vital activity as well as duration. Moreover, it reveals this in three different directions, in that of self-preservation, in that of preservation of offspring, and finally in the way, not only of not hindering others, but of actually helping them. At the lower stages of evolution success along one of these three lines may involve failure along one or other or both of the others; but Spencer insists that "evolution becomes the highest possible when the conduct simultaneously achieves the greatest totality of life in self, in offspring, and in fellow-men."[25]

[24] *Data of Ethics*, Preface, p. viii.   [25] *Ibid.*, ch. iii, para. 8, pp. 25–6.

The next step in the argument is taken by equating the highest evolutionary stage with the morally best. "That which we found to be highly evolved conduct, is that which we find to be what is called good conduct; and the ideal goal to the natural evolution of conduct we recognise as the ideal standard of conduct ethically considered."[26] It seems, therefore, that Spencer's thesis is: (i) that the trend of evolution is in the direction of an increase in the quantity of life, both in the way of the preservation of the individual and in that of the preservation of the species, and these compatibly with the positive helping of the preservation of other individuals; and (ii) that conduct which promotes this threefold end, and is consequently in line with the evolutionary trend, is therefore morally good.

If this were all it would be true, as already argued, that no room at all has been left for the ordinary moral consciousness; but Spencer does not hold consistently to this precise formulation of the matter. If he did his position would carry the same implication as the theological type of moral theory, that is, that ethics is not a separate science, and that moral distinctions are derivative from what is not moral. In addition, Spencer's theory would imply that moral distinctions belong peculiarly to those endowed with the ability to follow out the implications of a scientific hypothesis, and therefore that the ordinary moral consciousness is to be ruled out of court, not only because it professes to be moral, but also because it prides itself on being ordinary.

So far Spencer's theory might be regarded as a form of utilitarianism, since it looks upon the effects of actions as determining their morality; but as yet it is not specifically hedonistic. Spencer, however, finds room for hedonism also. The good, he insists, is always the pleasurable. If you deny this, he says, you are committed to the absurdity of supposing that it is therefore either the painful or else the hedonistically indifferent as such. This argument may well seem unconvincing, an escape between the horns of the dilemma may appear to offer itself, but the conclusion, at any rate, is clear. "No school", he says [27], "can avoid taking for the ultimate moral aim a desirable state of feeling called by whatever name— gratification, enjoyment, happiness. Pleasure somewhere, at some time, to some being or beings, is an inexpugnable element

[26] *Data of Ethics*, ch. iii, para. 15, p. 44.　　[27] *Ibid.*, ch. iii, para. 15, p. 46.

of the conception. It is as much a necessary form of moral intuition as space is a necessary form of intellectual intuition."

Thus the ordinary moral consciousness and the appeals thereto are reintroduced. In places Spencer appears to ignore this aspect of the matter and speaks as if the transition from the highest evolutionary stage to the position in which this is identified with the good is an immediate and direct transition. But his considered view is that there are really two intermediate points, namely, (i) that the good is always the pleasurable, and (ii) that life is worth living, that it yields a balance of pleasure over pain, and that therefore the more of life there is the more there is of pleasure and the less of pain. In other words, the scientific hypothesis of evolution is taken as revealing by implication, not the moral end indeed, which is discovered by moral intuition or the ordinary moral consciousness, but certainly the precise ways in which it is to be realised, that is, what is right and what is wrong.

How, then, is this contention different from the utilitarianism of Bentham and Mill? It is distinguished by Spencer himself as rational utilitarianism as opposed to empirical; and the point is that, whereas according to Bentham and Mill the precise lines of moral conduct are inductively discovered through experience of what produces happiness and what does not, moral laws are properly to be discovered by deduction from the evolutionary hypothesis. In a letter to Mill himself Spencer illustrates the matter by pointing out that in earlier times in astronomy events were predicted empirically or inductively on the basis of accumulated observations, whereas at a more developed stage they are deduced from the law of gravitation; and Spencer regards himself as performing a like service for ethics by deducing what precisely is right from the theory of evolution.[28]

Thus in what may be regarded as its final form Spencer's theory allows to the ordinary moral consciousness authority in regard to the nature of the moral end,[29] but on no other

[28] Cf. Spencer, *Data of Ethics*, ch. iv, para. 21, pp. 57–8.
[29] Our first formulation of Spencer's doctrine did not even allow this; and Professor Moore has pointed out that it may not be allowed even by the second. In both formulations, Moore suspects Spencer of having committed what he calls the naturalistic fallacy—in the first formulation, by assuming that good means " more evolved ", and in the second, by assuming that it means " pleasant ". But, as Moore admits, Spencer's language is not consistent, his thought therefore is probably confused, and although he may certainly have been influenced by the naturalistic fallacy, he is not committed to it (e.g., as against Moore's quotations

matter, and he still reserves to the man of science the determination of the lines of conduct along which it can be realised.

When Spencer's theory was introduced it was remarked that it lay rather off the line of logical development of utilitarianism in general. The implication was that a development in utilitarian theory can be traced historically; and, in fact, that does seem to be true. The original position has suffered successive modifications for a variety of reasons, and this fact must be recognised, although, of course, the recognition of it does not imply that these modifications were all justified.

One obvious line of development which can be traced is that by which utilitarianism as an ethical theory has been set free from the doctrine of psychological egoism. Tentative movements in this direction were apparent in John Stuart Mill, particularly at those points in his discussion where he found room for Hartley's principle of association and also for internal sanctions. In Mill, however, the divorce was never complete, and to the end he remained a psychological egoist. It was left to Sidgwick to expound the utilitarian theory independently of the background of egoism which had been common to his predecessors.

A second but not so clear line of development may be traced in the positions adopted regarding the nature of the consequences which render actions right or wrong. The general principle is of course "the greatest happiness of the greatest number"; but differences are apparent in the precise interpretation of that phrase. For Bentham there were seven circumstances relevant to the determination of what is the greatest amount of happiness in any given case. Then Mill introduced the idea that pleasures differ in quality. The test was that people acquainted with different kinds of pleasure prefer one kind to another; and to Mill any such preference was inexplicable except in terms of pleasure. They preferred the "higher" because they found them the more pleasant. Yet Mill was prepared to admit that in such cases "more pleasant"

---

to show the influence of this fallacy, compare Spencer's reference to moral intuition, already quoted, which suggests that " the good is pleasant " is a synthetic proposition). And Moore himself admits (para. 29) that Spencer is not so clearly guilty of the fallacy as his French disciple, Guyau. Cf. Moore, *Principia Ethica*, ch. ii, paras. 29–33. It is interesting to note that, according to Moore (ch. iii, para. 36), Sidgwick was the first hedonist clearly to avoid the naturalistic fallacy and to point out that at the basis of utilitarianism there is an intuition that pleasure is the sole good.

did not necessarily mean "more intensely pleasant" or "equally pleasant for a longer time", or any other comparative based upon one of Bentham's seven relevant circumstances. On the other hand, the "higher", on Mill's presuppositions, was necessarily the "more pleasant" in some sense. Thus Mill began to speak of differences in kind, as if quality were an eighth relevant circumstance to be added to Bentham's seven. This, as we saw, may well be an attempt to keep more closely to the facts, but it does not help the theory in the slightest. Moreover, the question must be raised, What else can be meant by "more pleasant" if every interpretation based upon Bentham's seven relevant circumstances is excluded? It seems then to have no meaning whatsoever; and if that is so the matter must be probed more deeply. Is Mill right, it must be asked, in interpreting the judgment, "I prefer this higher pleasure", as meaning "I find it the more pleasant"? Is the preference, in other words, based upon the amount of pleasure at all, in whatever way that amount is measured? Is it not possible that a smaller amount of pleasure (smaller in respect of any and every relevant circumstance) is preferred because, although on the whole it is less pleasant, it is yet higher? If this is so, then Mill's introduction of a variety in the kinds of pleasure is really an appeal to a non-hedonistic criterion.

Thus, if we may use the word "utilitarianism" to denote those ethical theories which find the fundamental moral judgment in that which refers to consequences,[30] there is within utilitarianism a movement away from hedonism. In Sidgwick this movement was arrested, and Mill's recognition of different kinds of pleasure was explicitly rejected as inconsistent and untrue. But this did not end the matter, for in Professor G. E. Moore's *Principia Ethica* (1903) the tendency which was extremely hesitant in Mill was allowed to come to fruition, and the result was a type of utilitarianism which was not hedonism, but is denominated instead "ideal utilitarianism". Moreover, Moore's contribution to the discussion is marked, not only by a novel conclusion, but also, as a preliminary to that, by a very careful and painstaking analysis of moral terms and judgments. He finds his starting-point in a distinction between two quite different ethical questions which have

---

[30] " The chief reason for adopting the name ' utilitarianism ' was, indeed, merely to emphasise the fact that right and wrong conduct must be judged by its results." (Moore, *Principia Ethica*, p. 106.)

often been confused. "I have tried in this book," he says, "to distinguish clearly two kinds of question, which moral philosophers have always professed to answer, but which, as I have tried to shew, they have almost always confused both with one another and with other questions. These two questions may be expressed, the first in the form: What kind of things ought to exist for their own sakes? the second in the form: What kind of actions ought we to perform?"[31] Now it may certainly be admitted that Professor Moore is right. A very large proportion of earlier ethical discussion suffers from a failure to distinguish these two questions; and an indication of this state of affairs is to be found in the fact that the predicates "right" and "good" are for the most part used indiscriminately and the word "virtue" is taken as a synonym of both. This does not mean, however, as perhaps Professor Moore is at times inclined to imply, that such discussions are without value. For, although the two questions were not clearly distinguished, the moralists concerned contrived to talk more or less coherently on their subject, because to a large extent some of them confined themselves in effect to one question or the other. None the less, it is true that their doctrines might have gained both in breadth and in depth had it been realised that there were really two questions and not just one.

But if the questions are different they are also related. The first kind of question is concerned with propositions of the type "A is good in itself, has intrinsic value". The second is concerned with actions or with propositions of the type "Act X is right or my duty". But, says Moore, this *means* that act X is good as a means, that it is productive of something good in itself. "What I wish first to point out is that 'right' does and can mean nothing but 'cause of a good result', and is thus identical with 'useful'."[32] This tenet, however, is one which Moore tends to take for granted, and he never treats it as open to serious doubt. His whole discussion takes place within the assumptions that we can ask questions regarding intrinsic goodness, that these are or include the fundamental ethical questions, and that all other ethical questions resolve themselves into two parts, (i) questions of the former sort, and (ii) questions regarding the causes which will have intrinsically

---

[31] Moore, *Principia Ethica*, Preface, pp. vii–viii. Cf. also p. 24, " It is precisely this clearness as to the meaning of the question asked which has hitherto been almost entirely lacking in ethical speculation."

[32] *Ibid.*, p. 147.

good things as their effects. "With regard to actions," he says,
"we may ask *both* how far they are good in themselves, *and*
how far they have a general tendency to produce good
results." [33] "But," he adds, "that these are the only questions
which any ethical discussion can have to settle, and that to
settle the one is not the same thing as to settle the other—
these two fundamental facts have in general escaped the notice
of ethical philosophers." [34]

There is indeed one argument which Moore offers in defence
of his definition of "right". "It is plain," he declares, "that
when we assert that a certain action is our absolute duty, we
are asserting that the performance of that action at that time is
unique in respect of value. But no dutiful action can possibly
have unique value in the sense that it is the sole thing of value
in the world; since, in that case, *every* such action would be the
sole good thing, which is a manifest contradiction. And for
the same reason its value cannot be unique in the sense that
it has more intrinsic value than anything else in the world;
since *every* act of duty would then be the *best* thing in the world,
which is also a contradiction. It can, therefore, be unique only
in the sense that the whole world will be better, if it
be performed, than if any possible alternative were taken.
And the question whether this is so cannot possibly depend
solely on the question of its own intrinsic value. For any action
will also have effects different from those of any other action;
and if any of these have intrinsic value, their value is exactly as
relevant to the total goodness of the Universe as that of their
cause." [35] Clearly, however, the critical step in this argument
is that taken in the first sentence, where, without proof—and
Moore holds that his definition of "right" is demonstrably
certain [36]—it is assumed that in its connotation the word
"right" carries a reference to intrinsic value of the same kind
as that denoted by the word "good". It is not *proved*, it must be
repeated, that the word "right" does carry this reference, but
if the point is granted the "proof" which follows adds little
compared with what has been initially assumed. Moore
nowhere considers that this assumption can be questioned;
but it is plain that there are two other possibilities, (i) that
"right" carries with it no reference at all to value, and (ii)
that it carries a reference to value but not of the same kind as

[33] Moore, *Principia Ethica*, p. 24.   [35] *Ibid.*, p. 147.
[34] *Ibid.*, p. 24.   [36] *Ibid.*, p. 147.

that denoted by "good", that it refers to a value which cannot be added to, subtracted from, or computed against, the value of things which are intrinsically good.

None the less, it can well be admitted that a definite advance has taken place when it is seen that there are at any rate two ethical questions and not simply one.

Having made this preliminary point, Moore goes on to argue that there is a further distinction which applies to both these types of ethical question. In the case of questions concerning intrinsic goodness there are, according to Moore, two quite different things we may have in mind. We may intend to ask either, What is meant by "good"? How is it to be defined? or, What things are intrinsically good? Similarly, when we make inquiries about right actions, we may mean either, How is "right" to be defined? or, What actions are right?

Moreover, he tells us that the two questions about intrinsic goodness have not always been clearly distinguished. In fact, more frequently than not they have been confused. He himself holds that "good" is simple and indefinable, just as "yellow" is simple and indefinable; yet many ethical philosophers have failed to see this. The reason for their failure has been that these philosophers have thought themselves able to define "good", when, really, what they were defining was not "good" itself, but something which was good. In more technical language, they have failed to see that "good" is simple and indefinable because they have unwittingly committed what Moore calls the "naturalistic fallacy", that is, the mistake of defining "good" in terms, not of itself, but of something which is good. "'Good' then," he says, "is indefinable; and yet, so far as I know, there is only one ethical writer, Prof. Henry Sidgwick, who has clearly recognised and stated this fact."[37]

Now it can also be admitted that a definite advance has taken place whenever these two questions have been clearly distinguished, for, obviously, an ethical theory which confuses them is less adequate as an ethical theory than one which distinguishes them. Besides this, however, the confusion is not only a fault in itself but is also the source of other faults; and in fact, according to Moore, this confusion is largely responsible for a great group of ethical theories which regard pleasure as the sole good. If "good" is defined as "pleasant" it clearly follows that unless a thing is pleasant it cannot possibly be

[37] Moore, *Principia Ethica*, p. 17.

D

good. But, as Moore points out,[38] such a statement, although it may seem of the first importance, is really insignificant, for, *ex hypothesi*, it bears precisely the same meaning as the statement that unless a thing is pleasant it cannot possibly be pleasant. The fact, however, that what appears to be both a significant and a most important conclusion, turns out to be an identical proposition, suggests that in reality "good" has been used to connote something other than "pleasant". On the other hand, if "good" does not *mean* "pleasant", although it may still be true that pleasure is good, it is no longer clear that it is the *sole* good. Indeed, it can only be maintained that it is the sole good on the basis of moral intuition; but there can be no logical proof that this intuition is true, and it is always open to someone else to declare, so far as *his* moral intuition is concerned, either that pleasure is not good, or that there are other things good besides pleasure. The final appeal, in other words, is to the moral consciousness.

As we have seen, it was in this way that avoiding the naturalistic fallacy Sidgwick did maintain that pleasure is the sole good. Moore, however, will not allow this. Pleasure, he admits, is good; but by itself it is not nearly so good as other things which are not pleasure. And he proceeds to make a classification of the kinds of things which are good. His first point is that there are organic wholes. What does he mean by the term "organic"? "I shall use it," he says, "to denote the fact that a whole has an intrinsic value different in amount from the sum of the values of its parts."[39] Thus pleasure, though not in itself a great good, has yet the power of adding to the value of a whole of which it is part much more than its own intrinsic value in isolation. There are then two points in Moore's answer to the question, What things are good? In the first place, he does not allow that pleasure is the sole good, and suggests that many other things are also good. Secondly, he points out that the intrinsic values of the parts are no guide to the value of the whole of which they are parts. And these two points taken together suggest that it would be an almost impossible task to give an exhaustive list of the kinds of things which are intrinsically good. "There are," he says, "an *immense variety* of different things, *all* of which are intrinsically good; and though all these things may perhaps have some characteristic *in common*, their variety is so great that they have

---

[38] Moore, *Principia Ethica*, p. 38.   [39] *Ibid.*, p. 36.

none, which, *besides* being common to them all, is also *peculiar*
to them."[40] At any rate Moore does not attempt to give such
a list, but restricts himself to a discussion of the "Ideal", that
is to say, that which is good in itself in a high degree.[41] And
the conclusion he reaches in this limited inquiry is a comparatively simple one. "By far the most valuable things," he
holds, "which we know or can imagine, are certain states
of consciousness, which may be roughly described as the
pleasures of human intercourse and the enjoyment of beautiful
objects."[42]

These, however, it must be stated, are only two, though
doubtless the greatest, of many possible goods. But in his smaller
book entitled *Ethics*, which was first published in 1912,
Professor Moore does decide that *all* intrinsic goods have two
important characteristics in common, although, he is careful
to insist, neither of these characteristics is peculiar to intrinsic
goods. "There do seem to be two important characteristics,
which are *common* to absolutely all intrinsic goods, though not
peculiar to them. Namely (1) it does seem as if nothing can
be an intrinsic good unless it contains *both* some feeling *and also*
some other form of consciousness; and, as we have said before,
it seems possible that amongst the feelings contained must
always be some amount of pleasure. And (2) it does also seem
as if every intrinsic good must be a complex whole containing a
considerable variety of different factors—as if, for instance,
nothing so simple as pleasure by itself, however intense, could
ever be any good."[43]

So far, then, Moore's conclusions are these: (i) that "good"
is indefinable; (ii) that there is no one thing which is the sole
good; (iii) that the intrinsic value of a whole is not necessarily
equal to the sum of the values of its parts; and (iv) that all
intrinsic goods have in common, but not peculiar to them,
the characteristics (a) that they are complex wholes, and (b)
that two of the factors constituting these wholes must be some
feeling and some other form of consciousness.

So much, then, for the first main division of Moore's discussion, that which deals with intrinsic goodness.

The second main division is concerned with what might be
called instrumental goodness. Strictly speaking, however, its
subject is really rightness; but, as we have seen, Moore defines

[40] Moore, *Ethics*, p. 248.   [42] *Ibid.*, p. 188.
[41] Moore, *Principia Ethica*, p. 184.   [43] Moore, *Ethics*, p. 249.

"right" as "productive of good". A right act, according to him, is by definition one which is not productive of less good than any alternative, and a dutiful act is one which is productive of more good than any alternative.

All this, of course, amounts to an answer to the question, What does "right" mean? And we have already seen that although Moore claims to have proved this conclusion he has done so by assuming either the whole of what is in question or at least the greater part of it.

This, however, does not complete the inquiry, for there remains a further question in this division of the subject, namely, What kinds of action are right? or, in other words, What conduct is a means to good results? These two questions however, are properly treated as having the same meaning, if and only if Moore's definition of "right" is a true definition, a matter on which he would not have the support of every moralist.

It is not proposed to follow Moore into a detailed description of what kinds of action are right. Indeed he admits that we cannot make universally true statements that certain acts are right; and the important point for ethical theory is the reasons he advances for this limitation in our knowledge.

In the first place[44] since the rightness of an act depends upon the nature of its consequences we cannot be sure that any given act is right unless we can accurately estimate the value of *all* its consequences; and, clearly, that is a task which lies completely beyond us, for it is only within the *near* future that we can tell what the consequences are going to be. We cannot possibly follow them out indefinitely into the future; and therefore when we say that act A is right we are, at the most, making a statement which is *probably* true, because it is based upon the merely probable assumption that if act A is preferable to act B so far as its nearer consequences are concerned the later consequences will not contain grounds for reversing that decision. In other words, our opinion regarding what is right is merely a probable opinion because it is based upon a merely probable discounting of more distant results.

But, in the second place, even if that discounting were perfectly certain, our opinion concerning which acts are right would still be no more than probable, since our estimation of even the near results is itself simply a probable estimation. We

---

[44] Cf. Moore, *Principia Ethica*, pp. 152-4.

may have a perfect knowledge of all the laws which can possibly determine the results of act A, yet we can never be sure that certain of these laws will be in operation in this particular case, nor that certain others will not. "An ethical law has the nature not of a scientific law but of a scientific *prediction*."[45]

Moreover, it is worth adding on Moore's behalf, when an agent has made the probable statement that act A is right, and when in fact he has performed act A and has found the exact consequences accruing which he had expected to accrue, his judgment that, after all, act A *was* right is still no more than probable. It is merely a probable statement for two reasons. In the first place, the assumption which discounts the later consequences of act A is still only a probable assumption, and must remain in that category no matter for how long the agent observes it in this case to have been justified by the issue. But, in the second place, even if these later consequences could be certainly and demonstrably discounted, the judgment that act A was, after all, right is still only probable, because although the agent has by experiment verified his probable judgment about the consequences of act A, he has not verified, and never can verify, his probable judgment about the consequences of act B and the other alternatives. Consequently it is an implication of Moore's position that every judgment to the effect that some act or another is right is always and must for ever remain a merely probable judgment.

Whether this theory gives a true account or not, it is possible, so far as we have yet seen, to act upon it. For if the probable near consequences of act A are intrinsically good to the degree $2x$ and those of act B to the degree x, we shall probably do what on Moore's theory is the right thing if we perform act A. Yet the case need not be so simple as this. It may be that while the probable near consequences of act A are good to the degree $2x$ and those of act B to the degree x, the consequences of act B are more probable than those of act A. Does this fact, then, alter the moral situation? According to Moore, it does—in certain cases. "A less good, that is more likely to be attained, is to be preferred to a greater, that is less probable, if the difference in probability is great enough to outweigh the difference in goodness."[46] But this is nothing else than the beginnings of Bentham's hedonistic calculus applied, not to pleasure, but to goodness; and the same difficulty is present,

[45] Moore, *Principia Ethica*, p. 155.   [46] *Ibid.*, p. 166.

that of knowing whether a given difference in probability is sufficient to outweigh a given difference in goodness. How can one possibly weigh a difference in goodness against a difference in probability?

In this way, then, Moore has answered both questions which fall within each of his two main divisions of the subject of ethics, that is to say, both questions regarding intrinsic goodness and both questions regarding rightness.

There remains, however, one further point. It was maintained at an earlier stage in our argument that ethical theories differ according as they regard as fundamental one or another of three different types of ethical proposition—that which speaks of motives as morally good or bad, that which speaks of actions as right or wrong, and that which speaks of consequences as good or bad. Now Moore's discussion is one of the first to distinguish these kinds of judgment and to subordinate one to another. It is evident that on his view the third is more fundamental than the second, and that that is so because "right" simply means "productive of good". Indeed, his discussion is almost entirely taken up with these two kinds of ethical judgment, and the subordination of the one to the other.

He does, however, refer briefly and almost parenthetically to the first type of moral judgment, that which deals with the moral goodness of motives. He refers to it under the guise of the moral goodness of virtues or moral dispositions, and he maintains that when we speak of this moral goodness we are really speaking of one or the other of the kinds of goodness already considered, intrinsic goodness and instrumental goodness. "A virtue," he says, "may be defined as an habitual disposition to perform certain actions, which generally produce the best possible results."[47] And he adds, almost at once, "if they are really virtues they must be generally good as means". He holds, however, that the majority of virtues are dispositions to acts which are externally right, and therefore that, although they may be instrumentally good, they are not intrinsically so. But virtues do sometimes consist of dispositions, not just to act in a particular external way, but to be moved by certain motives, and in these cases, according to Moore, "we may say that wherever a virtue does consist in a disposition to have certain motives, the exercise of that virtue *may* be intrinsically good; although the degree of its goodness may vary indefinitely

[47] Moore, *Principia Ethica*, p. 172.

according to the precise nature of the motives and their objects".[48]

Moore is careful to point out, however, that this exercise of a virtuous disposition is not at all the sole good, is not even the only great good; and, of course, in any given set of circumstances it may be outweighed by the goodness of the consequences which will probably follow upon some alternative act towards which there is no habitual disposition.

[48] Moore, *Principia Ethica*, p. 177.

CHAPTER IV

THE ETHICS OF IDEALISM

UTILITARIANISM, AS WE saw, provides a link between the eighteenth century and the twentieth, and enjoyed in the nineteenth what has been perhaps its greatest period of influence. This does not mean, however, that its sway was undisputed. On the contrary, even in the nineteenth century there was growing opposition in the form of a school of thought which looked to Kant and Hegel for its inspiration, and which, so far as ethics is concerned, is conveniently focused in the work of Thomas Hill Green (1836–82). Indeed, in the latter half of the century these two schools were concerned to state their respective points of view in explicit contradistinction the one from the other; and the situation is symbolised by the somewhat parallel careers at Oxford and Cambridge respectively of Green and the last of the great nineteenth-century utilitarians, Henry Sidgwick, who was Green's junior by two years. In their different spheres and in different ways, both exercised a powerful influence, and each found it necessary to relate his thinking to that of the other.

Green's philosophy of morals is contained in his *Prolegomena to Ethics*, a work which, on account of his early death, never received a final revision at the hands of its author. As a result it suffers from frequent repetition and faulty arrangement, so that the essential elements of Green's ethical thought tend to be obscured. On the other hand, this obscurity cannot be entirely attributed to faults of expression which might well have proved only temporary but have in fact turned out to be permanent. There is a natural and inherent complexity about Green's ethical teaching, for to his own mind it appeared in intimate connection with other conclusions which are ordinarily regarded as falling outwith the strict limits of ethical science. The whole of the *Prolegomena* does not fall within the science of ethics; and in fact there are at least four other topics with which the author feels it necessary to deal. In preparation for the ethical part of Green's doctrine there is a discussion which belongs partly to metaphysics and partly to psychology. Then when, after this long introduction, the subject of morality is properly broached a great deal of the reader's attention is directed by Green towards some account of the principles at work in moral progress and the manner of their working; and finally a question is raised regarding the place of moral theory, that is, of ethics itself, in the development of our conception of the moral ideal. In all this the precise results of Green's analysis of the moral consciousness are imbedded, and occupy a smaller and perhaps less prominent place than is customary in a work on ethics. Certainly they are apt to appear incidental to the onward march of Green's impressive argument. Yet it is with them that we are chiefly here concerned.

None the less, some account must be given of the context in which these results are set forth, and, in the first place, we must notice what Green has to say about the eternal consciousness which in being conscious of objects is conscious also of itself, distinguishing itself from these objects. His argument is that both the concept of a knowledge of nature and the concept of nature itself presuppose as their logical condition this eternal self-consciousness which can be a consciousness of a succession in time without itself being in time either as an event or as a succession of events. The argument is reminiscent of Kant's analysis of the logical conditions of the world of experience which he makes in the *Critique of Pure Reason*, with the exception that Green has no place in his system for unknowable things-in-themselves. Both nature and a knowledge of nature are inconceivable apart from the working of this eternal self-consciousness; and the fundamental reason for this assertion is that both a system of events and a knowledge of the system involve a unity in spite of the obvious plurality, involve, that is to say, something which distinguishes itself from the events, is not, like them, simply another event in time, but is present to each and all of the events which are in time. And this "something" is what Green calls the eternal self-distinguishing consciousness.

Yet, in spite of all this, it does ordinarily appear as if our knowledge consisted of a succession of states of consciousness. We are conscious of A, then of B, of C, and so on, and the one consciousness is before or after the other. Yet, as Green would point out, neither the terms of this succession nor the succession itself can be described as knowledge, as knowledge of A in relation to B in relation to C. The states of consciousness in succession may contribute to knowledge and render it possible,

may contribute, that is to say, to bringing A, B and C within
the ambit of our knowledge, but they cannot be identified
with the knowledge itself. The latter presupposes the eternal
self-consciousness which is present to each and all of the terms
of the succession, but is itself neither a term nor a succession of
terms. We may describe our growth in knowledge by reference
to a succession of such states of consciousness, but although that
succession may be involved in our growth of knowledge it is not
itself the knowledge, nor can it ever of itself produce knowledge.
In the last resort, our growth in knowledge is intelligible only
as the progressive realisation in us of the eternal self-distinguishing consciousness. And one consequence of this is that, since
our knowledge is not a term in any causal series of events, nor
the effect of any such series, it is therefore free. In knowing
we are free, for our knowledge is the work of the eternal
consciousness.

We are accustomed, however, to think of our freedom as
freedom in doing rather than as freedom in knowing, and it
is natural then to ask whether the eternal consciousness, which
is the source of freedom in knowing, is present also in those
actions we regard as human. And to this question Green's
answer is, as a matter of fact, in the affirmative. Just as knowledge is inconceivable apart from the action of the self-distinguishing consciousness, so specifically human action is inconceivable apart from the same consciousness. Moreover,
just as, in the case of knowledge, this truth is obscured by the
fact that there are events which contribute to knowledge, are
apt to be confused with knowledge, but are strictly not to be
identified with it, so, in the case of human action, there are
events which contribute to action, are apt to be confused with
it, but are really not at all the same thing as action. These
latter events are what Green calls wants. A want is a natural
phenomenon arising as a result of certain natural causes, and
it may quite well have as its effect a movement towards its
own satisfaction. But all these—the want, its causes and its
effects—fall within the realm of natural phenomena, and fall
short of distinctively human action. The entire process from
cause through want to ultimate effect is a natural process and
lacks that deliberateness which is present in even the most
spontaneous of human actions. By deliberateness is not here
meant deliberation between alternative possibilities of action,
although the particular case where there is a choice between

different possible courses may well display more clearly what is present even in spontaneous action so long as it is human. By deliberateness is meant that characteristic of his actions in virtue of which a man regards himself as responsible for them. Thus in discussing Esau's purchase of a mess of potage in exchange for his birthright, Green declares that "if the action were determined directly by the hunger" (that is, by the mere want) "it would have no moral character, any more than have actions done in sleep, or strictly under compulsion, or from accident, or (so far as we know) the actions of animals."[1] The sign that in Esau's action more is involved than mere hunger is that "he imputes it to himself, and it is morally imputable to him—an act for which he is accountable, to which praise or blame are appropriate".[2] And this quality which human actions have and natural processes have not, is what we denote by the word "deliberateness". It is more clearly recognised where there is a perceptible period of deliberation between alternatives, but it is present also in spontaneous human action. "It is not necessary", says Green, "to that putting forth of the man or self in desire which constitutes an act of will, that there should have been beforehand any conscious presentation of competing objects of desire, with consequent deliberation as to which should be pursued."[3]

Green has another way of putting the matter. It is that, whereas a mere want acts upon a man, in action he himself enacts. "His willing is not a continuation of any of those desires, if they are to be so called, that were previously acting upon him. It is that which none of these had yet become; a desire in which the man enacts himself, as distinct from one which acts upon him. Whether its object—the object to which the moral action is directed—be the attainment of revenge, or the satisfaction of a bodily want, or the fulfilment of a call of duty, it has equally this characteristic. The object is one which for the time the man identifies with himself, so that in being determined by it he is consciously determined by himself."[4]

There is then a definite difference between a natural process which includes a want as one of its terms and a moral action proper, a difference which may be described in terms of the distinction between enacting and being acted upon, or in terms of the presence or absence of what we have called deliberateness,

---

[1] Green, *Prolegomena*, bk. ii, ch. i, para. 96. [3] *Ibid.*, bk. ii, ch. ii, para. 147.
[2] *Ibid.*, bk. ii, ch. i, para. 96. [4] *Ibid.*, bk. ii, ch. ii, para. 146.

or in terms of the presence or absence of the element of responsibility; and the question is, Does this difference, however described, involve the eternal consciousness which is involved in knowledge? The answer is that it does, and that the action of the self-distinguishing consciousness makes all the difference.

When the eternal self-consciousness comes into play it puts an end, as it were, to natural process, it allows it to go no further without the consent of this consciousness itself. And it gives or withholds its consent by considering and holding up over against itself the object which would satisfy the natural want, by distinguishing itself from it, and then by either identifying or not identifying itself with that object as its own personal good. If this identification is made there arises what Green calls a motive as distinct from a mere natural want, and it is motives and not wants which move to distinctively human action. Moreover, according to Green, a want "only becomes a motive, so far as upon the want there supervenes the presentation of the want by a self-conscious subject to himself, and with it the idea of a self-satisfaction to be attained in the filling of the want".[5]

This account of the matter is for Green a true account so far as it goes, but it does not go quite far enough. For one thing, it suggests that the eternal consciousness in a man may simply refrain from identifying itself with any object as its personal good, whereas Green would probably say that in waking life it is continually so identifying itself, whether with a new satisfaction to be realised or with a present one not to be sacrificed (as when a man resists the enticement of new prospective delights and chooses to continue "in the same old way"). But whether that be so or not, the account of the matter requires still to be amplified in one particular direction. For it must also be stated that in human action the self-distinguishing consciousness does not simply identify itself with a certain satisfaction as its own good, but it does so identify itself with that satisfaction as not only being what it is, but as also making possible or ruling out, as the case may be, other satisfactions. "In reflection upon our motives", says Green,[6] "we abstract the predominant desire from that qualification, whether in the way of added strength or of abatement, which it derives from the belief on the part of the desiring subject that its satisfaction

[5] Green, *Prolegomena*, bk. ii, ch. i, para. 88.　　[6] *Ibid.*, bk. ii, ch. ii, para. 127.

involves the satisfaction or frustration of other desires. But it is in fact always so qualified." This means that more is involved than mere self-identification; there is present also an element of choice and comparative evaluation. The self-distinguishing consciousness identifies itself with this rather than that as its personal good. That is to say, the idea of better as well as the idea of good is present in the action of this eternal consciousness. "That a man should seek an object . . . as one without which in his then state he cannot satisfy himself—and this is to will— implies that he presents himself to himself as in a better state with the object attained than he is without it." [7]

Indeed Green goes further even than that, for he believes [7] that the idea of a better implies some notion of the best, of complete or perfect satisfaction. [8] Thus, he has been paraphrased, "the notion of complete satisfaction, as somehow and somewhere *possible*, is the regulative idea guiding all practical endeavour after even temporary satisfactions". [9]

Now this analysis has revealed two things in human action which are really two aspects of the same thing: (a) a consciousness which identifies itself with objects and yet distinguishes itself from them; and (b) a consciousness of a "whole of satisfaction" or a complete satisfaction, comparable to the *world* of knowledge. Moreover, these two aspects betray the action of the eternal consciousness which is present in knowing, and justify us in regarding men as free in action as well as in knowledge. By freedom, of course, Green does not, and cannot, mean an undetermined choice. A free choice is determined by the eternal consciousness so far as it is realised in us, determined, that is to say, by our character. And the exercise of this freedom is revealed in the existence of desire, will, practical reason, which, according to Green's usage, are different names for the action of the self-distinguishing consciousness in identifying itself with some object as in the circumstances its personal good.

This may appear an odd usage of the word "desire", as synonymous with "volition"; but Green insists that we must distinguish desires proper from what are admittedly often called desires, namely, mere solicitations in which the agent is

[7] Green, *Prolegomena*, bk. iii, ch. i, para. 178.
[8] Cf. Green, *Prolegomena*, bk. iii, ch. ii, para. 180; also bk. iii, ch. i, para. 172, where Green tells us that " the practical struggle after the Better " has its spring in the idea " of there being a Best ".
[9] Lamont, *Introduction to Green's Moral Philosophy*, p. 62.

acted upon; and he holds that it is the agent's reaction to these which alone is specifically human. This he treats as the same thing as will, although he recognises that owing to the circumstances which confront the agent the adoption of what was before a mere solicitation may be prevented from appearing as an overt act.

In all this, however, Green has been giving an account, not of morality, but of human action in general, and of that in a metaphysical context. What he has said covers the whole field of practical endeavour and the specifically moral quality which some actions have has not been dealt with. In a sense, of course, Green *has* been treating of moral action, for he has been treating of actions for which the agents are morally responsible, for which they are responsible, that is to say, from the moral point of view as opposed, for example, to the legal. Yet so far as the argument has proceeded, it is not clear that all such actions would accept one or other of the moral predcates "right" and "wrong", "morally good" and "morally bad", nor has Green tried to discover the underlying ground for some actions being judged good, and others bad, in a moral sense. And it is to his treatment of these questions that we must now turn.

We have already seen that in all human action, according to Green, the eternal self-consciousness identifies itself with some object as its personal good, in which, for the time being at any rate, it seeks satisfaction. It is not, however, concerned with this object in isolation from other possible objects, but in identifying itself with one it is aware that it is thus rendering some further satisfactions possible, and others impossible. Throughout the practical life, moreover, it is seeking not just one satisfaction at the expense of others but complete satisfaction, not only the good, but nothing less than the best. All this being so, it is clear that although in every action the agent seeks his own personal good he may seek it either in a direction which will actually promote, or in a direction which will actually hinder, his complete satisfaction, his attainment of the best. In other words, he may be guilty of miscalculation or not. And the question arises whether for Green this is the source of moral distinctions.

The answer is that on the whole it is so. He refers, for example, to "the question of the distinguishing nature of the moral good, or that other form of *the same question* . . . in

which it is enquired, how the true good differs from the merely
apparent";[10] and a little later he adds: "Regarding the good
generically as that which satisfies desire . . . we shall naturally
distinguish the moral good as that which satisfies the desire of a
moral agent, or that in which a moral agent can find the
satisfaction of himself which he necessarily seeks. The true good
we shall understand in the same way. It is an end in which the
effort of a moral agent can *really* find rest."[11] Again he says
that the search of the self-determining spirit after some satisfaction of itself is the source both of vice and of virtue; and, he
adds, "it is the source of vicious self-seeking and self-assertion,
so far as the spirit which is in man seeks to satisfy itself or to
realise its capabilities in modes in which, according to the
law which its divine origin imposes on it and which is equally
the law of the universe and of human society, its self-satisfaction
or self-realisation is not to be found. Such, for instance—
so self-defeating—is the quest for self-satisfaction in the life of
the voluptuary. . . . It is one and the same principle of his
nature—his divine origin in the sense explained—which makes
it possible for the voluptuary to seek self-satisfaction, and thus
to live for pleasure, at all, and which according to the law of its
being, according to its inherent capability, makes it impossible
that the self-satisfaction should be found in any succession of
pleasures. . . . He is living for ends of which the divine principle
that forms his self alone renders him capable, but these ends
. . . are not in the direction in which that principle can really
fulfil the promise and potency which it contains."[12] "The
self-objectifying principle," he elsewhere insists, "cannot
exert itself as will without also exerting itself as reason, though
neither as will nor as reason does it, in the vicious life, exert
itself in a direction that leads to the true development of its
capacity."[13] And, finally, "it is through the operative consciousness in man of a possible state of himself better than the
actual, though that consciousness is the condition of the possibility of all that is morally wrong, that the divine self-realising
principle in him gradually fulfils its capability in the production
of a higher life. With this consciousness, directed in the right
path, i.e. the path in which it tends to become what according
to the immanent divine law of its being it has in it to be—and it

---

[10] *Prolegomena*, bk. iii, ch. i, para. 171 (italics mine).
[11] *Ibid.*, bk. iii, ch. i, para. 171 (italics mine).
[12] *Ibid.*, bk. iii, ch. i, para. 176.
[13] *Ibid.*, bk. iii, ch. i, para. 178.

is as so directed that we call it 'practical reason'—rests the
initiative of all virtuous habit and action."[14]

Now the clear intention of all these statements is that vice
is a rational activity made possible by the presence in us of the
eternal self-distinguishing consciousness. It is action governed
by reason—otherwise, on Green's principles, it would be
involuntary—but by reason under a misapprehension, making
a mistake, and not according to a true idea, "such an idea as
our reason would have when it had come to be all which it has
the possibility of becoming, and which, as in God, it is".[15]
Vice, then, is a miscalculation of what is good, and virtue a
pursuit of good in the direction in which it truly lies. Morally
bad action presupposes a disharmony between reason in us
and reason as it really is, in God; and there seems no other
account of vice open to Green, who has identified will, desire
and practical reason.

Yet, it would appear, this is not the whole truth of the matter
as Green sees it. While he holds that "there is essentially or in
principle an identity between reason and will" he recognises,
in the same sentence, that these may "become divergent in the
actual history of men (in the sense that the objects where good
is actually sought are often not those where reason, *even as in
the person seeking them*, pronounces that it is to be found)".[16]
And this is no casual admission on Green's part. "To us,"
he says deliberately, "who view the process piece-meal,
ourselves representing certain stages in it, it is natural to treat
the development of practical reason, i.e. the gradual filling
up and definition of the idea of human perfection, as a separate
process, upon which the corresponding conformation of will
may or may not ensue."[17]

These admissions open up new possibilities in Green's
account of virtue and vice, and it is therefore necessary to
inquire how, and in what sense, he can make them; how, and
in what sense, he can allow that will and practical reason may
thus diverge. For, after all, the implication seems to be that,
at any given stage, the eternal consciousness may have realised
itself in a man more completely *qua* practical reason than *qua*
will or desire.

The first step in this subordinate inquiry is taken when we

[14] *Prolegomena*, bk. iii, ch. i, para. 178.
[15] *Ibid.*, bk. iii, ch. i, para. 177.
[16] *Ibid.*, bk. iii, ch. i, para. 177 (italics mine).
[17] *Ibid.*, bk. iii, ch. i, para. 179.

explicitly acknowledge that of which every reader of the *Prolegomena* must at least be dimly aware, namely, that Green speaks of the moral ideal, the Best, in two different ways, sometimes as complete satisfaction, sometimes as complete realisation. What, then, is the relation between these two descriptions, and which is the more fundamental of the two? The answer is that so far as the content of morality is concerned the idea of self-realisation is perhaps the more important, but that for the formal theory of morality the notion of self-satisfaction is the more fundamental. Having answered the question, however, we must now offer some explanation of the answer.

When Green lays it down that vice consists of seeking satisfaction where in fact it is not to be found, his reader is inclined at once to object. "Surely," he is tempted to say, "surely, this account misses the essential character of vice. I may certainly seek satisfaction along the wrong lines; I may, for example, go to the theatre thinking mistakenly that I shall enjoy the play; but is it plausible to say that that miscalculation shares and displays the essential nature of wrong-doing?" Now it is not clear whether Green can avoid completely the force of this criticism, but it is true that he holds vice to be usually of a somewhat more intricate nature, being the failure, not just to satisfy existing desires and interests, but rather to develop potential interests and abilities, in the development and satisfaction of which alone complete satisfaction is to be found. Most characteristically, then, vice is not the failure to achieve even temporary satisfaction, but rather the failure to achieve complete satisfaction in spite of almost any amount of success in achieving temporary satisfactions, a failure which is due to not taking into account the inherent potentialities of the moral agent. Thus virtuous conduct involves self-realisation.

On the other hand, the moral value of self-realisation is that along this line and only along this line is complete satisfaction to be found. Were it not so, self-realisation would have no place in Green's system. "In virtue", he says "of this principle [self-consciousness] in him man has definite capabilities, the realisation of which, *since* in it alone he can satisfy himself, forms his true good."[18] Thus, for moral theory the notion of self-satisfaction is quite fundamental, and self-realisation is merely a means to that as end. For the moral and social reformer self-realisation may be the guiding principle, but in the system of the

---

[18] *Prolegomena*, bk. iii, ch. ii, para. 180 (italics mine).

moral philosopher its whole importance is derived from the notion of complete satisfaction.

At this point, however, another question crops up, for it may well be doubted whether the idea of self-realisation can be a real guide to anyone, be he moral reformer or not. Self-realisation is simply the realisation of the capabilities of the self, but, as Green himself admits, "we cannot fully know what any capability is till we know its ultimate realisation".[19] Consequently, if the task of the social reformer or, for that matter, of the moral agent is to realise capabilities which are so far wholly unrealised, the moral agent is faced with a task in which it is impossible to know where to begin. As a matter of fact, however, the moral capabilities of man, that is, his potentialities which determine his moral good, are not in an entirely undeveloped state. They have realised themselves so far, and have expressed themselves in human legislation, in social and political institutions, in public opinion, in customs and in habits of action; and by reflection on these, Green holds, "we can form at least some negative conclusion in regard to the complete realisation".[20] These offer confirmation of the idea of the good as common, and an examination of them suggests two directions in which development may take place, (i) by extending the area of the common good till none are shut out, and (ii) in the more precise determination of the common good. Primarily, of course, each man's job is "to fulfil the duties of his station".[21] The least we ought to do is to keep "to the path in which human progress has so far been made";[22] and whether any particular individual will be able to take the development a step further still will depend "on his special gifts and circumstances".[23]

But, whether or not we are able to take this step forward, we can scarcely avoid being aware of what the self-distinguishing consciousness has so far achieved as embodied in social institutions, laws and customs; and of these Green gives a clear account. They are, as it were, stepping-stones to higher things, the accumulated achievement so far of the eternal consciousness seeking without respite the supreme good. It is as if in its search for self-satisfaction this consciousness had taken notes of the results of its experience, of deceptive avenues which are apt to

[19] *Prolegomena*, bk. iii, ch. i, para. 172.
[20] *Ibid.*, bk. iii, ch. i, para. 172.
[21] *Ibid.*, bk. iii, ch. ii, para. 183.
[22] *Ibid.*, bk. iii, ch. i, para. 176.
[23] *Ibid.*, bk. iii, ch. i, para. 176.

allure and finally disappoint, and of paths apparently un-
promising yet in the result none the less fruitful; and these notes,
the records of its experience, are to be found in law, institution
and convention. "The particular duties which the categorical
imperative enjoins will *at least* be all those in the practice of
which, according to the hitherto experience of men, some progress is made towards the fulfilment of man's capabilities, or
some condition necessary to that progress is satisfied."[24]

Now, as we have said, we can hardly avoid being aware of
what the eternal consciousness has so far achieved; and it is
with this awareness that our wills may conflict. The individual's
growing experience of the habits, customs and institutions of
contemporary society is in effect his learning what the eternal
consciousness has already learned regarding the ways of complete satisfaction; and yet the individual's will may not conform
itself to what he has learned. Green describes the individual's
conviction of what is truly good as "the echo in him of the
expression which practical reason has so far given to itself in
those institutions, usages and judgments of society, which
contribute to the perfection of life";[25] and he says that "in
the individual the idea of what is good for him in his actual
state of passion and desire—the idea which in fact he seeks to
realise in action—is apt not to correspond to his conviction of
what is truly good".[26] The individual, he says later, "knows
the better—knows it, in a sense, even as better for himself, for he
can think of himself as desiring what he *does not* but feels that he
should, desire—but he prefers the worse. His will, we say, does
not answer to his reason".[27]

Thus we see how Green can find room in his system for a
conflict between will and reason, by introducing his idea of
institutions and laws as the record of past experience on the part
of the eternal consciousness. It may still be questioned, however,
whether in this Green has really avoided contradicting his
identification of will and reason, and whether his principles will
really allow him to say of the individual that "he prefers the
worse". The truth seems to be that in spite of his special
account of laws and customs Green cannot consistently speak of
a conflict between will and reason as if they were two separate
faculties; and, it might be argued, Green appears in the end to
see this. "We see," he says, "that it is only some *better* reason

[24] *Prolegomena*, bk. iii, ch. ii, para. 197.   [26] *Ibid.*, bk. iii, ch. i, para. 179.
[25] *Ibid.*, bk. iii, ch. i, para. 179.   [27] *Ibid.*, bk. iii, ch. i, para. 179.

with which in vicious action a man's will conflicts, while there is
an exercise of reason by him which is the very condition of his
viciousness."[28] And this might be taken as suggesting that the
conflict is as much within reason itself as between reason and
will. The individual, the argument would run, knows the conclusions which the eternal consciousness has so far reached, but
he has not himself appropriated them. He is like the schoolboy
who, having overheard his more industrious mates, knows that,
but not why, the three angles of a triangle are equal to two
right angles. The individual's conviction is one of custom and
convention rather than of insight, and the conflict is between a
true conclusion for which he has not grasped the reason, and a
false one to which he holds more firmly. He is in society, that is
to say, but not yet of it.

When all this has been said, however, it must be confessed that,
whether legitimately or not, Green does seem to speak of something more like what we ordinarily mean by a conflict between
reason and will. He speaks of the two as "modes of the eternal
principle";[29] and he holds that an agent "can think of himself
as desiring what he *does not*, but feels that he *should* desire". Now
it depends on what Green understands by this word "should"
which he has emphasised. If he means what he says, if "knowing
that one should" means more than merely being sensitive to a
critical public opinion, more than not feeling at home in one's
particular society, then no doubt Green does allow a conflict
between the different modes of the eternal consciousness. And
there may be brought forward in support of this interpretation
the very statement that a man's will may conflict with "some
better reason", for he defines the latter, not as a point of view of
which the man is aware though not convinced, but as the man's
"capacity for conceiving a good of his own, so far as that
capacity is informed by those true judgments in regard to human
good which the action of the eternal spirit in man has hitherto
yielded".[30]

Now at an earlier stage of our general inquiry, it was laid
down that ethical theories fall into one or another of three
different classes, according as they take as the fundamental
ethical proposition that which predicates "morally good or
bad" of men and motives, or that which predicates "right or
wrong" of acts, or that which predicates "good or bad" of the

[28] *Prolegomena*, bk. iii, ch. i, para. 179.   [29] *Ibid.*, bk. iii, ch. i, para. 177.
[30] *Ibid.*, bk. iii, ch. i, para. 179.

consequences of acts; and a question naturally arises regarding the classification of Green's account of virtue within this general scheme.

This, however, is not an easy question to answer, not so easy as it has been in the case of other moral theories; and one reason is that, whereas to a large extent these other theories were content to concentrate on one of the three types of moral judgment as fundamental and to ignore the other two, Green's account of the matter attempts to do one thing which any adequate ethical theory must do, namely, it endeavours by considering all three types of moral judgment to set them forth in their proper relation one to another. The sentimentalists, for instance, concentrated on those moral judgments which deal with affections as their subject; and, without raising the question whether that kind of judgment is or is not the fundamental type of moral judgment, we can say that sentimentalism falls short by failing to consider the other kinds of moral judgment and to relate them to what we have called the self-conscious type. Green, however, does not fail in this way. All three types of judgment have a place in his system. Indeed, his very adequacy in this direction makes it difficult to discover which is really, in his view, the most fundamental.

In the first place, he recognises those judgments which affirm that certain acts are right and others wrong. These he comprehends as "the duties of a man's station", and he will not allow that these are unimportant or negligible.[31] Indeed, the duties of all stations taken together amount to the customs, institutions and laws of society, and Green does not teach at all that these are to be despised. On the contrary, they must be respected and obeyed; but, on the other hand, they are not self-authenticating.

Why, then, ought we to do the particular things that we ought to do? Green does not in fact put the question in this precise form. He approaches the matter from the other end, and in his argument these particular duties do not appear as the occasion which gives rise to the inquiry, but rather as the unforeseen conclusion to which the inquiry leads. Even so, however, it is clear that for him these particular duties derive all their force from the fact that they are what the eternal consciousness has hitherto achieved in its effort to realise itself. They derive their force from the fact that they are the fullest

[31] Cf. Green, *Prolegomena*, bk. iii, ch. ii, para. 183.

expression we have yet reached of what we may call the potentialities of the human soul, or, as Green puts it, of the moral
capability. This means that the obligatoriness of these particular
duties derives from the fact that they are expressions of the good
will, and therefore that the type of proposition which declares
that certain acts are right and others wrong is less fundamental
than that which qualifies a man's will as morally good or
morally bad.

But this does not close the matter. There remains the question
whether this latter type of question is ultimate. Is self-realisation
or, in other words, the creation of a good will a self-authenticating task and its own justification? The answer is that for Green
it is not. Certainly, in some contexts, he speaks as if, for the
purpose he has on hand at the time, the self-determining
spirit's satisfaction of itself and its realisation of its capabilities
could be treated as the same thing.[32] He does not, however, say
so in so many words, and it may only be that they lie in the same
direction. Moreover, when he does distinguish between them, as
in some contexts he seems compelled to do, he treats self-satisfaction as the ultimate and self-authenticating experience, which
justifies also the task of self-realisation through which alone
complete self-satisfaction is attainable.

Green begins this part of his theory with the point that the
good must be defined as that which satisfies desire; and the
moral good is therefore that which satisfies the desire of a moral
agent, that "in which the effort of a moral agent can really find
rest".[33] Now this appears to be a circular definition, but it is
not really so. The word "moral" has two different meanings
according as it is opposed either to "immoral" or to "amoral",
and by a moral agent he means what we ordinarily mean, a
moral agent as distinct from an amoral "agent", as one who is
capable of morality or in whom the self-determining consciousness is active, and who therefore acts under the regulative idea of
the best, complete and perfect satisfaction. This best or the moral
good is that which completely satisfies desire. By "moral good"
in this sense we *mean* complete satisfaction.[34] Yet a moment or
so later we find Green saying that "the moral good is the realisa-

---

[32] Cf. Green, *Prolegomena*, bk. iii, ch. i, paras. 175–6.
[33] Cf. Green, *Prolegomena*, bk. iii, ch. i, para. 171.
[34] Cf. Lamont's *Introduction to Green's Moral Philosophy*, p. 114: "The moral
good, then, is to be identified with full self-satisfaction." Later (p. 115), "we
are able to say that moral good is the absolute good or Best, and that it is the
pursuit of this Best which is the distinctive characteristic of the moral will".

tion of the moral capability".[35] By this, however, he does not
mean to contradict his definition, but rather to set down the one
means to that as end, the one matter which can fill that form.
To say that the moral good is the realisation of the moral
capability is another way of saying that complete satisfaction is to be attained only by realising the moral capability.
And so we find Green explicitly declaring that this realisation forms a man's true good *"since in it alone he can satisfy
himself"*.[36]

Thus, in the last analysis, what Green calls the good will and
what we should call the morally good will justifies the effort
after it because through its realisation men achieve what Green
calls the moral good and what we should call *the* good, the Best,
which Green defines as complete satisfaction. Consequently for
Green there would seem to be a more fundamental moral
proposition than the self-conscious type which predicates
"morally good or bad" of a man's will, namely, that which
says that X is good or rather a special form of that which says
that X is best.

This analysis seems plausible enough; and yet it has term-
inated in a very odd conclusion, namely, that Green's account
of virtue is a utilitarian account since it regards as the fundamental moral proposition that which holds that X is good.
This *is* an odd conclusion because both to Green and to his
readers the theory propounded in the *Prolegomena* is obviously
not utilitarianism. Consequently, we must try to discover in
what precise way Green's theory differs from that of utilitarianism; and this inquiry is perhaps best pursued by asking, What is
this X which, in Green's system, is *the* good?

It is, of course, self-satisfaction; but we must remember that
although Green's own language may not at all times avoid
ambiguity on this point, it is his constant conviction that what
is good is not the satisfaction which follows upon the successful
fulfilment of desire but, more strictly, that which fulfils or
satisfies desire. Green is quite clear on this point, and he
repeatedly charges Hedonism, which is a form of Utilitarianism,
with confusing these two things. The true account on his view is
that when a man regards certain objects as in line with the good
"he must indeed anticipate pleasure in their realisation, but the
objects, not the pleasure, form the actuating content of his idea

---

[35] *Prolegomena*, bk. iii, ch. i, para. 172.
[36] *Ibid.*, bk. iii, ch. ii, para. 180 (italics mine).

of true well-being. A transfer of his interest from the objects to the pleasure would be its destruction".[37]

The good, then, is that which completely satisfies, or that which satisfies a moral agent, for it involves not just the satisfaction of existing desires but also complete realisation. Green, however, has more to say of it than this. It is also in his view a common good shared with others. And this position is not unconnected with what has gone before, for if the good had been conceived of in terms, not of that which satisfies, but of the satisfaction or pleasure itself, it would have been something which could not possibly have been shared. Indeed, in passing, we may notice an embarrassment which inevitably besets those moralists who think of the good as pleasure, for, since their good is something which cannot be shared, it follows that either they must describe the moral life in a purely egoistical fashion, or else they must allow two entirely different moral principles, Self-love and Benevolence, which aim respectively at the agent's own pleasure and at the pleasure of others.[38] This dilemma, however, Green avoids by insisting that the good is not the satisfaction, but that which satisfies, and by so allowing himself to regard it as something which may be shared, a common good. That it is such a common good Green holds to be certain. We are naturally interested in others, and we can only be completely satisfied in society, and in a society in which others achieve a like satisfaction. Indeed, this characteristic of the moral ideal indicates one important direction in which moral progress may be achieved, by extending the area of the common good until it is nothing short of being universally common and the society in which it is realised embraces the whole of humanity.

Further, this common good, this idea of man's true good is characterised by Green as "for practical purposes . . . an idea of an order of life, more or less established, but liable to constant interference from actions prompted by passion or desire for pleasure; an order in the maintenance and advancement of which he conceives his permanent well-being to consist".[39] "When a man 'sits down in a calm hour'," he says, "to consider what his permanent well-being consists in, what it is that in desiring it he really desires, it is not indeed to be supposed

---

[37] *Prolegomena*, bk. iii, ch. iv, para. 234.
[38] Cf. Green, *Prolegomena*, bk. iii, ch. iv, para. 226.
[39] *Prolegomena*, bk. iii, ch. iv, para. 232.

that he traces the desire back to its ultimate source in his self-objectifying personality, or that he thinks of its object in the abstract form of that which will satisfy the demand arising from such a personality. But, if unbiassed either by particular passions or by philosophical prepossessions, he will identify his well-being with an order of life which that demand has brought into existence. The thought of his well-being will be to him the thought of himself as living in the successful pursuit of various interests which the order of society—taking the term in its widest sense—has determined for him; interests ranging, perhaps, from provision for his family to the improvement of the public health or to the production of a system of philosophy." [40] And so the good is conceived by Green as an order of life, as a social order, which alone can completely satisfy moral agents.

The precise nature of this good we cannot yet perfectly determine. We can only describe it as it has so far realised itself, and the complete description can come only through "that education of the conscience of which the end is the conviction that the only true good is to be good". [41] "The only good," says Green, "in the pursuit of which there can be no competition of interests, the only good which is really common to all who may pursue it, is that which consists in the universal will to be good—in the settled disposition on each man's part to make the most and best of humanity in his own person and and in the persons of others." [42] This means that Green has passed from the idea of the good as an order of life to the idea of the good as the good will. It means that the good will distinguishes itself from the bad as seeking to maintain and perfect itself in the agent and in others, and therefore that the object of the good will is the good will itself. And this development in Green's theory, although it may seem curious, is none the less in line with what has gone before, for if the existing order of life—the laws, customs and institutions of today—derives its value from the fact that it is what the eternal consciousness has so far achieved in its effort to realise itself, it is only to be expected that the perfect order of life will likewise derive its superior value from the fact that it is the expression of a will which has perfectly achieved self-realisation. The ultimate good is then the good will itself. In the last resort, the good must be conceived as "a spiritual activity in which all may partake, and

[40] *Prolegomena*, bk. iii, ch. iv, para. 234.   [41] *Ibid.*, bk. iii, ch. iv, para. 244.
[42] *Ibid.*, bk. iii, ch. iv, para. 244.

in which all must partake, if it is to amount to a full realisation of the faculties of the human soul".[43]

There are, however, two points to be made regarding this conclusion; first, that it seems to conflict with the analysis of Green's account already given, according to which the fundamental moral proposition is of the form, "X is the good"; and second, that it seems to involve not only a circular argument but a self-contradiction in affirming that the object of the good will is the good will itself. At an earlier stage in the inquiry we met with a somewhat similar circle, namely, that contained in the statement that the moral good is that which satisfies the moral agent; and we saw that the word "moral" was being used in this case in two senses. Is it then possible that a similar solution may apply in the present case? The answer is that it is. The good will under the imperfect circumstances which alone we know, that is to say, the morally good will is characterised by devotion to an ideal,[44] and this ideal is of course *the* good. So far the matter is plain enough; and indeed it is not essentially altered if *the* good is now further determined as the good will, for by this characterisation we do not at all return to our starting-point—the good will which is the absolute good is *not* the morally good will which we know, but is instead the perfect realisation of that in us and in all others[45] freely exercising itself without hindrance. The ultimate and true good is this perfect realisation, and the morally good will which we know is characterised by devotion to this good as the ideal. Moreover, the perfectly realised will is good because only in the exercise of it can the desire of a moral agent be completely satisfied. Thus, when we say that at the root of Green's system there is the proposition "X is best" or "X is *the* good", we mean that the good will is *the* good, but by the good will we do not mean my will or anyone else's, we do not mean the present realisation of the eternal consciousness in me or in another, but the ultimate realisation in all. This is in a sense outwith me; in another sense it is immanent, for it is simply the perfect development of inherent potentialities.

Thus, for Green, acts are right in so far as they represent

---

[43] *Prolegomena*, bk. iii, ch. v, para. 286.
[44] Cf. Green, *Prolegomena*, bk. iii, ch. iv, para. 244.
[45] "The good has come to be conceived with increasing clearness . . . as a spiritual activity in which all may partake, and in which all must partake, if it is to amount to a full realisation of the faculties of the human soul." *Prolegomena*, bk. iii, ch. v, para. 286.

the hitherto achievement of the eternal consciousness in its effort to realise itself, that is to say, in so far as they are the expression of a morally good will. A morally good will, in turn, is morally good in so far as it is a will devoted to *the* good. And *the* good is ultimate, being the perfect realisation of the eternal consciousness, the ideally and absolutely good will. Moreover, such a will is *the* good because only in its free exercise can a moral agent really satisfy himself; but, after all, this is not, on Green's principles, a significant statement, for the good *means* that which satisfies the desire of a moral agent.

Clearly, Green travels quite another course than that taken by utilitarians, and we must now attempt to say precisely in what respects he differs from the utilitarian school.

In the first place, he does not agree that in acting morally we consider and compare the various results of the alternative courses of action open to us. Rather, we meet a claim or a demand which comes immediately from without, from the social order in which we live, but which in the last analysis comes from within, arising as it does from the agent's "self-objectifying personality"[46] which demands its self-realisation.

Secondly, the ultimate criterion of morality is not goodness, an abstract quality which may exist in many things, nor the comparative of goodness which also may exist in many, but *the* good, the best, which is one, an ideal which may be served by many acts but is not the result of any one of them. The utilitarian's good results, or better results, or best possible results, are many, whereas Green's ideal is one, the good will fully realised in all, a well-being into the consideration of which "the opposition of self and others does not enter".[47] Moreover, not only is the good such that it may be served by many actions but produced by no one of them, but also when realised it is not other than actions, it is rather itself a spiritual activity.

Thirdly, however, this ultimate criterion is an empty one. Whereas Moore's goodness, for example, is a simple unanalysable predicate, Green's good is something complex which we cannot comprehend except in so far as it is already realised. Consequently, while it theoretically remains the ultimate criterion, practically we have to recognise another, and this practical criterion of morality is the correspondence of an act with the laws or customs of society, or its being a step in

[46] *Prolegomena*, bk. iii, ch. iv, para. 234.
[47] *Ibid.*, bk. iii, ch. iv, para. 235.

advance of these. The practical criterion of the morality of an act is the consideration whether it proceeds from a morally good will, that is, from a will which has realised its potentialities at least as far as the eternal consciousness in man has realised itself in the surrounding society.

By this reference to a morally good will, however, Green— and in this he advances beyond the earlier sentimentalists whom we have already considered—does not intend to separate a motive from the act to which it leads, saying that the act is right if the motive is morally good. Rather he regards the separation of motive from act as a false abstraction which may be corrected from either end. On the one hand, a motive is either a volition and includes the "act", or else it is a mere solicitation to which moral distinctions do not yet apply. From the other side, an act or the external part of it may seem right and my duty, and may claim as it were to be performed by me, but only because the volition which includes it will be morally good, that is, will partially realise the good will, *at least* so far as it has already been realised. The moral demand is immediately from without, but ultimately from within.

In summing up, then, we must say that for Green the proposition that act A is right is manifestly less fundamental than that which affirms that volition X is morally good. Moreover, since he defines "good" as that which satisfies desire, the only meaning which Green can give to "morally good", as we ordinarily understand it, is "being a partial realisation of the good" or "being an approximation to that which can satisfy a moral agent"; and *the* good, that which *would* satisfy a moral agent is the good will, which is itself a spiritual activity. Sometimes, indeed, he speaks of the morally good will, not as a partial realisation of the good, but as an effort towards it, as devotion to an ideal which is the good; and, in fact, he is compelled so to speak, since the ordinary moral consciousness sometimes speaks of an act having a quality of moral goodness and sometimes of the act aiming at an objective good, for example, the good of others. But, if to say that something is the objective good of others means more than simply that it satisfies *some* desire, if in other words this way of speaking has a moral relevance, this objective good can only be, on Green's principles, either the good itself (which is at least unlikely at this stage of history) or else a partial realisation of it. Consequently, the two ways of speaking of the morally good will ((a) as a partial realisation of *the* good will, and (b) as a will devoted to *the* good will as an ideal and making an effort towards it) really amount to the same thing. And if we still protest, arguing that there are surely involved two different principles and not just one, since the moral goodness of the agent is clearly different from the objective good which the agent seeks to confer upon someone else—if we argue along these lines Green will reply that the only thing really good whether in the agent or another is the good will itself, and, further, that into the consideration of this matter the distinction between self and others does not enter.

Thus in the end Green says:

(1) that the fundamental moral proposition is of the self-conscious type since an act is right if it proceeds from a morally good will, but that we must be careful not to treat the motive in isolation and as separable from the act to which it leads;

(2) that moral goodness and goodness are really the same thing, unless by goodness we mean merely the characteristic of being able to satisfy *some* desire, for in that case goodness has no moral significance;

(3) that the only permissible distinction between "morally good" and "good" is that which takes the former as a partial realisation of the latter, and that the distinction which differentiates between the good I do to others and the moral goodness I myself acquire in doing it is not permissible since it rests upon the false distinction between the agent and others.

Although Green's is the classical exposition of this point of view, there are others who also accept the main points of his theory, as, for example, Bradley, Muirhead and Mackenzie. Thus in his *Elements of Ethics* Muirhead starts from the fact that at first sight there appear to be two moral standards, the moral law and the moral end, and he raises the question which of these is prior. His answer to this is in harmony with Green's, for, "while the conception of end . . . is prior", he says, "being that on which the other rests, yet the conception of law comes first in time".[48] In other words, although the content of morality may come to us in the form of law, it is the moral end which ultimately imposes duties upon us, and without that end there would be no duty and no law. Law itself is in morality

---

[48] Muirhead, *Elements of Ethics* (2nd ed.), para. 28, p. 66.

an inadequate concept; and there are, in fact, three stages by which reflection seeks a more adequate conception. In the first place, the law is regarded as fundamental and also as external. Even in the ordinary practical life, however, the inadequacy of this idea is quickly apparent, and there are two main ways in which an effort may be made to surmount these difficulties, either by casuistry, that is, by extending and particularising the law in an effort to make it cover all possible situations, or, on the other hand, by taking some external law (as, for example, that which imposes obedience to king or pontiff) as containing the first and absolute duty. But it is found that the reflective moral consciousness can rest in neither of these positions; and so there follows the second stage in which the law is regarded as fundamental still, but is internal. This is, of course, the intuitionalist theory; and it is in such theories that conscience has a large part to play. We need not here inquire into what we mean by conscience. Different accounts have been given; but, according to Muirhead, [49] they have this in common that they regard conscience as a distinct faculty of the soul (however the different theories may choose to characterise this faculty), and therefore by implication as external to the self and its other parts. Now Muirhead's fundamental objection to an external law as the final moral form is that its authority depends on sanctions and superior power, and that therefore it cannot intrinsically justify itself to the moral agent, but must in the last resort appeal to non-moral considerations. But in the same way, according to Muirhead, if morality is to be finally described as the law of conscience, that law, being external to the self and its other parts, cannot justify itself to these except in a way (by the pains of an evil conscience, for example, which disobedience entails) that is amoral, if not immoral.

It is therefore necessary to carry the analysis of the moral judgment a step further and confess that the ultimate moral standard is an end. This, however, does not conclude the ethical investigation, for different accounts can be given of the nature of this moral end. But, says Muirhead, running through these various theories there are two main tendencies, which are radically distinguished the one from the other by their respective answers to the question whether in man it is reason or feeling that is fundamental. According to some of these theories it is feeling that in human life is directive, and the

---

[49] Muirhead, *Elements of Ethics* (2nd ed.), para. 35, pp. 82ff.

function of reason is simply to discover adequate means to given ends; and so there naturally arise the different forms of hedonism. On the other side, there are those who argue that "the predominating element in the self is reason, which, as essentially opposed to desire, asserts itself in the authoritative and categorical demands of the moral imperative".[50] This is the assumption behind cynicism, stoicism, and other forms of asceticism; and the moral end is held to be self-conquest.

Now Muirhead objects to hedonism that it blurs the distinction between right and wrong, and in this way falls short of morality. In this respect the theory of self-conquest is much nearer the truth; and yet Muirhead is unable to accept it, for it draws such a distinction between truly moral action and other kinds of human action as to make the former an utter impossibility for men in that all action from desire is denounced as immoral. In other words, the fault of both theories is that they make reason and desire external to one another, the one by making desire master and reason a mere servant, the other by describing reason as the uncompromising opponent of all desire.

The truth, as Muirhead sees it, is that desire is involved in all reasoning and reason in all desire; and that the moral end is the realisation, not of something given by desire independently of reason, nor of something given by reason independently of desire, but of the self itself. This self-realisation is neither the realisation of any or every desire nor the suppression of all desire, but the realisation of what may be called lower desires in subordination to the realisation of what may be called higher desires, in all of which, both high and low, reason is involved as apprehending a personal good. All conduct, indeed, involves this apprehension and pursuit of a personal good, and "conduct which is judged to be absolutely, i.e., morally, good is conduct whose end is the highest good, which again may be described as the realisation of the highest self. The *summum bonum* is to realise the *summus ego*".[51]

Moreover, the *summum bonum* is a common good; and for this insight Muirhead believes that credit is due to the exponents of evolutionary hedonism such as Spencer and Stephen, who completely rejected the traditional view, which might well be described as the atomic view, of society (each counting as one and none as more than one), and in its place put as a more

[50] Muirhead, *Elements of Ethics* (2nd ed.), para. 54, p. 122.
[51] *Ibid.*, para. 65, p. 163.

adequate account an organic view of society, according to which it is impossible fully to understand an individual life in abstraction from its social context.

In all this, it is clear, Muirhead is in close agreement with the findings of T. H. Green; and so far as their general ethical approach is concerned both affirm, in the last resort, that the fundamental ethical proposition is of the type "X is a morally good action", since for both the *summum bonum* is that kind of action in which the self completely realises itself. The only thing unconditionally good is the good will.

To a very considerable extent, Bradley, also, is in sympathy with this point of view. Like Muirhead he sees the idealist solution as a middle course between the two opposite errors of hedonism (pleasure for pleasure's sake) on the one hand and the ethics of self-conquest (duty for duty's sake) on the other. For Bradley these two theories are opposite extremes, and yet their respective exponents are guilty of the same mistake, the error of abstraction. The hedonist abstracts the content from the form and seeks a complete whole where indeed it can never be found, in an endless series of pleasures. The theory of self-conquest, on the other hand, abstracts the form from the content, and portrays the moral life as a conflict between the good will, which is the only thing absolutely good, and the empirical self, which is the seat of all desire. Thus morality is something absolute and universal, but at the same time something unreal because it is not also particular and therefore has no content. And so it appears that both these theories, hedonism and asceticism, while suffering from the same defect of abstractness, fall wide of the truth in opposite directions, and therefore a more adequate theory must be found in the middle ground which lies between them.

A general and more satisfactory account of the matter, which is true so far as it goes, Bradley finds in the theory of self-realisation; in the theory, that is to say, which describes the moral end as the realisation of the self, of the whole self, and not simply of desire in isolation from reason nor of reason in opposition to desire. "Must we not say," he asks, "that to realise self is always to realise a whole and that the question in morals is to find the true whole, realising which will practically realise the true self?"[52]

Moreover, although Bradley has severely criticised what he

[52] *Ethical Studies* (2nd ed.), p. 69.

calls the theory of "duty for duty's sake", declaring that it "carries with it little or no plausibility",[53] and although he has attributed to that inadequate theory the dictum that there is nothing absolutely and unconditionally good except the good will, yet when he comes more positively to characterise the moral end of self-realisation he accepts this latter insight as an essentially true one and holds that self-realisation consists in good activity. In expounding the ascetic theory, he had interpreted the moral consciousness as affirming "that the end is for me as active, is a practical end. It is not something merely to be felt, it is something to be done. . . . The moral consciousness assures us that the activity is an end in itself. . . . The end does not fall outside the doer. I am to realise myself. . . . In short, the good is the Good Will. . . . There is nothing which is good, unless it be a good will. This is no metaphysical fiction. It is the truth of life and of the moral consciousness".[54] Thus Bradley puts it in his exposition of the ascetic theory, and although his rejection of the theory is uncompromising, he himself does not depart from this true insight upon which the theory is based. And when he comes to develop a more adequate account of morality he largely builds upon the same foundation. "We find," he says, "the deliverance of the moral consciousness in the emphatic maxim that nothing is morally good save a good will. This maxim we shall forthwith take to be true, and so proceed."[55] "Acts," he later declares, "so far as they spring from the good will, are good, and a temper and habits and character are good so far as they are a present good will, result from it and embody it; and what issues from a good character must thus likewise be morally good."[56]

Further still, Bradley considers the atomic view of society as quite untenable. He regards society as an organism, and the isolated individual as a mere fiction of theory. Morality, he insists, is the progressive realisation in us of the good will, which is a social will and the will of society, which exists in individuals, but not in isolated individuals who do not exist. And this account of morality he entitles "My station and its duties".

Up to this point there is an unmistakable resemblance between Bradley's theory and those of Green and Muirhead; but Bradley does not regard the account he has given as cover-

---

[53] *Ethical Studies* (2nd ed.), p. 148.
[54] *Ibid.*, p. 143.
[55] *Ibid.*, p. 228.
[56] *Ibid.*, p. 230.

E

ing the whole of morality. It may be said to cover *real* morality, provided such a phrase is not misunderstood. It means that aspect of morality which is the realisation in me of the existing social will. But, clearly, morality is more than this. It is not only the perfection of my will in accordance with the judgments and institutions of existing society. It is also the perfection of society itself, of its institutions and its judgments. Besides the *real* social morality there is an *ideal* social morality, an ideal social will, which consists in the perfection of existing imperfect social customs, institutions and opinions.[57] And in this, too, Bradley is not out of harmony with Green and Muirhead. Indeed, a doctrine of social progress is essential to all their theories if they are to avoid the criticism that, professing to give an account of the absolute moral standard, they have been content to study the moral standard as it is to be found in any particular society at some particular time. Without the doctrine of progress they would write themselves down as relativists.[58]

Besides this, however, there is another respect in which real morality falls short of the whole. In addition to it, there is not only an ideal social morality, but also an ideal non-social morality. This can best be described in Bradley's own words. "The realisation for myself," he says, "of truth and beauty, the living for the self which in the apprehension, the knowledge, the sight, and the love of them finds its true being, is (all those who know the meaning of the words will bear me out) a moral obligation, which is not felt as such only so far as it is too pleasant."[59] And, later, "to me it is a fact that the moral consciousness recognises the perfecting of my intellectual or artistic nature by the production of the proper results, as an end in itself, and not merely as a means. The pursuit of these ends, apart from what they lead to, is approved as morally desirable, not perhaps by the theory, but, I think, by the instinctive judgment of all persons worth considering."[60] Bradley explicitly affirms that this non-social ideal is good in itself, and he explicitly rejects, as contrary to the facts, the *theory* that it is only good as a means to a social ideal.

[57] Cf. Bradley, *Ethical Studies*, p. 222: " We can see no reason for supposing this presented ideal self to be anything beyond the idealisation of what exists in human nature, the material idealised being more or less cosmopolitan, and the abstraction employed being more or less one-sided."

[58] Cf. Muirhead, *Elements of Ethics*, para. 85, pp. 217–18.

[59] *Ethical Studies*, p. 222.

[60] *Ibid.*, p. 223.

But now, of course, there arises the awkward question of the relationship between these three aspects or elements of morality, and this question Bradley does not attempt to avoid. In reply to it, he has several points to make, that a conflict between any two of these aspects is a case of colliding duties, not a contest between a moral claim and a claim that is not moral, and, further, that such cases are not scientific but practical questions: "moral science has nothing whatever to do with the settlement of them; that would belong, did such a thing exist, to the moral art . . . they arise from the complexity of individual cases, and this can be dealt with solely by practical insight, not by abstract conceptions and discursive reasoning."[61] Bradley's last word is this, that the ideal social aspect and the ideal non-social aspect of morality are based upon what he has called real morality (my station and its duties), and are related to it and to each other in the same way as within it different duties, which may collide, are related.

It may be asked whether in introducing the ideal non-social aspect or element of morality Bradley has not departed from the type of theory we have hitherto expounded as the ethics of idealism. And, certainly, it must be admitted that it is not in the interests of theory that he recognises this aspect. The quotations already given show that in making this recognition he is not following out a theory, but is paying attention to the facts, to the facts, that is, of the moral consciousness. Consequently, if in the end he is found to betray the ethics of idealism, it is not an over-abundant enthusiasm for the theory that has compelled him to play this part, but a fearless honesty in seeking a truly adequate and comprehensive theory.

What then is the fact? It is that the pursuit of truth and beauty is morally good. While admitting this, however, Bradley is not blind to the distinction between moral excellence on the one hand, and intellectual or artistic excellence on the other. "A man need not be a good man," he says, "just so far as he is a good artist; and the doctrine which unreservedly identifies moral goodness with any desirable realisation of the self can not be maintained."[62] On the other hand, he will not allow that morality stops short, as it were, and fails to cover in some way the whole extent of life. He cannot admit that where truth and beauty are relevant, morality is not so. Rather, although morality and self-realisation are not identical, there is a moral aspect of all self-realisation. "Whatever has been brought under the control of the will, it is not too much to say, has been brought into the sphere of morality."[63]

Further, it is a fact for Bradley that the moral ideal to which truth and beauty give rise cannot, without doing violence to the facts, be regarded as a social ideal. It is itself a non-social ideal, and it is good in itself and not just as a means to some social end.

It may be doubted, however, whether, if this is a fact, Bradley has room for it within his own theory. Certainly, we may agree with him, the task of ethics is confined to the elicitation of the moral principle, and does not include the application of it to particular cases where the various duties to which it gives rise appear to collide. That, we may agree, is a matter not for the moral philosopher but for the man of practical insight. But, we may well ask on this occasion, is Bradley's recognition of the non-social ideal equivalent to the recognition of fresh duties falling under the original moral principle, or is it rather in effect the recognition of another moral principle altogether? On the face of it, Bradley seeks to avoid this latter conclusion by holding the whole field of morality together under the term "self-realisation". Yet words do not finally dispose of the matter. For one thing, we may simply raise, without here attempting to answer, the question whether this non-social ideal is adequately regarded as a form of self-realisation. But, secondly, even if it is, it must be asked whether "self-realisation" means the same when applied to the non-social ideal as it does when applied to real and ideal *social* morality. And the answer seems to be that it does not. In the one case, the self that is realised is a self that is what it is in virtue of its place in the social organism; whereas, in the other case, the self to be realised is what it is in itself, although of course that may depend upon what its place *has hitherto been* in the social organism. What in the one case is immorality, namely, independence of the social will, may become in the other case morality itself. It may, of course, be that a restatement of the theory would avoid this difficulty; but at any rate it is clear that, as it stands, the ethical theory of idealism cannot be accepted as the last word.

[63] *Ethical Studies*, p. 217.

CHAPTER V

THE NEW INTUITIONISM

In our last chapter we saw that if Bradley was right in regarding the pursuit of truth and beauty as at once a non-social and a morally good activity, then the ethical theory of idealism could not stand without more or less drastic revision. In the present chapter, however, we are to consider a school of ethical thought which finds fault at a deeper level with all idealistic ethics such as Green's, and regards it as guilty of a more fundamental error.

The first document of this modern school came from the hand of H. A. Prichard and consisted of a paper in *Mind* (January 1912) entitled, "Does Moral Philosophy Rest on a Mistake?"; and this was followed in 1928 by Prichard's inaugural lecture, *Duty and Interest,* on his appointment to the White's chair of Moral Philosophy at Oxford, and in 1935 by a paper in *Philosophy* (January) under the title, "The Meaning of ἀγαθόν in the Ethics of Aristotle". These are all comparatively brief contributions, and one aspect of their subject is dealt with in another, *An Ambiguity of the Word "Good",* by Mr. E. F. Carritt.[1] Together they may be taken as containing the pre-eminently negative and critical side of this modern school's ethical thought; but, although there may be inconsistencies as between one author and another, and perhaps as between one contribution and another of the same author, the conclusions are not simply negative but are such as to form a quite distinct ethical position.

Prichard's main contention in his initial article is that in the past ethics has for the most part failed, not by giving the wrong answer to the right question, but rather by asking the wrong question. He argues that the ethical problem, as conceived by moral philosophers, has taken the form, Why ought I to do act A which is taken to be my duty?; and, he says, the answer has been given by reference *either* to the agent's happiness or advantage, *or* to some goodness (either in the results of the action or in the action itself when done).

[1] Annual Philosophical Lecture, Henriette Hertz Trust, British Academy, 1937.

Now it is maintained that the former type of answer is quite beside the point. Whether an act is advantageous to the agent or not has nothing at all to do with the question whether or not it is the agent's duty. "Though we may find ourselves quite unable to state what it is that does render an action a duty, we ordinarily think that, whatever it is, it is not conduciveness to our advantage; and we also think that though an action which is a duty may be advantageous it need not be so."[2] In this connection Professor Prichard takes Plato to task for his reply to the Sophists and his manner of dealing with their favourite contentions. They had argued that the ordinary moral code was not really obligatory on anyone, for the actions it enjoined were not really to the agent's advantage. Plato's answer to this was an attempt to show that, after all, they *were* to the agent's advantage; whereas, according to Professor Prichard, he should have said something like this: "These thoughts or convictions may or may not be true. But they cannot be false for the reason which you give. You do nothing whatever to show that they are false by urging that the actions in question are disadvantageous; and I should do nothing to show that they are true, if I were to show that these actions are, after all, advantageous."[3]

So much, then, for the first main type of ethical theory. And in passing we may be tempted to suppose that in criticising it Professor Prichard is but whipping a dead horse and that the second main type is by far and away his more serious rival. But, on the contrary, both Professor Prichard and Mr. Carritt believe that it is difficult to state this second type with any degree of plausibility[4] without slipping imperceptibly into a manner of speaking which implies the first type; and in fact Professor Prichard maintains that within the first class there fall such well-known names as Plato, Aristotle, Butler, Mill, and T. H. Green[5], to which Mr. Carritt would add the names of Professor Moore and Mr. H. W. B. Joseph.[6]

[2] Prichard, *Duty and Interest*, p. 10.
[3] *Ibid.*, p. 16.
[4] Cf. Carritt, *An Ambiguity of the Word ' Good '*, p. 26, where he says that the confusion between the two different types of ethical theory is largely responsible for any plausibility attaching to the " insistence that in ethics the idea of good is fundamental while that of obligation or duty is secondary to it and derivative ".
[5] Cf. Prichard, *Duty and Interest*; also " The Meaning of ἀγαθόν in the Ethics of Aristotle ", *Philosophy*, January 1935.
[6] Cf. Carritt, *An Ambiguity of the Word ' Good '*.

The reason why it is so easy to confuse the two types of theory is, according to Mr. Carritt, that there is an ambiguity in the word "good". For, quite apart from its instrumental and exemplary uses ("a good razor" and "a good thunderstorm" are the examples Mr. Carritt respectively gives of these non-ethical usages), the word "good" may mean "conducive to someone's advantage" (my good, or doing good to others), or it may denote a moral quality as in the phrase "a good man" or "a good act". This, of course, is not a new distinction. It is involved in the distinction between things which are good because someone desires them and things which are desirable because they are good; and it was this that Mill ignored when, to the lasting amazement of successive generations of moralists, he declared that "the sole evidence it is possible to produce that anything is desirable is that people do actually desire it". [7]

But even if this confusion is avoided, and a theory is set forth consistently to the effect that the reason why act A is my duty must be either that the results of act A are good (not necessarily advantageous), or that act A itself is morally good, this solution to the traditional ethical problem is not satisfactory any more than the other solution which connects rightness with the advantage of the agent. For if it is said that it is the goodness of the results which gives rise to the obligation that can only be so if it is assumed that the goodness of these results means or implies that they ought to be; whereas, in truth, it cannot properly be said that anything ought to be— "ought" applies only to actions. On the other hand, it can no more easily be maintained that it is the goodness of the act which gives rise to the duty, for that is the goodness of the motive, and, since "I ought" implies "I can" and motives are not within our control, rightness and moral goodness fall hopelessly apart. [8]

The contention is then that the word "good" has two usages; (a) in which it stands for a quality of actions or results, what may be called an absolute or objective usage; and (b) in which it means "conducive to someone's advantage", what may be called a relative or subjective usage. It is also contended that, according to the answers which ethics has traditionally

[7] *Utilitarianism*, ch. iv.
[8] Cf. Prichard, " Does Moral Philosophy Rest on a Mistake? ", *Mind*, January 1912.

given, the reason why we ought to do those actions we ordinarily think right is either that they are good in sense (a), or that their results are good in sense (a), or that the actions are good in sense (b). To these we might seek to add a fourth reason, that the results are good in sense (b); but in our definition of this sense the reference to results is already present, and to say that an act is good in this sense is not to say that it has a certain quality, but that its effects have a certain quality. Nor can we use "good" in sense (b) to denote a quality of the act itself, since, as Professor Prichard points out, "something's giving us enjoyment is *not* a quality of it, and when we say that something *is* pleasant, we are not attributing to it a certain quality but stating that it has a certain effect". [9]

There are then three possible answers to the ethical problem as traditionally posed; and it is further contended that no one of these is in the end tenable. Moreover, the intuitionists do not suggest that a fourth and more adequate answer is possible. Rather, Prichard's point is that the whole enquiry is vitiated from the start because the question asked is a wrong question. It implies that the concept of duty and the ethical judgment that act A is right are subordinate to, and derivative from, some other concept, such as that of good, and judgments of the type that something X is good (in any of its senses). He contends that that implication is false, that "ought" or "right" cannot be derived from anything but "ought", and that, on the contrary, the idea of right is for ethics a fundamental concept which stands upon its own feet. And with this affirmation there begins the positive part of the intuitionist theory.

Before passing on to this side of the theory, however, it will be well to attend at once to an ambiguity in its negative part; and perhaps this will best be introduced by a consideration of the line of argument to be found in Mr. Carritt's book, *The Theory of Morals*, which was first published in 1928. In this book, after introducing the subject of moral theory, the author proceeds to consider the theory which is to be found, he thinks, at the lowest reflective level, the theory of hedonism, and this, both as a moral and as a psychological doctrine, he completely rejects as in effect an attempt to explain morality away. It asks, Why ought we to do right actions? as if there must be some more fundamental reason for doing an act than simply

[9] " The Meaning of αγαθόν ", *Philosophy*, January 1935, p. 36.

that it is right. "If any one ask us, 'Why ought I to do these acts you call my duty?' the only answer is, 'Because they *are* your *duty*', and if he does not see this we cannot make him, unless by informing him about matters of fact; if he sees they are duties, he can no more ask why he ought to do them than why he should believe what is true. To answer, 'Because they are the best policy', would not answer the question why he *ought* to do them."[10]

That manner, then, of dealing with the ethical problem is finally abandoned; and this means for Mr. Carritt, not just that an inadequate answer to the ethical problem has been rejected, but also that the ethical problem itself has been reformulated in a more accurate fashion. "Once it be granted", he proceeds, "that we have duties, and that the obligation to do something consists neither in liking to do it nor in liking its consequences, whether these be natural or ordained by human or divine laws, it may seem consequent to ask what the nature of our duties is. The greater part of ethical writing has been occupied with attempts to answer this question, or, in other words, to define right conduct."[11] This task he describes as the task of finding "in all the acts we think right some other common quality which makes us think them so"; and, he adds, "such an attempted definition can be refuted if we discover that we think some acts right which do not contain this quality or some wrong which do".[12]

Now it is precisely to this task that Mr. Carritt addresses himself, and in succession he rejects the suggestions that an act is right because it consists in following nature, because it aims at or achieves the greatest happiness of the greatest number, because it seeks the moral good of others, because it involves self-sacrifice or self-realisation, or because it promotes the common good. Moreover, consistently with what he has already laid down, he rejects each of these definitions because it is too wide or too narrow or both.

Having done this, however, he pauses in his argument to take stock[13], and in so doing he makes two odd sets of statements.

(i) He points out that even if all right acts did have *all* of these suggested characteristics "it would still need to be decided which, if any, of these consequences is our reason for

[10] *Theory of Morals*, p. 29.
[11] *Ibid.*, p. 30.
[12] *Ibid.*, p. 30.
[13] *Ibid.*, ch. viii.

judging the act right".[14] "We are not asking", he adds,
"what are the actual consequences of a right act, but whether
any of these consequences constitute its rightness: the agent's
pleasure, or the greatest pleasure of others,"[15] and so on. But,
strictly speaking, this is *not* what Mr. Carritt has been asking.
He has not been asking what constitutes rightness, but what
other characteristic right acts have in common in virtue of
which they are right—whatever rightness itself may be. In
other words, we must carefully distinguish the question, What
is rightness? from the other question, What characteristic or
characteristics, if any, do all right acts have in common in
virtue of which they are right?; and we must note that it was
the latter question which Mr. Carritt posed when he disposed
of hedonism.

Indeed, we must even distinguish two meanings within this
latter question, because the relationship of rationality (the
relationship which consists in an act being right *because* it has
the common characteristic) may be either a matter of presumption or a matter of moral insight. Thus I may find that
acts A, B, C . . ., which are right, all have characteristic X,
and I may then *presume* that they are right *because* they have
characteristic X; or I may find that they all have characteristics X, Y, and Z in common, and then I may *presume*, with
greater confidence, that they are right *because* they have
characteristic X and characteristic Y and characteristic Z. In
these cases the proposition which states the connection is a
universal empirical proposition which may be rebutted by
finding right acts which do not have the characteristic or
characteristics denoted by the predicate. On the other hand,
I may see as a moral agent that all right acts must have
characteristic X and that all acts having it are right; and in
this case the proposition which gives expression to this insight
of my moral consciousness asserts a necessary synthetic connection between rightness and characteristic X. Such a
proposition can be rebutted only by a direct appeal to the
moral consciousness on the point, although of course the appeal
would be more critical if I could discover an act F which was
judged right by the moral consciousness in spite of the fact
that it did not have characteristic X, for then I might fairly
insist that the moral consciousness make up its mind which of
two mutually inconsistent affirmations it would retain. These

[14] *Theory of Morals*, p. 69.   [15] *Ibid.*, pp. 69–70.

two questions then fall to be distinguished from one another, and also from the question, What is rightness itself?

(ii) The second odd set of statements follows a paragraph or two later where Mr. Carritt declares, "The truth appears to be that the rightness of an act cannot be deduced, as all the preceding theories assumed, from the 'goodness' of the result, whether achieved or aimed at. None of these theories escaped the false distinction of means and end. Nearly all moralists since Plato have attempted, and none of them with success, to prove that certain acts are right, either the acts commonly thought right in their day or some slightly emended code of their own. And this they have generally tried to do by deducing the act from the conception of a good or end which it is to achieve. But there is no such proof of moral judgments. You cannot prove to a man that he has duties, or should do his duty, or that justice is a duty, or that this act is just. All you can do is to give him fuller information of the consequences and antecedents of what he is doing and then ask him to agree with you that it is right or wrong. If he know the situation and consequences as well as you do and still differ, one of you must be wrong, yet there is no proof."[16] And yet, according to the original statement of the problem[17] to which the theories considered were attempted answers, the question was not one of proving that we have duties, but was rather of the form. Granted that we have duties, what characteristic have they in common in virtue of which they are duties?

Now, since it is from goodness that attempts have been made to *deduce* duties, we are required in the interests of accuracy to add a fourth question to the three questions already distinguished, and this fourth question is of the form, What is goodness, and what, if anything, does it imply?

In other words, there are four ways in which rightness may be connected with goodness: (a) by an empirical generalisation to the effect that all right acts have some characteristic, X, which involves goodness, and that X is therefore *presumed* to be the reason why certain acts are right; (b) by a necessary and synthetic judgment on the part of the moral consciousness that right acts have such a characteristic X, and that X is therefore *seen* to be the reason why certain acts are right; (c) by holding that rightness *means* some connection with goodness, as when Professor Moore maintains that "right" simply means

[16] *Theory of Morals*, pp. 71-2.   [17] *Ibid.*, p. 30.

"conducive to a good or the best possible result"; and
(d) by holding that goodness means or implies something
necessarily connected with rightness, such as "ought-to-
be-ness".

These distinctions do not of course invalidate Mr. Carritt's
argument, for if, as he tries to show, there are right acts which
are not the producing of the most good possible (no matter
where we suppose goodness to reside, whether in happiness or
moral perfection and so on), then, not only theory (a), but also
theories (c) and (d), are disproved, and doubt is cast upon
theory (b).[18] None the less we are to recognise that it is not
only one type of ethical theory but really four possible types
which are questioned by the argument. The theory that goodness means or implies something necessarily connected with
rightness involves, in its most plausible form, the judgment
that what is good ought to be; and this is rejected by Prichard,
who strongly insists[19] that, properly speaking, "ought" always
applies to acts and never to states of affairs. The theory that
"right" means some connection with goodness has, as its most
plausible form, that given to it by Moore when he defines
"right" as the "cause of the best possible result"; and this
theory Sir David Ross rejects on the ground that, whether or
not being the cause of a good result is the indispensable characteristic of all right acts, at any rate "right" does not just mean
"cause of a good result"[20], and that on the contrary "'right'
is an irreducible notion".[21] Further, as we have just seen,
both these theories, along with that which asserts an empirically universal connection between rightness and goodness
are disproved if Carritt is right in his contention that, no
matter what things we regard as good, there are right acts
which do not produce, either in effect or by intention, the best
possible results. This contention also casts doubt upon the
theory which asserts a necessary synthetic connection between
rightness and goodness. Strictly speaking, this latter theory
cannot be disproved, but it can be, and is, rejected by the new
intuitionism when it holds that in morals we begin and end
with the intuitive judgment that act A is right, and that if a

[18] Doubt is cast upon this theory because if two verdicts of the moral consciousness are mutually incompatible *both* are doubtful until the moral consciousness
makes up its mind between them.
[19] "Does Moral Philosophy Rest on a Mistake?" *Mind*, January 1912, p. 24.
[20] *The Right and the Good*, pp. 8–9.
[21] *Ibid.*, p. 12.

general description of right acts clashes with such particular judgments it is the former that must be given up.[22]

We are now in a position to summarise the negative and critical side of the theory. It holds (i) that to identify duty and interest is really to abandon morality; (ii) that "right" does not mean "cause of a good result" or anything else in which goodness is directly involved; (iii) that rightness does not mean anything, such as "ought-to-be-ness", which is meant or implied directly or indirectly by goodness; (iv) that the moral consciousness does not affirm a necessary and synthetic connection between rightness and goodness; (v) that in fact some acts are right which neither aim at, nor achieve, the best possible results; and to these we must add (vi) that although in points (ii) to (v) we have spoken and perhaps thought mainly of goodness as residing in results of one kind or another, each of these points may be taken as applying also to the goodness of acts, that is, to moral goodness, and that in any case the dictum that "I ought" implies "I can" is fatal to any theory which regards rightness as dependent upon moral goodness.

We may now turn to consider the positive side of the new intuitionism, what it has to say for itself as a moral theory and not just in criticism of other theories. The first point is that since "right", "duty" and "ought" are words which stand for something irreducible and unanalysable the idea of duty must be taken as simple, and since duties cannot be deduced, derived or proven from anything other than duties themselves the idea must also be taken as fundamental. This is not to say that the idea of right is *more* fundamental than other ethical notions, such as that of goodness, but it is to say that at least it is not less fundamental. The point is simply that the judgment that act A is my duty can be neither analysed into, nor derived from, other judgments no one of which is a judgment that some act is my duty.

That being so, the question next arises whether there is any quality or characteristic with which rightness is synthetically connected, whether the connection is necessary or empirically universal. Now Mr. Carritt holds "that every right act must afford some satisfaction to somebody", and by this he means "satisfaction other than (and prior to) the satisfaction of

[22] Cf. Muirhead, *Rule and End in Morals*, p. 17, and Carritt, *Theory of Morals*, para. 63, p. 70.

a right act having been done ".[23] But this point is qualified in
two ways. In the first place, it is with hesitation that Mr.
Carritt commits himself to it, and it must therefore be regarded
as a tentative rather than a final answer. In the second place,
he is also careful to point out that "it does not follow that
the act which gives the greatest quantity of satisfaction is, as the
utilitarians hold, the right one";[24] and for this reason, too, the
point must be regarded as tentative and not as a final answer. It
is description, not explanation. It points to a quality which
happens to accompany rightness, but it is not the satisfactori-
ness which makes the act right.[25] It would appear that some
further investigation is required in search of peculiarities
attaching to the satisfactions which are associated with right
acts; but Mr. Carritt confesses that he himself finds nothing
along this line. "Some satisfactions," he can only say, "are
due, are in the circumstances the ones we ought to give; others,
not."[26]

Is there, then, any single characteristic which all right acts
have, and in virtue of which they are right? The answer is that
there is none. And Sir David Ross warns us that we must not be
disconcerted by this reply. We may feel prejudiced against any
such theory, partly because we feel that an adequate and complete theory of morals would succeed in laying down a single
principle in virtue of which all acts are right that are right,
and partly because we may suppose that an ethical theory which
does not recognise such a single principle cannot be easy to
apply. These considerations, however, are beside the point.
Referring to the ideal utilitarian position that an act is right
if and only if it is productive of the best possible results in the
given situation, Sir David Ross declares: "The view which
admits only one intuition . . . gratifies our natural wish to
reach unity and simplicity in our moral theory. We have a
natural wish to reach a single principle from which the rightness
or wrongness of all actions can be deduced. But it is more
important that a theory be true than that it be simple. . . .
After all, there is no more justification for expecting a single
ground of rightness than for expecting a single ground of goodness, and agathistic or generalized Utilitarianism recognises
a variety of goods without succeeding in finding, or even feeling

[23] Carritt, *Theory of Morals*, para. 38, p. 41; cf. para. 51.
[24] *Ibid.*, para. 38, p. 41; cf. para. 51.
[25] *Ibid.*, para. 51-2, p. 54.
[26] *Ibid.*, para. 38, p. 41.

any need to find, a single ground of the goodness of them all. It is, to my mind, a mistake in principle to think that there is any presumption in favour of the truth of a monistic against a pluralistic theory in morals, or, for that matter, in metaphysics either."[27] Moreover, he adds later on, "the fact that it would be easier to recognise our duty if it depended on factor *a* only than it would be if it depended on factors *a*, *b*, and *c* has no tendency whatever to prove that in fact it depends on *a* alone."[28]

If, then, there is no presumption in favour of there being only one moral principle, are there in fact several principles the presence of any one of which is sufficient to render an act right? To this question the intuitionist answer is that there are, but that the matter requires more careful statement. It will be remembered that in the negative part of this theory the point was made that the fundamental ethical proposition is a particular judgment, and that in morals we begin and end with the intuitive judgment that act A is right. "When we criticize a particular moral judgment", says Mr. Carritt, "as being inconsistent with a principle, it is ultimately with other particular judgments that our comparison must be made."[29] By this, however, intuitionists do not mean that the act which is thus intuitively judged right is a sheer particular. If that were meant, then, although it might be possible by a process of induction to come to the conclusion that it was the presence of characteristic *a* in all these sheer particulars which made them right, none the less that generalisation could never be a safe guide in practice. To act by its light would be to tamper with some of the evidence that should test it; and it would be necessary instead to leave it to the ordinary moral consciousness in any later situation to accept some sheer particular as the right act in that situation. Further, it is easy to see, a collision of duties in such circumstances would be quite impossible. It would seem, however, that what the intuitionists mean is that the moral consciousness judges, not that the sheer particular A is right, but that act A having characteristic *x* is right. Thus "when I reflect", says Sir David Ross, "on my attitude towards particular acts, I seem to find that it is not by deduction but by direct insight that I see them to be right, or wrong. I never seem to be in the position of not seeing directly the rightness of a particular act of kindness, for instance, and of having to read

[27] *Foundations of Ethics*, pp. 82–3; cf. p. 319.   [28] *Ibid.*, p. 91.
[29] *Theory of Morals*, para. 63, p. 70.

this off from a general principle—'all acts of kindness are right, and therefore this must be, though I cannot see its rightness directly'."[30] "When we consider a particular act as a lie, or as the breaking of a promise, or as a gratuitous infliction of pain, we do not need to, and do not, fall back on a remembered general principle; we see the individual act to be by its very nature wrong."[31] Now what Sir David Ross is arguing against in these passages is the existence of a deductive process in our recognition of right acts, but in so arguing he makes it clear also that it is not sheer particulars we recognise as right. It is rather "particular acts in virtue of a particular character they possess";[32] and his language in the quotations just made plainly implies that this is his view. Thus I recognise act A, which is a particular case of keeping a promise, as right, but I recognise it so as the keeping of a promise. My recognition is an intuitive recognition, and that intuition is, we may suppose, progressively clarified until I see that in general promise-keeping is somehow right.[33]

In all this, however, the intuitionist is saying nothing that the ideal utilitarian, for example, could not also say. It would be a mistake to suppose that, whereas, according to intuitionism, we start with semi-particular intuitions, such as "Act A, which is x, is right", and gradually come to see that all acts having characteristic x are somehow right, the ideal utilitarian holds *either* that we start with the general intuition that all acts having characteristic x are right and deduce from that particular duties, *or* that we directly recognise sheerly particular duties and from such recognitions come to hold, by a process of induction, that all acts having x are right. On the contrary, the ideal utilitarian may well agree with the intuitionist position on this matter. He need not do so, but at any rate if he does not, his theory is not being presented in its most plausible form. For consider the alternatives. On the one hand, it can hardly be argued that we start with a general ethical intuition or principle ready made. On the other hand, we cannot reasonably suppose that our starting-point consists of sheerly particular ethical judgments, for that would rule out rational morality altogether. It would mean that all ethical principles would be empirical generalisations, and it would be impossible to act morally on principle, for that would be comparable to altering

[30] *Foundations of Ethics*, p. 171.   [32] *Ibid.*, p. 170.
[31] *Ibid.*, p. 173.   [33] Cf. Ross, *The Right and the Good*, pp. 32–3.

the cases which are the evidence for or against the hypothesis. To this extent, then, ideal utilitarianism need not contradict intuitionism; but when the centre of attention passes from the form to the content of the intuitions the two theories do decisively part company. For, while the ideal utilitarian holds that the only characteristic which renders acts right is that they are productive of the best results possible for the agent in the situation, the intuitionist holds that there are several characters any one of which may render an act right, and that these different characteristics cannot be reduced to the single principle of ideal utilitarianism.

In particular, Sir David Ross gives a list of several principles which set forth the different types of duty we intuitively recognise.[34] They are: (i) duties which rest upon previous acts of the agent, and are either (a) duties of promise-keeping or (b) duties of reparation; (ii) duties which rest on previous acts of others, namely, the duties of gratitude; (iii) the duty of justice, that is, the duty to secure as far as possible a distribution of happiness according to merit; (iv) the duty of beneficence, to which ideal utilitarianism would reduce every other duty; (v) the duty of self-improvement; and (vi) the duty of non-maleficence. In his later book *Foundations of Ethics* Sir David is prepared to alter this list in some respects.[35] He seems more willing to admit that some of these duties may be only special cases of the general duty of utilitarianism. Yet, if that is to be allowed in certain cases, he holds no less vigorously that there are principles of duty which cannot be so reduced, especially the duties of promise-keeping, of making reparation, and of showing gratitude. Into the reasons for these modifications, however, we need not here inquire, since they concern the details of the theory rather than its central tenet. The important point is that, whatever be the precise principles recognised, Sir David Ross still insists that there is a plurality of principles and still resists the attempt to reduce them to a single principle.

Now it might appear that any such theory lays itself open to serious criticism. For if there is more than one ultimate ethical principle, may it not be that in certain practical situations these principles will be found in conflict? If I have a duty to produce as much good as possible and also a duty to keep any promise I have made, may it not happen that

[34] Cf. Ross, *The Right and the Good*, p. 21.
[35] Cf. Ross, *Foundations of Ethics*, pp. 286 ff.

on some occasion I shall be unable to follow the one principle without flying in the face of the other? And, if that is so, it may well be asked which principle ought to be observed. The point of this criticism is not that in such cases it will be difficult to discover which act is really the agent's duty—if that were all that is intended there is reason to suppose that ideal utilitarianism is not much better off in this respect, since it does not recognise a single principle of goodness[36]—but rather that in such cases we should be faced with two incompatible duties and that would involve that the moral consciousness is guilty of a self-contradiction.

There are, however, two main ways of avoiding this conclusion. The first is that favoured by Kant, who lays it down that there are two different classes of obligation, imperfect obligation and perfect, and that in cases of conflict the former must always yield to the latter. For example, it is right that if an agent can either produce the most good possible or else keep a promise he has made, he should in all circumstances fulfil the perfect obligation of promise-keeping and leave the other imperfect obligation unfulfilled. Yet, strictly speaking, the distinction between perfect and imperfect obligation only meets the criticism as based upon the *difficulty* of applying a plurality of moral principles, and does not meet the criticism as pointing to a *self-contradiction*, unless indeed the distinction is understood as involving that all imperfect obligations, however elliptically we may normally express them, are really of the form "I ought to do acts having characteristic *x*, *provided* I can do so without failing to meet my perfect obligations". Let us assume, however, that the defence is really intended in this second and more adequate form, and let us see with what success it is attended. Certainly, it does avoid the necessity of saying that the moral consciousness is guilty of self-contradiction, but it does so only on one condition, namely, that there is no more than one perfect obligation, for, if there were several, the same difficulty would arise in this more restricted sphere. Even to this limited extent, however, it may be doubted whether the defence has really succeeded, for, as Sir David Ross has pointed out,[37] the difficulty may arise again within a single principle of perfect obligation, since I may not be able to keep one promise without breaking another. In any case, it seems

[36] Cf. Ross, *Foundations of Ethics*, pp. 89–90.
[37] *Foundations of Ethics*, p. 173.

quite plain that in so far as the defence does succeed, it does so only by itself contradicting the moral consciousness, for we do not believe that every promise in all possible circumstances ought unconditionally to be kept.

The alternative line of defence is that which the modern school of intuitionism adopts. According to it, although there are several moral principles, which we may denote as *a*, *b*, *c*, the presence of any one of these, say, *a*, in an action is not sufficient to render that act obligatory. What it does do is to render it *prima facie* right. In other words, the act *tends* to be right in virtue of having characteristic *a*; and it is quite possible that in the same situation some other act also tends to be right in virtue of having characteristic *b*, and another in virtue of characteristic *c*. When that happens, the act which is really right is that of which the tendency to be right is strongest. Now it is Sir David Ross to whom is due this use of the phrase "*prima facie* obligation"; and he confesses his own dissatisfaction with the terminology as it stands.[38] On the one hand, it says too much, "it suggests that what we are speaking of is a certain kind of duty, whereas it is in fact not a duty, but something related in a special way to duty".[39] On the other hand, it says too little, it suggests that we are simply referring to an apparent fact in the situation, which may not be a real fact after all. He mentions Professor Prichard's suggestion of the word "claims" as a substitute for "*prima facie* obligations"; but he considers it also as unsatisfactory, (a) as referring to the fact from the side of the patient and not the agent, and (b) as suitably covering only *prima facie* obligations to others. These considerations may seem to lack any great importance as being concerned with a choice of words; but we must remember that the school is seeking to stress certain facts in the moral situation which have hitherto for the most part been overlooked, and it is therefore necessary that the language be carefully chosen so that the precise intention of the school may be accurately passed on. That being so, it is interesting to observe that in his second book Ross accepts Carritt's suggestion of the word "responsibility". The fact to be denoted by the phrase "*prima facie* obligation" is something which in many cases may be described from one end as a claim, and in all cases from the other end as a responsibility.

[38] *Foundations of Ethics*, pp. 84–5.
[39] *The Right and the Good*, p. 20.

What advantages, then, does this theory have over its rivals, such as ideal utilitarianism? The answer, according to its exponents, is that it accords more closely with the facts, with the judgments of the ordinary moral consciousness. Consequently, one may expect to find that the two theories come most actively to grips in the consideration of particular moral situations, actual or imagined; and, as a matter of fact, one of the most thorough-going attacks upon the intuitionist position is contained in three articles in *Mind*[40] by Mr. Pickard-Cambridge, written from the utilitarian point of view and devoted largely to a consideration of particular cases.

Many of the cases cited by Mr. Pickard-Cambridge refer to the keeping of promises, and of these there are some in which the author seeks to reduce the intuitionist theory to moral absurdity by insisting upon a literal, and, it must be admitted, somewhat unreasonable interpretation of the words of the promise. Thus, for instance, he puts the case in which A has promised to call for B and to go for a walk with him. Before the promised time of fulfilment arrives, however, B falls ill and is unable to leave the house. Now, says Mr. Pickard-Cambridge, if intuitionism is a correct account of morality, A will still be under an obligation to fulfil the first part of his promise.[41] Yet surely it is clear that the arrangement was made under the implicit condition "if A and B are fit and able to do what they propose doing". And, in arguing otherwise, "Mr. Pickard-Cambridge is insisting on the letter of the promise and forgetting the spirit".[42] "My reference to the spirit of the promise", Sir David Ross continues, "is simply a reference to the obvious fact that most promises, like most statements of any kind in ordinary life, are made without any attempt, and without any necessity, to state in full all their implied conditions and qualifications, since conversation would be very tedious if all of these were insisted upon. . . . To argue that one who takes the non-utilitarian view of promises is bound to interpret them according to the letter and not to the spirit is really to misinterpret the nature of ordinary speech."[43]

In other cases there are possible two alternative general results, for either the intuitionist and the ideal utilitarian will agree as to which act is obligatory, or else they will disagree.

[40] January, April and July, 1932.
[41] " Two Problems about Duty ", *Mind*, April 1932, pp. 164-5.
[42] *Foundations of Ethics*, p. 96.
[43] *Ibid.*, p. 98.

Which, then, of these two possibilities is significant in the present connection? At first sight it might seem to be the latter; and yet, on second thoughts, it is clear that where the ideal utilitarian and the intuitionist disagree as to which of several possible acts is the right one, it is just as likely, or almost as likely, that the same disagreement will occur as between one utilitarian and another and as between one intuitionist and another (unless indeed they are allowing their moral judgment on particular cases to be influenced by their ethical theory), so that the consideration of such cases is inconclusive. Further, even if a particular case could be found regarding which all utilitarians agreed that act A was right, and all intuitionists that act B was right, this also would fail in advancing the discussion. For any genuinely ethical difference of opinion is a difference of opinion about the theory which adequately covers the facts, and not a difference of opinion about the facts to be covered. Disputed facts can neither conclusively support nor conclusively condemn any hypothesis. Where there is not only a divergence between two theories, but also a corresponding difference of opinion as to whether act A or act B is right, the dispute cannot possibly be settled in any direct fashion, except by the entirely unsatisfactory method of counting heads. The first thing to be done is to go over the case again and again until agreement is reached as to which act is really right.

The crucial cases, then, are those in which it is generally agreed on both sides that act A is the right act, for that common ground supplies an admitted fact by reference to which the differing theories can be tested. A question, however, arises as to the manner in which this test is to be applied. On the one hand, the argument, from the utilitarian side, for example, may be of the form "Granted on all sides that act A is right, if intuitionism were a true account act B would be thought right by intuitionists". Now, if the intuitionism in question were of the kind which recognises perfect and imperfect obligations, and if B were an instance of the former, A of the latter, this argument would be effective—except that the intuitionist would doubtless admit that act B *was* right, which is contrary to the supposition. As against the newer type of intuitionism, which lays down no rule of thumb but regards the agent as under the necessity of estimating and comparing the different urgencies of several *prima facie* obligations, just as for the utilitarian he must estimate and compare the different degrees of goodness to be found in several different sets of results, the argument is not nearly so effective. Indeed it is difficult to see how the argument can be put without begging the question, for, *ex hypothesi*, the intuitionist and the utilitarian are in agreement that act A is right. In effect, what the utilitarian is trying to do in such an argument is to transform the case into one of the kind in which there is disagreement regarding which act is right, and, as we have seen, to do that is to render the case inconclusive.

To be effective, then, the test must be applied in another way. The argument must proceed, not from moral theory to particular moral judgment, but from particular moral judgment to moral theory. It should, in other words, endeavour to exhibit the real grounds of the common moral choice of act A as right. Further, if this attempt is to be of value in relation to the controversy between intuitionism and utilitarianism, it must not simply concern itself with a situation in which all the alternative acts are instances of producing something good or something bad, and in which none of the possible acts is an instance of the special *prima facie* obligations recognised by intuitionists. For in such a case intuitionism and utilitarianism would be at one. Both accept an obligation to produce as much good as possible, and their main difference is that whereas the utilitarian accepts no other obligations, the intuitionist recognises several. The case, therefore, must contain at least one of these special obligations which the intuitionist recognises and the utilitarian does not.

Here again, however, there are two possibilities. Let us suppose that act A is the keeping of a promise, and that act B, besides being the breaking of this promise, is also the producing of x units of good. It is possible, then, either (a) that both sides will agree that act A is right, or (b) that both sides will agree that act B is right. If it is agreed that act A is right, the utilitarian account of the matter is, of course, that act A is productive of more good than act B; whereas the intuitionist holds that we would ordinarily pronounce act A right even if it were productive of slightly less good than is represented by x units.[44] Stated thus, however, the intuitionist's position is a trifle ambiguous, for it is not quite clear whether he is referring to this particular case in which it is agreed that act A is right, or

[44] Cf. Ross, *The Right and the Good*, pp. 34 ff.

to another particular case which differs only very slightly from this one but regarding which the utilitarian and the intuitionist may well disagree, not only concerning the true theory, but also concerning the facts. The case which is potentially more conclusive, however, is that in which it is agreed that act A is right, but in which the utilitarian holds that act A is productive of more good than act B and that it is in virtue of that fact that it is judged right, whereas the intuitionist holds that it is productive of slightly less good than act B and that in any case its productivity of good is not the reason moral agents have for judging it right. In this connection the utilitarian holds that the intuitionist is wont to ignore certain good results of act A, for besides the gaining by the promisee of the promised benefit, there fall to be considered also (i) the pleasure caused to him by the fulfilment of his expectation; (ii) the heightening of the promiser's reputation for trustworthiness, with the greater power to do good which this will bring in its train; and (iii) the benefit to society caused by his increasing the general confidence that promises will be kept.[45] As against this, the intuitionist may hold that if he ignores some of the effects of promise-keeping, it is because the moral consciousness sees fit to ignore them also, and they are, therefore, or need be, no part of the ground which makes act A the right act. In other words, it is the apprehension of something else which leads to the recognition of act A as right; and intimately connected with the judgment that act A is right there is something, Z, which on the intuitionist theory is not to be identified with a comprehensive appreciation of the goodness of the various results.

Now the existence of this something, Z, seems to be beyond question; and it makes its presence felt in the other case, (b), in which it is agreed that act B is right. For there the intuitionist has good ground for pointing out that along with the moral judgment that act B is right, there generally goes something like a moral regret that the path of duty should prevent the keeping of a promise.

So far, then, as the consideration of particular situations is concerned, the issue seems to turn on what account is to be given of this something which we have denoted Z. For the intuitionist himself it is an appreciation of the fact that act A as the keeping of a promise is in its own right *prima facie* obligatory. When compared with the other acts it may turn

---

[45] Cf. Ross, *Foundations of Ethics*, p. 92.

out to be the act which is morally obligatory on the agent in the given situation, but in itself it is at any rate *prima facie* right. And it is with the awareness of this that the intuitionist identifies the preliminary, Z, which precedes the judgment that act A is right, and gives rise to a moral regret when the decision is that act B is right. It is possible, however, to give some account of the matter from the utilitarian point of view, for it may be argued that we have so often selected promise-keeping as a right act on utilitarian grounds that by the principle of association we come to acquire a tendency to regard any keeping of a promise as *ipso facto* right. And, doubtless, when in some particular situation we decide on reflection that our duty is to break the promise this acquired tendency would be sufficient to arouse some feeling of uneasiness. Moreover, it does seem to be a fact that when in a certain kind of situation, S, we have been long accustomed to regard a certain kind of act, X, as our duty, and when we later become convinced that there was really nothing morally obligatory about acts of type X, in situations of type S, none the less when we then perform some alternative act in a situation, S, we cannot help feeling uneasy and uncomfortable in doing so. Thus, for example, an individual who, as regards alcoholic drinks, had been brought up in an atmosphere of total abstinence, might well be expected to feel uneasy when taking a drink, even if in the meantime he had become quite convinced that the only moral requirement was temperance, not abstinence. Of course it might also be reasonably expected that in due course that feeling of uneasiness would disappear, whereas the moral regret at promise-breaking does not disappear. But, it must be noted, the two cases are not exactly parallel, for in the one case the acquired tendency (to regard the taking of even a single drink as wrong) is subject to a continuing resistance and weakening, while in the other case the acquired tendency (to regard the keeping of promises as right) may be weakened once in one particular situation, and subsequently reinforced on several occasions before further resistance is required. Indeed it is likely that the latter tendency will be more often confirmed than not, and this would be sufficient to account, in conformity with the utilitarian theory, for the persistence of the uneasy feeling.

Now this explanation, given from the utilitarian point of view, is, it must be admitted, a possible explanation. That is to say, the processes and facts of which it makes use are processes and facts which actually occur in human experience; and the only question is, Are they properly identified with the particular facts in human experience to which the intuitionist has drawn attention? Is the something, Z, simply an acquired tendency to regard certain kinds of action, such as the keeping of promises, as *ipso facto* right? It will be remembered that John Stuart Mill made a somewhat similar use of the principle of association in explaining how from desiring pleasure only men come to desire such things as money. There is, however, an important difference between the two cases, for desire is simply a fact, and an acquired desire is just as much a fact as an original desire. A judgment, on the other hand, besides being a fact, is also either true or false. How then does an acquired tendency to make judgments of a certain kind stand in regard to the question of their truth or falsity? Such a tendency might be a flair for grasping the relevant points in situations of a certain kind, but that interpretation would be easier to apply if it were allowed that the something, Z, is a comprehensive appreciation of the results of an act, whereas, whatever it is, it is agreed that it is not that. The tendency, then, must be a tendency to *assume* that acts of a certain type are right; and it is clear that the assumption that act A is right has no bearing whatever on the question whether in fact act A is right. Rather this question can only be answered, on utilitarian grounds, by an estimate and comparison of the results of the various acts possible in the given situation. From the intuitionist point of view, however, the something, Z, is not a tendency to assume that act A is right, but an insight or awareness that act A itself tends to be right; and this *is* relevant to the consideration of the question whether in the given situation act A is actually right. Thus the issue between utilitarianism and intuitionism concerning the proper account of the something, Z, resolves itself into the question, Is the reflective consideration of whether act A or act B is right a consideration of the goodness of the various results, to which a tendency to assume that act A is right is just irrelevant, or is it a consideration of several *prima facie* obligations with a view to discovering which is the more incumbent, a consideration to which the recognition that act A is *prima facie* right is entirely relevant? Thus the issue between utilitarianism and intuitionism turns upon the question whether the something, Z, is a *subjective* tendency (to regard certain acts as right) or the awareness of an *objective* tendency (to be right); and that in turn depends on whether, when it reflects and does not simply allow it to be assumed that a certain act is right, the moral consciousness endeavours to estimate the goodness of results, or seeks to discover which of several *prima facie* duties is in the circumstances more of a duty than the others. To a consideration of this matter on its merits the argument will later return; and in the meantime it only falls to be noted that on both these questions intuitionism accepts the latter account as the true one.

CHAPTER VI

FURTHER ASPECTS OF INTUITIONIST THEORY

IT WILL BE noticed that there is a progress in the questions which intuitionism raises and seeks to answer. So far, two of these questions have been considered in turn, namely, What is the meaning of "right"? and What is it that renders right acts right?; and to these questions intuitionism gives definite and self-consistent replies. Having done so, it then proceeds to raise a further question, What is it exactly that is right?, and on this it does not speak so clearly with a single voice.

There are, however, two stages in this part of the inquiry, and concerning the first of these intuitionism does speak quite distinctly. The question here is whether that which is right is the "doing of something, A", considered simply by itself and in isolation from any particular motive which may give rise to it, or the "doing of something, A, from a particular motive, X." It is not, of course, doubted that, if done at all, the act must be done from some motive; but it is questioned whether the act which may be the bearer of the predicates "right" or "wrong" includes as part of itself some particular motive. On this point, intuitionists insist that an act as the potential bearer of the predicates "right" and "wrong" cannot possibly include a motive as part of itself.[1] In the first place, "I ought" implies "I can", and therefore, since motives are beyond our immediate control, what I ought to do cannot include some particular motive. In the second place, there is an additional argument which holds against one particular motive, the sense of duty, for the proposition that it is my duty to do act A from a sense of duty leads to an infinite regress (it is my duty to do act A from a sense that it is my duty to do act A from . . .), and it does so, because, as Sir David Ross points out[2], "the whole expression is in contradiction with a part of itself". Thus an act as potentially right or wrong cannot include a motive;

[1] Cf. Ross, *The Right and the Good*, pp. 4 ff.; *Foundations of Ethics*, pp. 115 ff.
[2] *The Right and the Good*, p. 5.

and Ross suggests that additional clarity would be gained in ethical discussion if we embodied this fact in the very language of ethics by using "'act' of the thing done, the initiation of change, and 'action' of the doing of it, the initiating of change, from a certain motive". "We should then talk of a right act", he proceeds, "but not of a right action, of a morally good action but not of a morally good act. And it may be added that the doing of a right act may be a morally bad action, and that the doing of a wrong act may be a morally good action; for 'right' and 'wrong' refer entirely to the thing done, 'morally good' and 'morally bad' entirely to the motive from which it is done."[3]

Moreover, this contention is important for intuitionism, not only on account of what it says in itself, but also on account of what it is taken to imply. Intuitionism in putting forward its own peculiar position is concerned to deal critically, not only with utilitarianism, but also with what we have already described as the sentimentalist theory, that which regards rightness as dependent upon moral goodness. Now moral goodness is a quality of will and attaches principally to motives. But if acts, as the bearers of the predicates "right" and "wrong", cannot include a motive as a part of themselves, it certainly follows that acts which may be right or wrong can be neither morally good nor morally bad. We may sometimes speak of a morally good act, but, if we do, we are using the word "act" in a sense in which we cannot speak of right or obligatory acts—if the two arguments already adduced are valid. Further, if acts which may be right or wrong can be neither morally good nor morally bad, it follows in turn that "right" cannot possibly *mean* "morally good", and also that moral goodness cannot be the quality of acts which renders them right—it cannot be the quality which renders certain acts right, for, if the argument is sound, it is not any quality of these acts at all.

Here, however, it must be said that the issue between intuitionism and sentimentalism is not so clear as that between intuitionism and utilitarianism, nor, in consequence, is it so plainly seen in the former case as it is in the latter whether or not intuitionism has successfully disposed of its rival. Even if it is allowed, not only that the two arguments against the obligatoriness of motives are valid, but also that the intuitionist's

[3] *The Right and the Good*, p. 7.

inferences from them are themselves valid, it may be argued that, in theory, just as the utilitarian regards the rightness of an act as depending upon the goodness, not of the act, but of its results, so the sentimentalist may hold that the rightness of an act depends upon the moral goodness, not of the act itself, but of its cause or motive. For all that the intuitionist has shown is that the act which is right cannot have moral goodness as one of its *qualities*; and it is therefore still possible in principle that the rightness of the act is dependent upon the moral goodness of the motive. But, if this were so, the intuitionist would be entirely wrong in his assertion that the doing of a right act may be a morally bad action. Yet, it may be asked, how can the rightness of an act, which I can therefore perform, depend upon the goodness of a motive which I just cannot choose to have? This question, however, merely serves to draw our attention to a further fact which intuitionism has considered only inadequately, if at all. It is that if an act is possible for an agent, that presupposes that the agent does have some motive for doing the act, and without such a motive the act would not be possible. Further, if several acts are possible, that presupposes that the agent does have several motives amongst which he can then choose. If this were allowed, sentimentalism might well hold that the right act in any situation is that suggested by the best motive by which the agent is or can be moved in the given situation. Thus, if I am tempted to go out and waylay my enemy, A, and have also a desire to continue my studies in peace, it *might* be maintained that if I choose the latter alternative as my duty I do so because it issues from a better motive.

As against all this, the intuitionist is not without reply. For one thing, it seems clear that the several motives among which it has been suggested an agent might choose conscientiously could not include a sense of duty, which is often regarded as the highest motive of all. If the sense of duty is one of the motives, it would appear, then although the agent might still choose amongst them he could not do so conscientiously. Further, and in fact, Sir David Ross urges, what we actually attend to when we find ourselves trying to discover our duty in some situation is "the nature of the possible acts, considered apart from the motive from which we should do them—their tendency to affect the welfare of other people, in this way or in that, their quality as fulfilments of promise or breaches of promise and the like". Certainly, he admits, a scrutiny of one's own motives is "a well-known part of the technique of moral deliberation", but not as tending to show what is one's duty. "Consideration of my motives will throw no light on *this* question; *this* question must be decided in the light of quite other considerations such as I have suggested above."[4]

There is clearly point in this argument; but it still remains a question whether or not Ross has done justice to the facts in so separating act from motive as to be able to say that the doing of a right act might be a morally bad action. The intuitionist may agree with the utilitarian, but on grounds drawn from theology, for example, that the right act has the best possible results, but that, though interesting, is strictly no concern of ethics. It belongs perhaps more to religious faith than to ethical insight. On the other hand, ethics does seem to have a genuine interest in the question whether rightness and moral goodness can really fall hopelessly apart; and it does seem that the new intuitionism has failed to bring its controversy with sentimentalism to the same pitch of conclusiveness as it has achieved in its dispute with utilitarianism—perhaps because its analysis of this part of the field is not so thorough. None the less, the intuitionist position is itself clear, that what is right, the act, cannot include a motive as part of itself.

So far then the intuitionist is clear and definite in his opinion concerning what exactly it is that is right or wrong. It can be described, he says, as an act, provided we use the word "act" to denote something which does not include a motive as part of itself. This answer, however, although it is undoubtedly important, is also largely negative; but in seeking to determine the matter more positively intuitionism is not nearly so sure of itself, and in particular we find that the position put forward in Ross's Gifford Lectures is openly and admittedly quite different from that adopted in his earlier book, *The Right and the Good*.

The starting-point here is the recognition that an act which may be right or wrong may be one or other of four different things: (a) the aiming at something, such as A's reception of a certain book; (b) the doing of something which is likely to have this result; (c) the doing of something which will actually have this result; or (d) the securing of A's reception of the book. Now in *The Right and the Good* it is the fourth possibility which proves acceptable to the author; and justifying the rejection of the other three there are three strains of argument. (i) The

[4] *Foundations of Ethics*, pp. 123-4.

first of these, which certainly tells against (a), and *may* tell against (b) and (c) also, is that this account of the matter reintroduces motive into the content of duty. To aim at something, it is said, is to act from a motive consisting of the wish to bring it about. (ii) The second strain of argument, which applies against (a) and (b), is that if I have promised to let A have the book in question, "I obviously do not fulfil my promise and do my duty merely by aiming at his receiving the book; I must see that he actually receives it", and "however likely my act may seem, even on careful consideration, and even however likely it may in fact be, to produce the result, if it does not produce it I have not done what I promised to do, i.e. have not done my duty".[5] "We get the curious consequence", Ross adds, "that however carelessly I pack or dispatch the book, if it comes to hand I have done my duty, and however carefully I have acted, if the book does not come to hand I have not done my duty. Success and failure are the only test, and a sufficient test, of the performance of duty. Of course, I should deserve more praise in the second case than in the first; but that is an entirely different question; we must not mix up the question of right and wrong with that of the morally good and the morally bad."[6] (iii) And the third argument, which holds against (c), is that what is obligatory is not the mere means, but the means plus end, the securing of A's possession of the book. And if we extend this consideration from special obligations to the general obligation which utilitarianism and intuitionism have in common, as Ross is willing to extend it, it is clear that in accepting the utilitarian's sole duty as one duty amongst several, the intuitionist gives a somewhat different account of it. It is no longer the obligation to do something which will have good results; it is the obligation to produce these results.

It appears, however, that on second thoughts intuitionism is not prepared to uphold this position that what is right is the doing of something, although, curiously enough, what is accepted in its place is not exactly any one of the three other possibilities noted above, but a fresh one altogether, namely, exerting oneself or setting oneself to bring about a certain change. Sir David Ross explicitly announces his recantation on this matter,[7] and he attributes his conversion to the close and conclusive reasoning of Professor Prichard in his lecture to the

---

[5] *The Right and the Good*, p. 43.   [6] *Ibid.*, p. 45.
[7] *Foundations of Ethics*, p. 148.

British Academy entitled *Duty and Ignorance of Fact*, given in
1932.

The first stage in this rational conversion is the recognition
that in any given set of circumstances the agent is confronted
by what in a sense are two situations, the objective situation
and the subjective situation. The former is the situation as it
really is, and the latter is the same situation as it strikes the
agent, and consists therefore of his thoughts and opinions
concerning it. Once this is recognised, it is not difficult to
see that ethics has a question to deal with in this connection, Is
a right act right with regard to the objective situation or with
regard to the subjective situation? Clearly, the argument runs,
there is something to be said for the former alternative. In morality we think ourselves to be dealing with, and reacting to,
reality, and not just our own thoughts about it. "When we are
in a difficult moral situation, what we *want* to know is not what
act we think likely to produce certain results, but what act
will produce certain results."[8] In the end, however, there are
certain considerations which tell decisively against the objective view. It means, for example, that we can never know
what is our duty, since we never know that we can produce
certain changes. It means also that we can never perform a
duty because it is a duty, that is, because we know it to be a
duty. Again, the objective view implies that my duty may well
be an act which I take to be contrary to duty, and also that
I may do my duty "though I do not even suspect that it will
have the effect which renders it a duty", as, for example, when
an agent cures a man's disease by doing something calculated
by the agent to render it fatal.

These considerations are taken as disposing of the objective
view, but at the same time it is recognised that the subjective
view is not without difficulties. On this view it will happen that
an act is right, not because it will in fact have certain effects,
but because the agent thinks it likely to have these effects; and
to this account of the matter there are two main objections.
(i) The first, which is never disposed of, is that there are
different degrees of probability, that presumably there is a
minimum degree requisite before an act becomes a duty, and
that consequently "there will be border-line cases in which
I shall be unable to discover whether the degree to which I
think the act likely to confer a certain benefit is sufficient to

[8] *Foundations of Ethics*, p. 147.

render it a duty".[9] (ii) In addition, the subjective view has an apparent defect in the fact that it would make the rightness of an act depend, not on some character it would have, but on our thinking it likely that it would have that character—which has really nothing to do with the act itself.

This latter difficulty is regarded as the more fundamental, and upon it the argument concentrates. How, then, is it to be met? In this way. Earlier in his lecture, Prichard had distinguished our being able to produce certain states of affairs directly and our being able to produce other states of affairs indirectly by first of all producing certain states of affairs directly which would have the others as their effects. But, on examination, it is clear that we cannot be sure of producing any state of affairs in the physical world. The most we can do, and all that morality can require of us, is that we exert ourselves or set ourselves to produce certain states of affairs. What is required is not an action, but a mental activity. "An obligation", says Professor Prichard, "must be an obligation, not to *do* something, but to perform an activity of a totally different kind, that of setting or exerting ourselves to do something, i.e. to bring something about."[10]

Does this, then, remove the difficulty we are seeking to remove? According to Professor Prichard, it cannot be doubted that it does nothing at all to remove it.[11] Sir David Ross, however, holds a different opinion. The difficulty, he argues, *is* removed, because now an activity will be right "not because of the activity's being thought to have a certain character but because of its actually being of a certain character, the character of being the setting oneself to bring about a certain effect".[12] And it seems certain that Sir David Ross is right. If I set myself to bring about A, the character my activity has as being the setting of myself to bring about A is a character which the activity really has, and not just one which I think it has—although it may well be that I am mistaken in thinking that this activity will actually bring A into being. "If our being bound to set ourselves to do some action", says Professor Prichard, "were a character which the activity would have, its existence would, no doubt, have to depend on the fact that the activity would have a certain character, and it

[9] *Duty and Ignorance of Fact*, p. 13.   [11] *Ibid.*, p. 25.
[10] *Ibid.*, p. 24.   [12] *Foundations of Ethics*, p. 156.

could not depend on our thinking that it would."[13] And this, of course, is true enough; but what character could the activity possibly be thought to possess which it did not actually possess? Certainly not the character of being the setting of ourselves to do such and such, for on this matter we can hardly be mistaken. We *know* at least what we are setting ourselves to do, although we may be quite wrong in our estimate of the chances of success, or, again, in our opinion regarding the fruits of success.

Thus Sir David Ross is right when he says that the problem has now been solved. But having got rid of one difficulty we now seem to be confronted by another, for in defining what is right as the setting of ourselves to do something have we not reintroduced motive into "the structure of that which we ought to do"? On the face of it, as Ross admits,[14] setting ourselves to bring about A is rather like being moved to action by a desire to realise A. But Ross's own conclusion is that in reality the two things are quite different, that always what we are morally obliged to do is to set ourselves to produce something, and *not* to set ourselves to produce something from a particular motive, and that in fact we may do what we ought to do from any one of several different motives.

It will be remembered that one of the reasons Prichard and Ross had for departing from the objective view of what is right, the view that it is the actual bringing about of A, was that if this view were accepted it would involve that a man might do his duty without ever realising that the act in question had a character which might render it obligatory, and even thinking that it had a character which rendered it wrong.[15] The objective view of what is right was finally abandoned by the intuitionists because it implied that a right act might be done *accidentally*. Thus in accepting the subjective account of what is right, the intuitionists ruled out completely the idea that a right act might be done accidentally. But in ruling out that idea they did not intend to rule out another idea which may be confused with it, the idea that a right act may be done without regard for its rightness, that is, may be done from a thoroughly bad motive. "An act", says Ross, "may be the act which the agent thinks to be his duty, and yet be done from an indifferent or bad motive, and therefore be morally indifferent or

[13] *Duty and Ignorance of Fact*, p. 27.
[14] *Foundations of Ethics*, p. 158.
[15] *Ibid.*, p. 150; also *Duty and Ignorance of Fact*, p. 11.

bad."[16] It is therefore important clearly to distinguish two propositions, (i) that a right act may be done accidentally, that is, without any awareness of its rightness; and (ii) that a right act of whose rightness the agent is aware may none the less be done from an entirely bad motive. These two propositions do not say the same thing; and in its final form intuitionism denies the one and approves the other. Moreover, it must be admitted, intuitionism is right to this extent, that the two propositions are *not* just different ways of saying the same thing; but it may still be that they are so connected that the contention that what is right is the setting of oneself to do something, which rules out the one proposition, also rules out the other. If what is right were the objective and actual bringing about of A it would certainly then be possible for an agent to perform a right act, while aware of its rightness, yet from a bad motive, that is, while aware of its rightness but not at all because of its rightness. But if what is right is the setting of oneself to do A, can it be maintained that an agent can do *that* from a thoroughly bad motive? For example, can we really set ourselves to produce a certain amount of good from a motive which is entirely bad? Or is it not rather the case that if the motive is a thoroughly bad one it must be that one sets oneself to do something, X, other than produce good, although one is aware that this setting of oneself to do X may involve, not indeed the setting of oneself to do A which is good, but the actual doing of A? If, on the other hand, it does involve the setting of oneself to do A, it seems arguable that the motive cannot be *entirely* bad, although, of course, the motive may well be mixed, and, secondly, the good part of it by itself may not be sufficient to lead to the act.

It seems that both Prichard and Ross may have committed the same error, though in different degrees, the error, namely, of regarding the setting oneself to do something as a psychical but objective event. Prichard seems to look on it in this way when he implies that it may have a character quite contrary to that which the agent supposes it to have. He does not see that it contains just what the agent puts into it, and that an agent cannot possibly be mistaken regarding what he is setting himself to do, although he may be quite in error regarding what this setting himself to do something will actually bring about. But is not Ross guilty of the same error when he fails to see that a man's motive inevitably colours what he sets himself to do? If his motive is mixed, is it not the case that he is really setting himself to do more than he might care to admit to other people? And if his motive is entirely bad, is it not the case that what he is really setting himself to do is, not something more than he would admit to other people, but rather something entirely different? Suppose, for example, that I set myself to pay a debt to A from a *thoroughly* bad motive, say, from fear of law-court proceedings and from no other motive whatsoever. In that case the sum of money I set myself to transfer to A, measured in pounds, shillings and pence, may well be exactly the same sum that I should set myself to transfer to him if my motive were a pure sense of duty. Yet it is surely clear that in the former case what I set myself to transfer is not the sum *due*, but whatever sum is necessary to prevent my appearance in a court of law, and that if I had any reason for supposing that a smaller sum would have the same effect I should have no hesitation in transferring the smaller and I should never dream of transferring the larger amount; and, if that is so, it does seem that my setting myself to do something in the one case is not indistinguishable from my setting myself to do something in the other case. Part at least of the difference is a difference in the inter-relationship of the elements concerned, and to deny any difference between my setting myself to do in the one case and my setting myself to do in the other is like denying any difference between my belief that A is in fact B and my belief that A is necessarily B. On the other hand, when I pay a debt from mixed motives, which is a much more frequent case than that of paying a debt from a thoroughly bad motive, then although my sense of duty may be extremely weak and in the direst need of reinforcement by some other motive, none the less it is operative, and consequently I do set myself to pay the sum due, whatever else in so doing I may set myself to do. And if there is anything in this line of argument, it does follow that, in its later form as well as in its earlier, intuitionism is less conclusive when dealing with the motives of right acts than it is when dealing with their consequences.

It is now necessary to retrace our steps to that point in the discussion at which the respective positions of Prichard and Ross began to diverge. The issue was whether or not the new and subjective view of what is right solved the difficulty which had

arisen regarding right actions, the difficulty that they seem to be
right, not on account of a character which they possess, but on
account of a character which they are only thought by the
agent to possess. On this matter, Prichard was of the opinion
that the difficulty remained, Ross that it had vanished. How,
then, does Prichard deal with the difficulty and what is Ross's
attitude to the solution? The former deals with it by making
certain points with regard to "ought", with which the latter is
in full agreement, only declaring that "this last part of Professor Prichard's theory, while both true and important, is not
necessary for the saving of the subjective view".[17] Thus the
divergence between the two protagonists falls into the background, and we are faced with a new development in intuitionism.

This development may be summarised in two sentences from
Professor Prichard's *Duty and Ignorance of Fact*. (i) "When we
make an assertion containing the term 'ought' or 'ought not',
that to which we are attributing a certain character is not a
certain activity but a certain man."[18] And (ii) "we are apt
to think that when we say of an action that we are bound, or
bound not, to do it, we are stating that it would have a certain
character, for which the proper term would be 'ought-to-be-
doneness' or 'ought-not-to-be-doneness'. And this tendency is
fostered by our habit of using the terms 'right' and 'wrong'
as equivalents for 'ought' and 'ought not'."[19] Now, if all this
were true, it would meet the difficulty it is intended to meet, for
the statement that I think A is x, not only asserts that A has
apparently the character x, but also that *I* have, without qualification, the characteristic of being of the opinion that A is x.
Therefore, if "ought" is a character of the agent, it may be held
to depend, not on an apparent, but on an actual, characteristic
of the agent himself.

Quite apart, however, from the success or failure of this
development in meeting the difficulty it is intended to meet,
there is the question whether the development itself is in
accordance with the facts; and to this question we must address
ourselves, taking in succession its two points, (i) that "ought"
is a character of agents; and (ii) that "ought" and "right" are
not equivalent terms.

[17] *Foundations of Ethics*, p. 156.
[18] *Duty and Ignorance of Fact*, p. 27.
[19] *Ibid.*, p. 26.

(i) To say that "ought" is a character of agents is on the face of it an unnatural way of expressing the facts of moral experience. More often our moral queries are of the form, Which act ought I to do? Which act is obligatory? rather than of the form, Who ought to do this act? Which agent is morally obliged to do it?[20] No doubt obligatoriness is not a quality of an act which it has independently of the fact that the act confronts a particular agent as one which he can do. The word "obligation" points rather, not to a quality, but to a relation which holds between a particular act and a particular agent faced by a particular situation. The moral fact is that in this situation, S, I, A, ought to do X. Further, if the existence of the obligation depends upon the fact that it is I rather than some other agent who am faced by the situation, it depends at least equally upon the fact that the act to which I am obliged is this particular act and not one of the alternatives possible in the same situation. Indeed, on reflection, this is so obvious that one is constrained to wonder what possible reason Professor Prichard could have had for regarding "ought" as a character of agents. His answer is that "since the existence of an obligation to do some action cannot possibly depend on the actual performance of the action, the obligation cannot itself be a property which the action would have, if it were done".[21] Again, according to Ross, "we cannot, strictly speaking, say 'such and such an act is obligatory', for the act is not there, to be either obligatory or anything else. Nor, again, can we say 'such and such an act would be obligatory if it were done'; for clearly its obligatoriness, if it has any, does not depend on its being done."[22] And to this it might be added that when the act is done its obligatoriness disappears, for it is no longer obligatory and the situation in which it was obligatory has materially changed. The argument is, then, that since when an obligation exists the action does *not* exist, and since when the action has been performed and does perhaps exist, the obligation has disappeared, therefore the obligatoriness cannot be a property or character of the action, and consequently it is not a property which the action has in virtue of having some other

[20] Cf. Prichard, *Duty and Ignorance of Fact*, p. 27: "What does exist is the fact that you, or that I, ought, or ought not, to do a certain action, or rather to set ourselves to do a certain action." But is this the normal moral situation? It is to be noticed that " ought, or ought not " disguises the more frequent query, " Which act is right? "

[21] *Duty and Ignorance of Fact*, p. 26.

[22] *Foundations of Ethics*, p. 56.

characteristic. So long as "right" or "obligatory" was defined as "productive of the greatest amount of good" it was possible to regard obligatoriness as a characteristic which an action would have if it were done; but when such false definitions are carefully excluded it is seen that the obligatoriness does not depend on the performance of the act, for it would still have been the obligatory act even if it were never performed, and therefore never came into existence to possess its property. Consequently, it is concluded, "ought" attaches, not as a property to actions at all, but as a character to agents. But this will not do. The assumption is that the word "ought" stands for a character of something, whereas the truth is that obligation is a character neither of actions nor of agents, it is not a character at all. It is a relation between them which is sometimes described or referred to from the one end, sometimes from the other. No doubt if the agent is only one of two (or more) terms between which the relationship holds, there is still a question regarding the precise nature and status of the other term (or terms); but *at any rate* it seems wrong to regard the obligation, not as a relation at all, but as a character of the agent. Moreover, it also seems wrong to regard it as depending simply and solely upon some other character of the agent, even if we include his opinions as characteristics. Professor Prichard expresses the obligation in the form, "*I* ought to set myself to do so-and-so, because *I* think that it would have a certain effect";[23] yet it seems certain that the ordinary moral consciousness would repudiate the incidence of this emphasis, and that for two reasons. (a) In the first place, I ought to do so-and-so not because *I* happen to think it would have a certain effect, but because in thinking so I am endeavouring to grasp the objective situation as thoroughly as I can. And (b) it is difficult to see how my thinking anything could of itself give rise to an obligation upon me; the moral claim is a claim made by reality upon me and presupposes certain knowledge on my part, which may be mixed up with mere opinion but in which in any case the important thing is not that it is *I* who know but rather what is known.

(ii) The second point in the development in intuitionism which we are considering was the contention that "ought" and "right" are not equivalent terms. Now it may certainly be that there are minor differences of usage between them. Thus,

[23] *Duty and Ignorance of Fact*, p. 27.

"ought" seems to refer to the obligation-relation no more from the one end than from the other (unlike "obliged", which refers to it from the side of the agent, and "obligatory", which refers to it from the side of the act), whereas "right" generally refers to it from the side of the act. Again, Sir David Ross has pointed out that where we are faced with a situation in which morally we may do act A or act B but not act C, we must say that both act A *and* act B are right, whereas our duty, what we ought to do, is "one or other of acts A and B".[24] But here we must note two meanings of "right", a negative use in which it stands for the mere contradictory of "wrong", and a positive use in which it stands for the contrary. Thus, when faced by a situation which seems to lay no moral claim upon me, I may well say that A is right—for example, a friend might assure me that I was quite right in doing what I did, even if I later discovered that unknown to me there were elements in the situation capable of giving rise to a moral claim. And in such a case "right" is being used in its negative sense, as the contradictory of "wrong". If then we return to the situation in which acts A and B present equal claims and act C a weaker claim, is it not in this negative sense that we say that acts A and B are both right? Ross, however, will not allow this and insists that both are right positively. Yet it would seem that in such a situation we should normally say that we do not know which is right positively, but that we should be right negatively (no one could blame us) in doing A, and again that we should be right negatively in doing B. And if we find this negative rightness of our conduct colder comfort in this case than in that in which we seem to be faced by no moral claim whatsoever, may that not be due to our awareness (in this case but not in the other) that if we knew the situation better we should be able to choose morally between acts A and B? If this is true, it is also important because it implies that we know that if there is a moral claim at all the claim of morality is in the last analysis and to a perfect knowledge of the situation one claim and not two equal but conflicting claims. Thus in the situation which Ross has set, either act A is right or act B is right, but certainly not both act A and act B. Is it then true to say that we ought to do one or other of these two acts? Surely it depends upon what precisely we mean. If we mean that in trying to discover which act is our duty we may ignore the other alternatives and confine

[24] *The Right and the Good*, p. 3.

our consideration to acts A and B, then we may certainly mean what we say and our judgment may well be true. But if we mean that our final duty in the situation is to do "one or other of acts A and B" that contention can hardly be true, for the simple reason that there is no act which can be described as "one or other of acts A and B". It may be that so far as we know the situation it is either our duty to do act A or our duty to do act B, but it cannot possibly be our duty to do "either act A or act B". And this, of course, is in line with our earlier conclusion that acts A and B cannot both be right in a positive sense.

We pass now, however, from minor differences to a much more important difference between "ought" and "right", which is alleged to exist by intuitionism in its latest form. For, following Professor Broad, Sir David Ross holds that "right" means suitable or fitting.[25] He recognises that many uses of the word in this sense are non-ethical, but he holds that none the less there is a moral suitability. In this sense he speaks of a right emotion (for example, grief in certain circumstances such as those occasioned by the loss of a friend);[26] and later he says that "an action done from a certain motive is undeniably right, or morally suitable to a situation, in a sense in which a mere action, irrespective of its motive, is not".[27] This characteristic of moral suitability, it is said, is a complex characteristic which includes a "generic quality of suitability which it shares with the rightness of an element in a beautiful whole"[28] along with a differential element which cannot be defined in terms of anything other than itself. Now if we call these elements x and y respectively, it is clear that neither x nor y nor x plus y either is or includes "ought", for "ought" still implies "can",[29] whereas an emotion or a motive may be right. Yet Ross holds that "the word 'right', when used in a context of moral thought seems to me to mean very nearly, but not quite, the same as 'obligatory' or 'what is my duty'."[30] But this is a contradiction unless Ross is using the phrase "very nearly" in a sense in which it would be true to say that the equiangularity of a triangle is "very nearly" the same thing as its equilaterality. For if "right" neither equals nor includes "ought" then the proposition that an agent ought to do the right act is a synthetic

[25] *Foundations of Ethics*, pp. 51 ff.
[26] *Ibid.*, p. 55.
[27] *Ibid.*, p. 159.
[28] *Ibid.*, p. 54.
[29] Cf. Ross, *Foundations of Ethics*, p. 45.
[30] *Foundations of Ethics*, p. 43.

proposition. And indeed we find Ross distinguishing three right acts in any situation, "the first suitable to the objective circumstances, the second to the agent's opinion on the non-moral question, the third to his opinion on the moral question", and then asking which of these three right acts is the one which the agent ought to do.[31] Yet surely this rightness to the objective circumstances, which does not even carry oughtness with it, is really just a hypothetical rightness, and what the facts warrant is not that some other act is in some sense right besides the obligatory act, but that if the agent's view of the situation were to change in certain definite directions it would be his duty to perform some other act. Moreover, the fact to which the definition of "right" as suitable really points is that no act is obligatory in a vacuum as it were; it is rather the right act for the agent *in the given situation*. In other words, obligation is not quite so simple as a two-term relation between an agent and an act.

It must be confessed, however, that this does not deal quite conclusively with the distinction which Ross has drawn between "right" and "ought", and that in particular the explanation we have just given clearly does not cover the use of "right" as characterising an emotion or a motive. We have already seen that intuitionism itself is not quite conclusive in supporting its contention that what is obligatory is always something which is quite separable from, and independent of, any particular motive; and that being so we shall certainly be dealing with the strongest part of the case for the alleged distinction between "right" and "ought" if we concentrate attention upon the supposed rectitude of certain emotions. For, it must be admitted, emotions are never, strictly speaking, obligatory. None the less, according to Ross, they are sometimes right, fitting or suitable, and that in a perfectly moral sense. Moreover, Ross rightly claims[32] that he has the support of two British moralists, Samuel Clarke and Richard Price, for this contention. Further, it is to be presumed, this moral rightness which is to be distinguished from oughtness is not to be identified with moral goodness, for then the difficulty would have arisen simply by using the wrong word to denote a perfectly authentic moral notion.

Let us, then, consider the case of grief. Suppose that a close friend of A's has just died, and that A himself is in consequence

[31] *Foundations of Ethics*, p. 162.   [32] *Ibid.*, pp. 52, 54.

deeply grieved. His grief, it is said, is right and fitting. Now by this two things are *not* meant, (i) that the grief is obligatory;[33] and (ii) that it is morally good, the sign of a sensitive character. The judgment is concerned neither with the determination of A's duty nor with the development of his character. The grief is simply judged fitting with regard to the situation—"its fittingness depends solely on the nature of the circumstances".[34] Yet if we take the word "solely" at its full value and abstract from everything else, it is difficult to see how grief can be judged right and fitting. It *may* be judged, but hardly right. Something more is required besides the grief and the objective circumstances, and the question turns on the nature of this additional factor. If, for example, I am driving to X and come on my journey to cross-roads, then no doubt it is fitting that I should take one road rather than another; but the fittingness arises, not just from the combination of my taking a particular road and the objective situation constituted by the cross-roads, but from these together with *my desire to arrive in X.* What additional factor, then, corresponds to that desire in the case in which A's grief is judged fitting in respect to the death of his friend? (a) It might be the moral consciousness itself, and this is the answer which Ross's position actually requires. *To the moral consciousness* A's grief in relation to the death of his friend is right and fitting, and this is involved in Ross's belief that "right" in such contexts denotes a *moral* suitability. But it would seem that if this something is the moral consciousness the judgment must be either that certain conduct was dutiful or that a certain type of character was good; and there does not appear to be any other judgment which the moral consciousness could make. None the less, whether by the moral consciousness or not, the judgment is made, and, further, it uses the word "right" in a way which is not so completely devoid of moral character or quality as when it is said that I have chosen the *right* road in order to arrive at X. Consequently, our treatment of this matter must remain unsatisfactory, unless we can point to something which would correspond to the desire to arrive at X, and which might easily be confused with the moral consciousness itself. (b) There is in fact, however, just such a factor, which is other than the moral consciousness and yet might readily be confused with it. It is the body of established principles and

[33] *Foundations of Ethics*, p. 55.   [34] *Ibid.*, p. 55.

customs of the surrounding society, and its equivalent is to be found in almost any society. It is not a specifically moral phenomenon, for its range varies from matters of considerable moral import to detailed points of social etiquette. Part of it, however, does cover part of the moral sphere, but these principles are not themselves moral insights. Rather, they are based upon moral insight. For if certain specific types of conduct are frequently judged dutiful by the moral consciousness, and if also they are more or less regularly followed in the given society, they gradually become established; and the token of this establishment is that in the society in question the pursuit of them comes to arouse a sentiment of approval, and the breach one of disapproval. In practice, this sentiment is, from the moral point of view, both a safe and an unsafe guide, safe in so far as the sentiment is based upon moral insight, unsafe because, by the nature of the case, even when based upon moral insight, it attends to the externals of conduct. Moreover, as has already been pointed out, it is not confined to the sphere of morality, for any practices, even morally indifferent ones, may become established and approved by this pseudo-moral sentiment. Further, when it does approve or disapprove, it is not concerned with what was the agent's duty, nor with the question of his capacity or incapacity for a particular course of action, nor with what he set himself to do. An agent may act conscientiously and yet win its disapproval, for it looks simply at his action from the outside and in relation to the objective circumstances. It then either approves or disapproves, and in doing so it judges the action right, fitting, suitable, appropriate, proper, or the opposites of these. In other words, it declares that the action is "the done thing" or not as the case may be. The word "propriety" may be defined as "agreement with established principles or customs", and these judgments of fittingness are in this sense judgments of propriety. Certainly, so far as their content is concerned, they seem to be objective judgments, giving expression to the facts, but, as in the case of the cross-roads, the judgments fail to convey a meaning if we abstract, in the one case from the desire to arrive at X, and in the other from the body of established principles of action and the sentiment which approves all actions done in conformity with them. The act in both cases seems to be right in relation to the circumstances; but on examination it appears that it is the act in relation to the circumstances which is right with regard to the desire to arrive at X in the one case, and the pseudo-moral sentiment in the other. An act, or in fact anything else, cannot be just suitable *simpliciter*; it is suitable or not from some particular point of view, such as a desire to reach X or a sentiment which approves certain types of action and disapproves of others. Thus the rightness which Ross distinguishes from oughtness is not a purely moral rightness after all, although in many cases it may be *based upon* genuinely moral insight. It is right that I should be grieved at the death of a friend, but it is also right that I should wear dark clothes at his funeral; and the rightness in both cases is one of propriety.

The main point of the new intuitionism which remains to be considered is the account it gives of goodness; yet for the most part this falls outwith our present purpose since the subject is the claim which morality makes upon us. In other theories this cannot be considered apart from goodness, for the claim of morality is made to depend upon, and derive from, the goodness of one thing or another. In the new intuitionism, on the other hand, rightness is made at last to stand upon its own feet; and, in a way, the whole point of this theory is that the claim of morality can be considered apart from an account of goodness.

Indeed, Mr. Carritt seems to go much further and to suggest that, so far from rightness being dependent upon goodness, it is goodness which depends upon rightness. "I am inclined to believe," he says, "though with some misgiving, that the word 'good' when applied to acts always means either 'right' or 'moral' (i.e. done because thought right by the agent) or virtuous (i.e. thought right but done from a kind of desire that usually leads to right acts), but that when applied to states or events, unless it means useful, it always means either 'satisfying desire' or 'the sort of state or event which we should think it our duty in normal circumstances to bring about were it in our power'."[35] Ross, however, would not go so far as this. He admits that certain things are good because there was a duty to produce them. He considers, for example, the case of a man receiving a promised benefit, and he concludes that "the rightness of the act will, as in the cases of reparation for wrongs and return for benefits, depend on the *nature* of the result to be produced, but not on its *goodness*, since it is good only because

[35] *Theory of Morals*, para. 64, p. 73.

there is a duty to produce it".[36] In the other cases, on the
other hand, in the case, for instance, of distributing pleasures
among others in proportion to their goodness, "it seems", he
says, "that a good man takes satisfaction in finding goodness
rewarded, independently of the thought that it was any one's
duty to produce this situation, and independently of the
thought that he ought to do what he can to effect in other
cases the rewarding of goodness".[37] Indeed, Ross goes even
further and asserts that the good man's "sense of a duty to act
justly seems to be properly said to rest on an obscure sense
that the happiness of the virtuous is a good in the sense of
being a morally worthy object of interest"—although, unlike
utilitarians, Ross still does not say that a duty is a duty because
it will, or is likely to, produce the *best* possible results in the
circumstances.

There is, however, another aspect of Ross's account of
goodness which may suggest the idea that for him goodness is
a less fundamental notion than rightness. It is that he regards
three things as good—moral activity, intellectual activity and
pleasure—and yet he notes a difference in this respect, that the
first two are good wherever they occur and whoever their
possessors may be, whereas the agent's own pleasure is not
good and gives rise to no *prima facie* obligation to produce it.
This leads him to distinguish two senses of "good", the one
applied to things which are worthy objects of *admiration*, and
the other applied to things, such as the pleasure of others,
which are worthy objects of *satisfaction*. The element common
to both is the idea of "worthy", which may be identified with
"right" and lead therefore to the suspicion that rightness lies
at the bottom of Ross's idea of goodness. But this, it appears, is
hardly true; it is true only of goodness in one sense, and not
of goodness in the other. "Nothing", he says, "can be a
worthy object of admiration—it cannot be right to admire
it—unless it is also good in itself; while the pleasures of others
are good, from the point of view of any man, *simply* in the
sense that it is right for him to take satisfaction in them."[38]

It may seem unsatisfactory to give two quite different
accounts of two senses of "good", which are both morally
relevant, and two quite different accounts of their relationship
to rightness; but Ross finds justification for this course in the

[36] *Foundations of Ethics*, p. 289.   [37] *Ibid.*, p. 288.
[38] *Ibid.*, p. 282.

fact that unless it is followed violence is done to two facts which emerge from moral experience and which relate to the peculiar position of pleasure as something good, namely, (a) that although we may have a duty to produce pleasure for others we have no duty to produce our own pleasure; and (b) that "we seem quite incapable of equating, in respect of goodness, any amount of pleasure with any amount of morally good action",[39] that, in other words, morally good action is always morally preferable to any amount of pleasure.

The final issue of the matter for intuitionism, then, is that there are two senses of goodness, both of which are morally relevant, and that while one is a fundamental moral concept, no less ultimate than rightness itself, the other is dependent upon rightness. But, as we have seen, the rightness upon which it depends is that which can be identified, not with oughtness, but with suitability, in other words, if our argument is sound, with the rightness of propriety. Now it can hardly be held that this is a completely satisfactory account of the matter; but it would be beside our immediate purpose to follow it further at present. It is enough to notice that in dealing with goodness and its relationship to rightness, intuitionism has drawn attention to certain facts which have not been sufficiently considered in ethical theory.

[39] *Foundations of Ethics*, p. 275.

PART TWO

REFORMULATION AND REVIEW

THE PROBLEM REFORMULATED

IN OUR LAST two chapters, by dealing with the modern school of intuitionism, we have brought our survey of ethical theories to a close. There are indeed other contributions to the subject which have not been considered, such as *The Limits of Purpose* by J. L. Stocks, a series of articles by W. G. de Burgh in the *Journal of Philosophical Studies* entitled "On Right and Good", and Mr. H. W. B. Joseph's book, *Some Problems in Ethics*. But, although these have been classed together by J. H. Muirhead as involving a more or less radical criticism of the new intuitionism or the anti-idealist reaction, as Muirhead has described it, and as constituting in some measure a return to the idealist position, nevertheless they do not occupy sufficient common ground to be regarded as a new and distinct school of ethical thought. These writers may certainly be described as thinkers "who, while they have been stimulated to a re-examination of the whole ground by the difficulties that have been raised from a deontological point of view, are not prepared to part with the elements of truth that are contained in idealistic Ethics as represented by the great writers from Plato downwards, and who, by paths of their own, seem to be finding their ways back to something with difficulty distinguishable from it";[1] but, in the interests of accuracy, a considerable share of the emphasis must still rest upon the phrase "by paths of their own" as indicating the diversity of standpoint to be found amongst them.

In any case, however, our primary purpose in the foregoing chapters was not to present an exhaustive list of the different kinds of ethical theory which have historically appeared. For it is just not the case that the student of ethics is confronted by a variety of answers to a fixed and definite problem. Rather the interplay of competing theories represents a movement of thought which takes strides towards a satisfactory solution of the problem largely by formulating ever more precisely the

[1] Muirhead, *Rule and End in Morals*, p. 52.

problem itself. In this respect the ethical problem differs at least in degree from those to which the existence of the natural world gives rise. For in the latter the facts to be covered by any theory are relatively fixed and indisputable. The emergence of new facts, of course, is always a possibility; but facts and theory are distinguishable and the inadequacy of a theory may be due, not only to an incomplete knowledge of the facts, but just as much to error in the theory itself. In ethics, on the other hand, the facts are themselves judgments, and the efforts of the moral philosopher are therefore directed towards purging these judgments of error and ambiguity, making explicit what in them is only implicit, and finally presenting them as a coherent whole with their logical relationships one to another made clear and definite. Inadequacy in a moral theory, therefore, consists in treating as a true judgment what is partly false, ignoring one which is true, or arranging the judgments in a manner which the logic of the moral consciousness disowns; and if these errors could be completely avoided, if all false judgments could be detected, everything implicit made perfectly explicit, and the judgments of the moral consciousness arranged according to their own inherent logic, the task of ethics would be completed. The essence of the matter then is the paradox that if the ethical problem could be stated with perfect precision the problem itself would be solved. And the truth contained in this paradox is that whereas in the natural world the facts *give rise* to a problem, in ethics the problem is to discover what are the facts.

There are, however, two modifications which suggest themselves to all this. The first is to the effect that there is a broader view of ethics according to which the discovery of the facts is only one of several problems, and the task of the moral philosopher cannot be separated from that of the metaphysician. But this contention may mean one of three things. It may mean that ethical truth follows from metaphysical truth in much the same way as the logical conclusion follows from its premises; but such a contention runs contrary to Kant's clear-cut distinction between the theoretical and practical exercises of reason and to our own modern recognition of the moral consciousness, and it does seem wrong in principle to seek to derive morality by a purely logical process from that which is not specifically moral in character. The suggested modification, however, may not mean this; and if it does not it will mean either that we cannot make the judgments of the moral consciousness perfectly explicit without entering the field of metaphysics, or else that if these could be made perfectly explicit they would prove exceedingly useful data for the metaphysician. Yet, even if either or both of these suggestions are true, it still remains the case that the task of ethics is to discover the facts.

In the second place, however, this conclusion does fall to be modified, or perhaps amplified, in another direction altogether. For, granted that the general task of ethics is to discover the facts in their proper relationship one to another, we must allow that at any one time in the history of ethical thought there may be special points at which the judgments of the moral consciousness seem to conflict and fail to hang together, or special points at which these judgments appear to leave gaps; and consequently, in a subsidiary sense, the problems of ethics at that time will be to resolve these difficulties and fill these gaps. The problem is still to discover the facts, but it is a problem defined by its place in the history of ethical thought.

Since that is so, it follows that we have now reached a stage in our inquiry at which it is fitting to take stock and to reformulate the ethical problem; and to that task we must now address ourselves. Our task is not simply to pick and choose amongst the theories which have historically appeared, but rather by grasping whatever there is of truth in them to concentrate attention upon those parts of the field which still resist the efforts of the philosopher to give a coherent account of the judgments of the ordinary moral consciousness.

In the first place, then, the field of ethics has become more or less clearly defined. It has become increasingly plain that ethics is concerned pre-eminently with a certain kind of judgment, the moral judgment, which cannot be derived from any judgment of a non-moral type. In particular, it is seen that moral judgments cannot be logically derived from metaphysical or scientific truths, such as the evolutionary hypothesis. The fundamental failure of evolutionary ethics was, not that it gave a wrong account of the ordinary moral consciousness, but that it tried to by-pass the moral consciousness altogether, and to derive morality from non-moral truth. In this way, however, we can achieve only the appearance and not the reality of a *moral* code. Moral judgments cannot be logically derived from non-moral judgments; and consequently it is not the duty of the moral philosopher, by the investigation of non-moral truth such as is contained in metaphysics and natural science, to produce a moral code. Such truths do not logically imply any moral judgments whatsoever, although the recognition of them by a moral agent may certainly give rise to the recognition of certain duties by the moral consciousness. Ethics, therefore, is concerned with the judgments of the moral consciousness, and not with judgments which may copy the form of such genuinely moral judgments but none the less are not judgments which commend themselves to the moral consciousness of mankind. This is part of Kant's meaning when he holds that moral philosophy is concerned with the practical, not the speculative, exercise of reason. All sorts of speculative investigations, metaphysical and scientific, may give rise to the recognition of a duty for example, but the recognition itself is not the logical conclusion of a speculative argument but an act of the moral consciousness, and it is only as such that it falls within the scope of ethics.

In the second place, it is more or less generally admitted that the moral judgments which together constitute the subject-matter of ethics represent an insight into reality, and do not simply report an impression made upon this, that or the other moral agent. In discussing the theory which we have denoted sentimentalism, we observed that, although its main significance for modern ethics lies in the fact that in opposition to intellectualism it took the self-conscious type of moral judgment as fundamental, the more important issue at the time, as between sentimentalism and intellectualism, was whether the moral consciousness was to be regarded as akin to the senses or feeling on the one hand, or to thinking on the other. That this latter issue has ceased to be the aspect of eighteenth-century thought most relevant to the modern discussion is silent evidence that the question whether the moral consciousness is akin to feelings or senses on the one hand or to thinking on the other has to some extent been settled. Not that this settlement is a matter of small importance. Indeed, the existence of ethics as a science depends upon it. For if moral judgments are simply a report of impressions made upon moral agents, then two seemingly contrary moral judgments may both be true. There are some judgments, such as judgments of taste, which merely report impressions made. Thus A may like cheese and declare that it is good, whereas B may actively dislike it and declare that it is bad. The two judgments appear contrary, but it is clear that both may well be true. In the case of moral judgments, on the other hand, we ordinarily regard such contrariety as an indication of falsehood in one judgment or the other or in both. That such is our opinion is seen from the fact that when these differences occur we think that there is something to argue about.

Now the implication of all this is that in the field of morals there is an objective truth, of which we may often fall short in our moral judgments, but at which we are at least aiming in making these judgments at all. If it were not so there could be no science of ethics, since there would be no possibility of presenting a single self-coherent system of moral judgments. Instead we should have on our hands nothing more than a whole host of unrelated judgments of private taste, and quite possibly of what *appear* to be mutually inconsistent propositions. But if judgments cannot really conflict, neither can they actually cohere. Both the claim of the moral consciousness to apprehend, however imperfectly, an objective truth, and the claim of ethics to be a science are decisive in favour of rationalism as opposed to mere sentimentalism, although of course it cannot therefore be maintained that the moral consciousness involves reason and nothing else.

It is to be noticed, however, that if one finds a moral judgment which is false, that discovery does not conflict with the general claim of the moral consciousness to give expression to an objective truth. Rather, it confirms this claim, for the claim itself is the condition both of truth and of falsehood in moral judgments. Where a judgment merely gives expression to a private preference of taste ("Cheese is good") it can be neither true nor false—although, of course, the judgment that I like cheese, being an objective judgment about the judge and not the cheese, may be either true or false. Thus the claim of the moral consciousness to apprehend an objective truth is not to be confused with a claim that each and all of its judgments are true. None the less, the former claim does seem to involve the contention that *by and large* its judgments are true, or, more precisely, that they contain *some* truth and are *not completely* false. And this point is involved in Samuel Clarke's thesis that what would be a real embarrassment to the claim of our moral consciousness to apprehend objective truth is the existence of a nation (or of an individual for that matter) whose moral judgments, not only conflicted in certain points with our own, but were "universally and directly contrary"[2] to them. It is inconceivable that the moral consciousness should claim to apprehend, however imperfectly, an objective truth, and at the same time allow even the possibility that all its judgments may be *completely* false. The claim, then, to apprehend an objective truth is a twofold claim, (i) that there is an objective truth there to be apprehended, and (ii) that this truth has already been at least partially apprehended; but it is not essentially a claim that this truth has been perfectly apprehended.

Moreover, this claim on the part of the moral consciousness to apprehend an objective truth is not to be confused with a claim that the peculiarly moral qualities are there in the objects independently of their apprehension by the moral consciousness. On that point the inherent claim of the moral consciousness is properly neutral. It may be that these peculiarly moral qualities are objectively there in that sense, but, on the other hand, it may not be so. What the moral consciousness does claim is that these qualities are there, not independently of the moral consciousness in general, but independently of the moral consciousness in this man or the other, and, therefore, independently of the peculiarities pertaining to this individual or the next.

Thirdly, however, it does seem clear that, whether the fundamental moral qualities do or do not belong intrinsically to the acts, states of affairs, or characters to which they are applied, that is, whether the moral qualities do or do not belong even if the acts, states of affairs, or characters in question are not the objects of a moral consciousness, they are at any rate necessarily connected with some at least of the qualities which do so belong. But it is only the *fundamental* moral qualities of which this can be said. For example, if "right" is dependent upon "good", if an act is right only if it is productive of a good result, the rightness of the act will not be necessarily connected with qualities which do belong intrinsically to the act; but in that event, the goodness, whether it belongs intrinsically or not, will be necessarily connected with some quality or qualities which do belong intrinsically to the result. Whether the fundamental moral quality belongs intrinsically or not to

[2] *Discourse*, i, 3 (Selby-Bigge, para. 497).

its act or state of affairs, its connection with all other intrinsic qualities of the same act or state of affairs is not one of mere contingency. Its connection with *some* of these qualities may be purely contingent. If it is a headmaster's duty to tell parents the truth about their sons, it may be quite accidental that it is the headmaster's duty to inform a particular parent, X, that his son's Latin is deficient; but the connection of the moral quality with one or some of the other qualities of the act or state of affairs is a necessary connection. If one were asked to give a rough general description of the moral consciousness one might be content to say that it is the awareness that certain kinds of thing have one moral quality and that certain other kinds of thing have another moral quality. It is, for example, the awareness that certain acts are right and certain others wrong; and what we have just been doing is to make explicit what is contained in this general description. It might be held, indeed, that the general account is compatible with a contingent connection between moral qualities and any or all amoral qualities of things; but it does seem clear that that is not what is meant. The statement that certain things are right or good is more akin to the statement that triangles have their three angles equal to two right angles than it is to the statement which informs us that the man with the red hat is wearing a yellow waistcoat. In other words, it is an insight rather than an observation. Thus with regard to the fundamental moral qualities, it seems to be the case that the moral consciousness affirms a necessary connection between certain moral qualities of things and certain other of their non-moral qualities, although of course it may not be easy to give a precise and accurate expression of the necessary connection. It may not be accurate, for example, to say that all lies are wrong, but none the less it is a necessary or rational connection, not a contingent one, which is affirmed.

This does not mean that *every* moral judgment which predicates a fundamental moral quality affirms a necessary connection between it and something else, but it does mean that all such contingent connections are derived from, and based upon, some necessary connection. That is to say, it is maintained that *fundamental* moral judgments which predicate a fundamental moral quality assert a rational connection. Thus it may be my duty to obey the commands of a political sovereign, and it may be that act A is commanded. Now in itself act A may be

such that it would not be my duty unless it were commanded;
and in this case, although act A may be right, there is no
necessary connection between its rightness and its other
characteristics. None the less, if rightness is a fundamental
moral quality, there is a necessary connection between obedience and rightness, and the judgment which affirms this
connection is the logical ground of that which asserts that act
A is right.

In the fourth place, it seems possible to maintain that there
is more than one fundamental judgment predicating a fundamental moral quality. This, of course, is not so certain as the
other three points, and indeed it cannot be asserted without
qualification. But what does seem certain is that none of the
historical suggestions of a single comprehensive fundamental
moral judgment predicating a fundamental moral quality can
be finally accepted. In each case the suggestion appears to
be an over-simplification of the facts of moral experience.
Thus it cannot be held with plausibility that, if rightness is a
fundamental moral quality, the only necessary connection between rightness and something else is that which obtains
between rightness and obedience to the command of God, or,
again, that, if rightness is a fundamental moral quality, the
only necessary connection between rightness and something
else is that which obtains between rightness and obedience to
the command of a political sovereign. Both suggestions fall to
the ground for the same reason, namely, that the characteristics of the things commanded are not all morally indifferent.
In the case of some of these things we should consider it right
to do them whether they were commanded or not; and in the
case of others, at least of those commanded by a political
sovereign, we can ask significantly whether in spite of their
being unquestionably commanded it is after all right to do
them. This does not mean that in the last analysis the whole of
morality may not be subsumed under the law of God; but it
does mean that, even if that is possible, our knowledge of God
and His law is not the logical ground of our knowledge of moral
distinctions. Rather it is much more likely that our knowledge
of moral distinctions is in some way the ground of our knowledge of God, and that without our knowledge of self-authenticating moral distinctions we should be incapable of knowing
God. At any rate, whether the whole of morality can be
subsumed under the law of God or not, it is not the case that

the only necessary connection between rightness and non-moral qualities is that between rightness and obedience to the command either of God or of the political sovereign. Again, if goodness is a fundamental moral quality, it is no longer plausible to hold that pleasure and only pleasure is good. Indeed, as Professor Moore has pointed out, this single comprehensive principle would hardly have had the long innings in ethical theory, which in fact it has had, were it not for the naturalistic fallacy by which "pleasant" and "good" have been regarded as synonymous terms. Nor is Kant's suggestion in much better case. Here it is rightness that is a fundamental moral quality, and the one necessary connection asserted is that between rightness and self-consistent universa-lisability. The moral consciousness, however, recognises certain acts as right, without even raising the question whether the maxims could without contradiction become the maxims of all moral agents; and indeed Kant did not succeed in applying this moral principle without introducing other moral principles in addition to that which alone he explicitly recognised.

At this point, however, a complication arises, for although it does not seem to be the case that the only fundamental moral judgment regarding rightness is that which affirms a necessary connection between rightness and self-consistent universalisability, none the less it may well be that self-consistent universalisability is a characteristic of all right actions. And here there are three possibilities. (i) It might indicate a necessary but in itself insufficient condition of rightness. (ii) It might indicate neither a non-moral quality which right actions must have in order to be right nor rightness itself, but an implication of rightness. (iii) It might indicate a characteristic, x, which, so far as we can discover, all right actions do in fact possess, but which, so far as the moral consciousness can see, is neither a necessary, nor a sufficient, *condition* of rightness. In this last case, the proposition that all right acts have characteristic x, would not be a strictly necessary and universal judgment, but would represent no more than an empirical generalisation which moral experience might at any time rebut. Such a judgment, unlike the other two, is not a judgment of the ordinary moral consciousness, but one which arises when the moral consciousness and its judgments are made an object of thought; and this judgment, along with similar judgments, may well be denoted *ethical* judgments as distinguished from *moral* judgments or judgments made by the ordinary moral consciousness. And it is well to recognise the existence of such judgments, lest our earlier contention that the aim of ethics is to present the judgments of the ordinary moral consciousness as a self-consistent and coherent whole should blind us to the fact that in order to accomplish that end the moral philosopher is compelled to make judgments which are ethical rather than moral. Although it is true that the main difficulty in ethics is to get the facts and their relationships one to another perfectly clear, ethics could not proceed without making the moral consciousness and its judgments an object of thought, and without making judgments about the peculiar ideas of the moral consciousness, such as "act", "freedom", "right", "good", and so on, and about the judgments in which the moral consciousness embodies these ideas.

We have, then, the field delimited, and delimited as a field of objective truth, and not just of objective truth but of necessary truth, consisting at bottom of rational connections and not merely of empirically observed juxtapositions. Moreover, from the history of ethical thought we have received warning against over-simplifying the field of morality; and we have noticed different kinds of judgment which may find a place in ethics, namely, the *moral* judgment on the one hand and the *ethical* on the other.

Now, in following the course of ethical thought, we have seen what is perhaps the main ethical problem gradually taking shape, the problem of the inter-relationship of the three peculiarly moral concepts—"right", "good", and "morally good". At first, as we saw, these were not precisely distinguished one from another, and indeed to a very large extent "right", "good", and "virtuous", were treated as interchangeable and synonymous. That they should have been so treated in the earlier days of ethical discussion is perhaps not a matter for wonder, for it is only gradually that we can separate and distinguish different yet kindred ideas; but in fact the result was not by any means such a great confusion as one might have expected, and behind the early treatment there lies the silent assumption that the field of morality is one field, and not two or more rather similar fields. Indeed, when the different methods of treatment *are* distinguished, they are regarded as different ways of treating one subject which are not only mutually consistent but are a strength and support one to another. Thus, in the course of his *Preface to Sermons*, Butler declares: "There are two ways in which the subject of morals may be treated. One begins from inquiring into the abstract relations of things; the other from a matter of fact, namely, what the particular nature of man is, its several parts, their economy or constitution; from whence it proceeds to determine what course of life it is, which is correspondent to this whole nature. In the former method the conclusion is expressed thus, that vice is contrary to the nature and reason of things; in the latter, that it is a violation or breaking in upon our own nature. Thus they both lead us to the same thing, our obligations to the practice of virtue; and thus they exceedingly strengthen and enforce each other."[3] In this way intellectualism and sentimentalism are treated as two paths by which the same truths may be reached; and the emphasis is upon the self-identity of the field. When the two theories come into conflict, the issue is almost invariably whether sentimentalism really in effect destroys morality by reducing it to a matter of private impression and private taste. Historically, the issue was not whether sentimentalism wrongly described morality, but whether in spite of the good intentions of its authors it described morality at all; and consequently we find that one of the ablest of the intellectualists, Richard Price, having reduced sentiments of approval to the status of merely external supports of real morality, does not hesitate straightway to introduce a moral sentiment as an internal and moral support. In Price, however, we do meet the beginnings of later ethical analysis, for he does distinguish in effect between virtue or moral goodness on the one hand, and rightness on the other. He holds that the only virtuous motive is the sense of obligation, and so, by implication at least, he subordinates the judgment that X is morally good to the judgment that act A is right.

In utilitarianism the process is taken a stage further, and virtue or moral goodness on the one hand is distinguished from rightness *and* goodness on the other. Thus John Stuart Mill takes notice of the objection which was sometimes made against utilitarianism that "it is exacting too much to require that people shall always act from the inducement of promoting the general interests of society", and answers that "this is to

[3] *Preface to Sermons*, Selby-Bigge, vol. i, para. 188.

mistake the very meaning of a standard of morals, and confound the rule of action with the motive of it". "It is the more unjust to utilitarianism," he says, "that this particular misapprehension should be made a ground of objection to it, inasmuch as utilitarian moralists have gone beyond almost all others in affirming that the motive has nothing to do with the morality of the action, though much with the worth of the agent. He who saves a fellow creature from drowning does what is morally right, whether his motive be duty, or the hope of being paid for his trouble; he who betrays the friend who trusts him, is guilty of a crime, even if his object be to serve another friend to whom he is under greater obligations."[4] Mere moral goodness or virtue is distinguished, not from rightness only, but from goodness also, and it is held that one may be present where the other is absent.

Another step, however, was still required to complete the analysis, for rightness had to be distinguished from goodness, so that, in its meaning at any rate, it was not simply subordinated to goodness. But the clear recognition of this distinction was long in coming. Even Professor Moore's *Principia Ethica* *defines* "right" as "productive of good"; and, although there is some indication that the author departed from this position in his later book, *Ethics*, it was not until the appearance of the new intuitionism that this distinction was clearly recognised and forcefully expressed. On the other hand, the matter cannot be said to have reached the stage of final settlement, for, as we have seen, there is still a question regarding the different meanings of "right" and other cognate terms, such as "duty" and "obligation".

Moreover, the careful distinction of one moral idea from another, although it is of the first importance if the subsequent discussion is to avoid confusion and ambiguity, is none the less a preliminary task; and there still remains a double problem: (a) the problem in the case of each of the three moral ideas of achieving the highest degree of generality in asserting the necessary connection of the moral quality in question with other non-moral qualities; and (b) the problem of setting the three different types of moral judgment in their proper relation one to another. These two problems are not entirely separate, and deserve to be treated as a double problem, since, for example, in solving the first of them with regard to rightness it

[4] *Utilitarianism*, ch. ii.

may be held that all right acts are right because productive of a good result, and that of course is already a considerable step towards a solution of one kind or another of the second problem.

We have already referred to Richard Price's adumbration of a solution to this second problem in a more primitive form, namely, as concerned with the relation between moral goodness and rightness. Attention has also been paid to Mill's system, which over-subordinates rightness to goodness, and makes virtue on the one hand and rightness and goodness on the other fall hopelessly apart in that the one can be present where the other is completely absent. The most complete and compact gathering together, however, of the different strands of moral experience is to be found in the ethical system of idealism. Here, as we saw, goodness and virtue are brought together, for the highest good is taken to be the good, that is, the morally good will, and rightness is related to this, being present in, and arising out of, the customs and institutions of present society which represent the hitherto achievement of the eternal consciousness seeking to perfect itself. Yet this ethical system cannot be taken as a final solution of the problem, for, in the first place, it may be questioned whether the idealist is right in connecting goodness and moral goodness by defining "good" as that which satisfies desire. If it is questionable so to define "good", it is still more questionable to define the highest good as that which completely satisfies desire, and to equate this with moral goodness. In the second place, it may be doubted whether justice is done in this system to the idea of "right", for on this theory certain acts are right because they are the hitherto achievement of the eternal self-consciousness. By saying that certain acts are right it is meant, in other words, that these acts are the ways, so far discovered, in which the eternal self-consciousness can so far realise itself and consequently approximate to complete self-satisfaction;[5] and this means that "right", as it finds a place in the idealist system, is given the same meaning as applied to acts as it ordinarily bears when applied, for example, to roads. By doing one's duty one is simply following the right path;[6] and so used the rule of right is not a categorical but a hypothetical imperative. An act is right, not on account of what it is in itself, but on account of

---

[5] Cf. Green, *Prolegomena*, bk. iii, ch. ii, para. 197.
[6] Cf. Green, *Prolegomena*, bk. iii, ch. i, para. 178.

the end which it has been found to serve as means. The obligation to fulfil the duties of one's station is that by doing so one will realise oneself to some extent, and so achieve a more complete satisfaction than would otherwise be possible. Moreover, it may well be true that the only man who achieves complete satisfaction is the perfectly moral man; but we hardly regard this as the very essence of conscientious living. Rather, if indeed it is the moral man alone who can achieve complete satisfaction, that will be an interesting fact about morality; but it will not exhibit the essence of morality. We ordinarily think that right acts are right independently of the presence or absence of the prospect of near or distant self-satisfaction. It may indeed be that out of moral experience there grows a faith that along this line real self-satisfaction is to be found, and it may be that without this faith men are apt to lose their grip upon morality itself—this is involved, for example, in the contention that where religious faith disappears morality may linger for a time but will ultimately vanish—but this is only to say that morality in itself is incomplete, that morality has ragged edges, and that unto him that hath shall be given and from him that hath not shall be taken away even that which he hath. None the less, the self-satisfaction is not of the essence of morality, and the element of faith is based upon, and built upon, moral experience as upon a foundation.

In these two ways, then, the ethical system of idealism fails to maintain itself as a final and complete solution to the problem.

The new intuitionism, on the other hand, has not reached the stage of presenting a complete and coherent system. Its main intention is analytic rather than synthetic, and it has to its credit the achievement of a thorough-going examination of the concept of right. Yet it is possible to make certain judgments regarding any attempted synthesis which would make full use of the fruitful analysis which has so far been given, and which would at the same time remain consistent with the results of that analysis. In the first place, "right" and "good" must stand for mutually independent ideas, and the one may be present where the other is absent—unless, indeed, Mr. Carritt's position is adopted which seems to subordinate "good" to "right";[7] and, in the second place, moral goodness and rightness must also be taken as mutually independent, and

---

[7] *Theory of Morals*, para. 64, p. 73.

again it must be recognised that the one may be found where the other is completely absent. There is indeed a connection between goodness and virtue for the latter is taken[8] as a special kind of goodness. It follows from this that the chasm between rightness and goodness could be bridged if a connection could be found between rightness and virtue; but in harmony with the tenets of the new intuitionism no such connection is possible, for with J. S. Mill it is asserted that a right act can be done from an entirely bad motive. At one point in the development of the new school it did indeed look for a moment as if such a connection were about to appear, for, as we saw, in his later book Sir David Ross, following Professor Prichard's *Duty and Ignorance of Fact*, gives up Mill's position that the bearer of the moral quality "right" is the series of objective states of affairs which we should ordinarily call an act, and holds instead that what is right is the setting of oneself to do something. It soon appeared, however, that to the mind of the intuitionists this modification to the original theory does not affect the question whether a right act can be done from a bad motive. We did, however, see some reason for re-examining this aspect of intuitionist doctrine; and indeed it does seem as if the progress of intuitionist thought from the question, What is the meaning of "right"? through the question, What things are right and what makes them right? to the question, What is it that is right? would naturally find its conclusion in the question, What is an act?

There are two main points here.

(1) In the first place, if moral goodness and rightness are held to fall hopelessly apart, if their connection is purely contingent and accidental even although it occurs, and even although it is likely to occur, in a majority of cases (for on any view it is hardly plausible to deny that the morally good man is more likely to do what is right than his less virtuous neighbour), if, in other words, it is maintained that the worth of the agent is one question and the rightness of his conduct an *entirely* different question, morality divides into two and it is difficult to see how on this theory its unity can again come into view. Of course, even if this unity were apparent, there would remain a question concerning the relation between rightness and goodness in general; but it does seem right in principle to approach this

[8] Cf. Ross, *Foundations of Ethics*, p. 290.

G

broader question by considering first of all the possibility of a connection between rightness and one special kind of goodness, namely, virtue.

(2) In the second place, the issue whether the worth of the agent is one question and the rightness of his conduct an entirely different question turns very largely upon the precise account of what it is that is right, that is, upon the definition of an act—for it is acts in one sense or another that are right or wrong. The issue turns upon the question what precisely an act is, and how it is related to motives and character in general. T. H. Green in his system of idealistic ethics does not raise the question whether a right act can be done from an entirely bad motive, but it is the case that for him the rightness of an act derives from the moral goodness of the will whose achievement it is; and it is because of this view of the matter (along with the dogma that there is nothing absolutely good save the good will) that ethical idealism can present a compact appearance and exhibit the moral field as one field and the judgments of the moral consciousness as a self-coherent system. The new intuitionists deny that the rightness of an act can depend upon, and derive from, the moral goodness of the will; but simply to deny that is not to imply that a right act can be done from an entirely bad motive. Yet, whether it be an implication or not, the new intuitionism does make this contention also. In doing so it drastically separates act and motive, and the result is that virtue and rightness fall asunder.

It is necessary therefore that we carefully consider the nature of acts, the bearers of the moral qualities right and wrong. But the realm of practice is a complicated realm, and there are doubtless several different elements within it any one of which might lay claim to being what is meant by an act. Doubtless, too, at one time or another, in one context or another, each of these is actually denoted by the word "act". The question which concerns us in the present inquiry, however, is not which of these has the best claim to be referred to by this word "act", but rather, given that the ordinary moral consciousness uses the word to denote the bearer of the qualities right and wrong, which of the various elements in the practical realm is it that the moral consciousness entitles an act and to which does it attribute these particular qualities. Our problem will be, not to say what "act" ought to mean, but to examine the usage of the moral consciousness in applying the words "right" and "wrong", with a view to the discovery of what it is precisely (the act) to which they are applied. It is not enough to say that our task is to discover what the ordinary moral consciousness means by the word "act", for that might mean that we were simply trying to find out what the ordinary man thinks the ordinary moral consciousness has in mind when it uses the word "act"; whereas what we *are* trying to discover is what the ordinary man ought to think the ordinary moral consciousness has in mind when it uses this word "act". And that we can discover only by examining the ways in which the moral consciousness uses the words "right" and "wrong".

THE NOTION OF RIGHT ACTION

WE MUST NOW address ourselves to the task of defining actions as precisely as possible, and, as we have already noticed, it is actions in which we are interested as the subjects of the moral predicates "right" and "wrong". The word "action" may be used in completely amoral contexts, but with such a usage we have no concern here. Further, the word may be used in a moral or apparently moral context, but again we are not here concerned with any such usages unless indeed the entities for which the word is made to stand are the bearers of the moral predicates "right" and "wrong". Our immediate concern, then, is with those things which are right or wrong; and, that being so, it might seem that it would be less ambiguous if we were to avoid the word "action" altogether, and refer instead, as Sir David Ross does, to "what it is that is right".[1] Apart from the awkwardness, however, of this circumlocution, there is some reason for retaining the word "action", since it is actions in one sense or another that are right or wrong, and not something which is not an action at all. We have already discovered some ground for supposing that both Prichard and Ross, in seeking to determine what it is that is right, tend to regard it not as an action but as a certain psychical event as such;[2] whereas, by its constant use of the word "action" as the subject of the predicates "right" and "wrong", the ordinary moral consciousness roughly delimits the area to which these predicates are applicable, and our present task is not to try to discover some other area altogether, in conflict with the persistent witness of the moral consciousness, but rather to define this roughly delimited area more precisely.

Moreover, we are to conduct this inquiry by examining the usage of the ordinary moral consciousness in applying the predicates "right" and "wrong". In this respect our task bears a certain resemblance to that which Kant set himself in the first *Critique*. There, at bottom, his inquiry was an attempt to discover the logical presuppositions of our ordinary

---

[1] *Foundations of Ethics*, chs. vi and vii.   [2] Cf. p. 163 above.

experience. Given that experience, he said in effect, what must be logically presupposed in order to render it possible? Similarly, we are to start from our moral experience and all the judgments which the ordinary moral consciousness makes (especially those in which it employs the predicates "right" and "wrong"), and, for the most part, we are to try to discover what precise definition of an act is logically presupposed by this experience and these judgments. The whole of ethics is based on the assumption that, by and large, moral judgments are true, and our immediate task is to find out what precise definition of action is required in order to make the most coherent sense of these judgments, and in particular of a certain class of these judgments, namely, those which employ the predicates "right" and "wrong" or their equivalents.

We cannot, however, undertake this inquiry until we discover first of all whether in using the word "right" the moral consciousness always means the same thing by it; and this, of course, involves an inquiry into the meaning or meanings of "right". In the history of ethics this question was slow in being raised, doubtless because ethics was, for the most part, concerned with the concept of good, and tended to regard "right" as simply meaning "productive of good". There were exceptions to this tendency, but their significance was not generally noticed and an adequate conception of right did not at once become a part of the common stock in trade of ethical science. Indeed, we find even Professor Moore defining "right" as "productive of the best possible results". As we have seen, however, one of the achievements of the new intuitionism was to break away from this assumption, for according to this theory the idea of right is ultimate and indefinable. It may be, it was initially admitted, that productivity of good is necessary and enough to render an act right, but at least the word "right" does not *mean* "productive of the best possible result". And this, it must be agreed, is perfectly true, since, if on this point the new intuitionism were in error, the proposition that a right act is productive of the best possible result would be an identical and insignificant proposition, of the same kind as that which affirms that X is X. Further, if we examine the notion we see that to say that an act is right just means that the act is right; and if we attempt to make the meaning clearer by the use of alternative expressions we can do so only by employing in place of the word "right" mere synonyms of "right", such as "dutiful" and "obligatory". Right is a simple, unanalysable, indefinable and fundamental concept.

But we noticed in the treatment of this matter by the intuitionists that, although this was a main contention of their theory, it was subject to certain modifications which tended to detract from the force of the contention and to obscure the original insight of the theory. These modifications consisted principally in this, that (a) a minor difference was recognised between "ought" and "right", and (b) as the account of rightness is developed in Sir David Ross's *Foundations of Ethics* and as it becomes identifiable with moral suitability and therefore applicable to emotions as well as actions, a wide and important difference is implied, if not admitted, between "ought" and "right".

(a) So far as the first of these points is concerned, we need not here repeat what was earlier said in explanation of the apparent minor divergence. It is sufficient to recall that we found reason to suppose that where "ought" and "right" are used strictly and in their full ethical sense they do not after all so diverge in meaning that I ought to do something which is not strictly right or that something is right of which it cannot truly be said that I ought to do it. It is true, however, that if one or other of these two words is employed in what is less or other than its strict and full ethical significance the two may quite possibly diverge in some more or less important respect, and there are uses of both terms which fall short in varying degrees of their strict and full ethical use. "Right", for instance, is sometimes used as the mere contradictory of "wrong", that is to say, with a negative intention, and so employed it may well be distinguishable from "ought" and "duty" which are positive conceptions. "Ought", in its turn, when not used to represent moral obligation, may indicate a merely legal obligation, or, again, it may be used instrumentally to signify a hypothetical imperative; while "obliged" may in addition introduce the notion of compulsion of one kind or another. But in all these uses the terms in question are employed in something less or other than their strict and full ethical significance, and such uses of them are distinguishable from their strict ethical employment. And in this latter employment they appear to be synonymous. At any rate, so far as we have yet seen, there is no such difference between them that one can apply to an act to which another cannot apply. It may not be right to do what legally I ought to do, or what I am obliged to do if I am to realise my fondest ambition, and it may be that I have no duty to do what is not wrong so far as I can see; but if morally I ought to do act X then act X is my duty and it is the morally right act in the situation.

(b) In the second place, we noticed a development in the intuitionist account of rightness which threatened a wider divergence between oughtness and rightness than the minor difference which intuitionism recognises and the existence of which we have just denied. The central point in this development is the identification of rightness with moral suitability; and one result of this identification is that rightness must be regarded as applicable to emotions, and so, by implication, as other than oughtness which is not so applicable. We saw also, however, that where rightness is equivalent to moral suitability or fittingness it is a derivative notion and only a partially moral one. Judgments which employ the word "right" in this sense are judgments of propriety. To say that act X or emotion A is right in this sense is not to express an insight of the moral conciousness, but to affirm that the act or emotion is in accordance with the external standards of contemporary society, which may in their turn be based upon moral insight. To say that act X is right in precisely the same sense in which it can be said that emotion A is right is to adopt this second-hand moral standpoint. Further, it is not a matter for wonder that the word "right" should be used in this derivative sense since, as a matter of everyday experience, our moral standpoint can easily become second-hand, since in many matters for most of us most of the time it *is* second-hand, and since it is perhaps less often that we directly face up to a situation and make an independent evaluation of the rights and wrongs inherent in it.

In this connection it is interesting to notice the argument of Lord Lindsay in his book *The Two Moralities*, where he contrasts the morality of "my station and its duties" on the one hand with the challenge to perfection or, as he alternatively calls it, the morality of grace on the other. There are aspects of this argument which will later claim our attention, but at the moment what is important to notice is the manner in which Lord Lindsay describes the former of these moralities. "The standard", he says, "of my station and its duties is based upon the fact of how most people concerned are prepared to behave."[3] "Moral rules . . . are of no use unless they are generally kept."[4] The standard, in other words, is not that which indicates how, purely and simply, we ought to behave, but is rather that which indicates how most are prepared to behave and how in fact in general they do behave. "We know," says Lord Lindsay, "that our effective practical code is one thing and an ideal code, to which we may from time to time profess allegiance, another. We know the conduct we expect of ordinary decent people of our sort; that is, conduct we expect of them as a matter of course, and our expectations are not usually disappointed. But if expectations were of ideal conduct in ourselves or in others they generally would be disappointed. Behaviour we can rely upon, as is this practically effective code, is imperfect. We know it to be so if only by our contrast between it and an ideal or abstract code. We know this in ourselves, in the contrast between the way in which we can fairly undertake that we shall normally act and the very different standard of our highest and most heroic moments. We know it by the contrast between the behaviour of the decent average man and the conduct of the saint. The standard of conduct embodied in moral codes and laws can never be higher than the conduct that the decent average man is prepared to act up to. But saints, we know, pay no regard to such limitations."[5] Now, since the emphasis in all this is not upon what ideally men ought to do, but upon what in any given society they are prepared to do and what they do in fact habitually do, the morality of my station and its duties, as it finds a place in Lord Lindsay's argument, is to be identified with what we have called the standard of propriety; and if this identification were to be called in question it is easily seen that the standard of propriety shares the peculiar characteristics of Lord Lindsay's morality of my station and its duties, namely, that it is based upon what men are in fact and in general prepared to do, that it is therefore a closed morality, that is, confined to a given historical society, and that it is necessarily imperfect, relative, and changeable.[6] None the less it is a real factor of which account must be taken. As we have said it is the standard followed by most of us most of the time. But in all this there is nothing inconsistent with the distinction

---

[3] *The Two Moralities*, p. 26.
[4] *Ibid.*, p. 22.
[5] *Ibid.*, pp. 24–5.
[6] Cf. Lindsay, *The Two Moralities*, p. 20.

which we have drawn between the standard of propriety on the one hand and that other standard to which reference is made whenever we apply to actions the words "right" and "wrong" in their full and proper significance.

Yet there is one aspect of Lord Lindsay's argument which does cast doubt upon the validity of this distinction. It is that aspect of his argument which suggests that the ease with which we adopt this standpoint of propriety (according to us—my station and its duties, according to Lord Lindsay's thesis) is not entirely due to moral lethargy on our part. It is, so the argument runs, the standpoint of the society to which we belong, and there is a sense in which society may be said to force its standpoint upon us. "Most of our actions," says Lord Lindsay, "are co-operative, at least in the sense that they assume the behaviour of other people and assume that that behaviour will be of a certain kind. . . . Other people's behaviour is necessarily an assumed background of ours, as our behaviour goes to make up a background to theirs. We all so much take that for granted that we hardly notice it. We are aware of it only, perhaps, when we change from one social atmosphere to another. . . . It is not just that such social atmospheres, created by the different moral codes which are practised in them, are pleasing or displeasing. They compel us to act differently. The actions which are wise in one social background are not wise in another. If you know that other people are ready to co-operate and help, you act in one way; if you know that they will do nothing of the kind, you act in another way. That is true even if you do not allow your purpose to be altered by what other people do or are prepared to do. Your ways of carrying it out are bound to be changed." [7]

Now this *does* cast doubt upon the validity of our distinction, for it suggests that we may not be at liberty to follow any standard other than, or at least more purely moral than, that of propriety, and therefore that, since "I ought" implies "I can", this other standard, if there is such a standard at all, cannot be a standard of rightness or oughtness. Much depends upon what precisely is meant when we say that our social atmosphere may "compel us to act differently". This affirmation, however, does not carry a single unmistakable significance. Indeed, it may mean one or other of three things: (i) that the social atmosphere, the existing social and economic

[7] *The Two Moralities*, pp. 20–2.

institutions, and in general the way in which people behave may determine, to some extent at least, the kind of practical situations with which an agent may be faced and the alternative courses of action which he may pursue in relation to them; (ii) that, given the alternatives open to an agent in any given situation, the social atmosphere *tempts* him to follow one rather than another; or (iii) that, given the alternatives open to an agent in any given situation, the social atmosphere literally compels him to follow one rather than another. But it is only the last of these, which is perhaps not the most plausible interpretation, that really casts doubt upon the validity of the distinction drawn between the standard of propriety and the standard of rightness proper. Consequently, it remains the case that the standard of my station and its duties, which Lord Lindsay identifies with the moral standard of rightness and oughtness, is really identifiable with the sub-moral or pseudo-moral standard of propriety, since essentially it is a standard which is practically *effective*, and, under the imperfect conditions prevailing in any historic society, whatever *is* falls inevitably under the judgment of what *ought to be*.

Our conclusion is then that if all employments of the terms "right", "ought", "obligation" and "duty" are excluded in which they are used in something less than their strict and full ethical significance, these terms are synonymous. At least, if one applies they all apply. That they are strictly synonymous would follow only if it were the case that no one of them is more fundamental than the others. But in fact that is the case. Doubtless I can say if I wish that if I ought to do act A then act A is right; but, clearly, there is no real movement of thought in this apparent inference, and I might equally well say that if act A is right I ought to do it. These different terms are, in other words, different names for the same fundamental, underivative and indefinable notion.

Admitting that, however, we may still ask if this indefinable notion is the notion of a quality or of something which is not a quality. At first sight it might appear that in truth it is a quality, and the use of such adjectives as "right", "obligatory" and "dutiful" might be adduced as evidence for this contention. Yet such linguistic evidence may be misleading. We may say, for example, that A is an uncle; but in spite of the form of words in which we have expressed our point we know that what we are asserting is that A stands in a certain relationship to someone else, and not that he is a particular kind of individual. Moreover, as a matter of fact, moral obligation consists, not of a quality of actions, but of a relation, a peculiar irreducible and indefinable relation in which actions stand to an agent. Doubtless they stand in this relationship in virtue of certain qualities which they possess, but the relationship and the qualities are mutually distinguishable. When we apply the ethical terms we are considering to actions, we refer, not to their qualities, not to the kind of actions these are, but to this peculiar relationship in which they stand, of being obligatory upon an agent, of being the agent's duty, of being actions which the agent ought to do and which it is right that he should do.

Now since our idea of duty is the idea of a peculiar relationship it follows that we can describe it from a variety of points of view. If A is uncle to B, we can refer to the uncle-nephew relationship, or to A as the uncle of B, or to B as the nephew of A. Similarly, we can refer to the fact of moral obligation as a relationship (A ought to do X), or we can think primarily of the agent as standing in this relationship (A is morally obliged), or we can think primarily of the act as standing in this relationship (X is dutiful, obligatory or right). And this, of course, may well obscure the truth that all these terms stand for the same fact.

Further, this moral relationship is more complicated than may at first appear, for it is a three-term relationship. Its complete expression is of the form, "A ought to do X in situation S". We do not have duties in a vacuum, nor are actions right in certain situations independently of the existence of some agent who may perform them.

No doubt, we often express the relationship in a way which seems to ignore, for example, the agent. We may say that it is right that debts should be paid; but what has happened here is that we have abstracted from the concrete reality of all possible agents. This process is quite legitimate, for many characteristics of an agent are irrelevant to his moral obligations. (A man's height and the colour of his hair, for example, are usually irrelevant to the duties he has to perform.) And in the case we are considering we have carried this process so far that the agent is reduced almost to x, a *mere* debtor, that is, any debtor so long as he is only a debtor. Indeed, we have gone even further, for the mere debtor is not explicitly posited in our expression, but is simply understood or presupposed by the situation. The situation which consists of a creditor presupposes a debtor. But without this presupposition and silent understanding the original statement that debts should be paid would be nonsense, for in its sensible form it clearly does *not* mean that I or anyone else who is not a debtor should pay all debts or any debts. Indeed, it does not even mean that any debtor should pay all debts or any debts, but only that he should pay his own. Similarly, although we may sometimes express moral obligations in a way which seems to ignore the situation and refer only to agent and action, the reference to the situation is none the less understood. I may say that I ought to keep my promises, and in this the only terms between which the obligation appears to hold are the agent (I) and the action (promise-keeping); but here the description of the action presupposes and understands a situation, namely, the kind of situation created by the making of a promise. Consequently, in spite of our frequently elliptical expressions of the fact, moral obligation is a three-term relationship.

It is worth noting, however, that this fact that the description of one term can silently presuppose another term carries with it an interesting implication or suggestion. For it seems to involve that the three terms are not wholly unrelated terms which are first brought together by the relation of moral obligation. Rather they are independently related in some ways. The description of an act can presuppose the situation, and it is easy to see that in fact situations do determine the acts which can be done in them. The description of a situation, too, can presuppose an agent, and here perhaps the explanation is not so obvious. Yet it is the case that agents partially determine the situations which confront them. A and B, for example, may be walking along a street and may pass a shop which belongs to C. A, being in debt to C, may then be confronted by a situation in which it is his duty to settle his debt to C. If B, on the other hand, has had no dealings with C, then, whereas for A C and his shop have become part of a practical situation, for B they remain simply part of his environment. But the significance of this point must await later discussion.

Enough has been said to support against contrary suggestions the thesis that "ought", "right", "obligatory" and "duty", used in their strict and full ethical significance, all refer to the same fact, and that this fact is an indefinable and irreducible relation holding between three terms—an agent, an act, and a situation. And this being so, we are free to proceed to a consideration of the nature of actions.

At the outset of this investigation we must remind ourselves that in ordinary usage the word "action" may be employed to denote several different kinds of thing, and that perhaps not all of these senses are relevant to the ethical inquiry concerning the idea of right action. In the present context, however, we are concerned only with the sense which is so relevant; and, consequently, as has already been said, our aim must be to discover and define that sense of the word which is presupposed by the judgments of the ordinary moral consciousness and in particular by those judgments in which the predicate "right" or its equivalents are to be found. All such judgments will be entirely relevant to this investigation; but at the outset it is clear that two of these judgments, both of which are universal judgments, are likely to prove of the very first importance. Indeed, to a large extent, the argument will represent an endeavour to discover what meaning of the word "action" is implied by these two universal propositions, namely, "It is always right for a man to do what he thinks right", and "'I ought' always implies 'I can'".

Here, however, it may be questioned whether in the former of these two propositions the word "right" is used on both occasions in its strict and full ethical significance. This is an important point, for, clearly, if as the proposition stands "right" is used on both occasions in this way, the proposition appears to contradict itself; and, as a matter of fact, one common explanation which seeks to avoid this contradiction is that "right" on the first occasion is not used in the same sense as it is on the second. It is held that the phrase "it is right" means, not strictly what it says, but rather that *nobody can blame a man* if he always does what he thinks right. Now if "right" is not used in its strict and full ethical significance it may mean one or other of two things, for (a) "right" may really mean "morally good" or, at any rate, "not morally bad", or (b) it may mean "not wrong". If, however, the former possibility is intended it is on the face of it hardly a plausible suggestion, for when we say that it is right for a man to do what he thinks right we are *not really* talking about the character which a man displays in acting, but are rather talking of the action itself. In others words, "right", if it is used for "morally good" or "not morally bad", is not being used in a secondary sense, but is instead being misused. And yet, on examination, it does appear that sometimes at least when we say that it is right for a man to do what he thinks right this is actually what we mean, especially when the reference is, not to agents in general, but to some particular agent. If someone asks me for practical advice I may well say, "It is right for you to do what you think right", and my meaning may be hardly distinguishable from what it would have been if I had said, "No one can blame you, you will not have behaved badly, if you do what you think right". On the other hand, even if we do sometimes mean this, yet when we make the general point that it is always right for a man to do what he thinks right, we do mean exactly what we say, *not* that no one can be blamed or that everyone has behaved well when he does what he takes to be right, *but rather* that it is always right for a man to act in this way. And because that *is* our meaning we can express it in other terms by saying that a man ought always to do whatever he takes to be his duty.

The other suggested interpretation was that when we say "it is right" in the judgment we are considering, we really mean "it is not wrong". But what circumstances can justify the contradictory, without justifying the contrary, of "wrong"? Surely only those circumstances in which, so far as the agent can see, two or more acts are, so to speak, equally right; but if these circumstances are lacking then if the contradictory of "wrong" is justified and is rightly used, so also is the contrary. And in this case the circumstances *are* lacking, for our proposition presupposes that the agent does think some act right rather than the other possible acts in the same situation.

Consequently, whatever else we may sometimes mean by this proposition or other propositions similar to it, we do sometimes mean to affirm precisely and strictly what the proposition says; and we are therefore entitled to proceed to a consideration of that sense of the word "action" presupposed by the judgments of the ordinary moral consciousness, and especially by the two universal propositions we have noted, "It is always right for a man to do what he thinks right", and "'I ought' always implies 'I can'". What, then, is an action, the kind of action which can be the bearer of the moral predicates "right" and "wrong"?

First of all there are several points which may be disposed of very briefly. An action, clearly, is something which defines itself in contradistinction from a state of stagnation. It involves movement and change, and it may be described as a succession of states of affairs. When, for example, I put my hand in my pocket, my action appears to consist of a succession of states of affairs, in each of which my hand is in one or another of a number of different positions.

But, equally clearly, every succession of states of affairs is not an action. The falling of rain, for instance, is such a succession, but normally it is not regarded as an action; and the reason is that normally it is not thought of as emanating from a person. An action, then, is not any succession of states of affairs, but only one which proceeds from a person. Moreover, the person must be conscious of the general change, although it is not at all necessary that he should know of all the detailed alterations involved. The latter condition could seldom, if ever, be fulfilled, but the former is quite essential. Thus, when a man turns in his sleep, he has not performed an action—at least, not in any ethically significant sense of the word; but he may have done so when he is conscious of the general change. Yet more than such consciousness is necessary, for the succession is not an action if it happens against the agent's will. Indeed, even when it conforms with it, it is not an action unless it is deliberately brought about by him, unless he has really chosen the change, that is, unless it is a succession willed by him. But, since to say that in order to be an action a succession of states of affairs must be willed by some person includes and covers the condition that the succession must proceed from a person, and also the condition that the person must be conscious of the general change, it is sufficient, so far as the points already raised are concerned, to define an action as a succession of states of affairs willed by a person. We have then arrived at a definition which seems to commend itself at a level not much higher than that of common sense; and in what follows it will either be modified or rendered more precise.

The first difficulty with regard to our definition which presents itself, is that it is ambiguous and does not sufficiently distinguish between two things, namely, the succession of states of affairs which is willed, that is, which is the content of the volition, and the actual succession of states of affairs which follows as a result of the volition. Although for practical purposes these are not usually distinguished, they are none the less always different, and on occasion the difference may be vital for ethics. They will always differ to this extent, that the latter will include extra states of affairs (intermediate ones of which the agent did not think, and which therefore he did not will), and further, that those states of affairs of which the agent did think, and which he willed, will actually possess many characteristics which the agent did not consider, and which therefore were not included in the content of his volition. The actual succession will differ, that is to say, from the willed succession in having extra states and characteristics; but on occasion they may differ in a more crucial fashion, for the former may have, not only extra states and characteristics, but even contradictory ones. The states of affairs willed may not actually ensue, and the volition may not make the intended alteration in reality, although of course it may be the cause of some alteration.

This is, perhaps, most frequently the case where the action consists in saying something, for it is notoriously easy to say the wrong thing with the best intentions in the world. Thus one may pass a remark believing that one is soothing an angry person, and the only result may be that the wrath becomes more violent than ever. But, of course, this divergence between the willed succession and the actual succession is not confined to acts of speech, for whenever a person acts it is always possible that what transpires will be different from what he is under the impression he is bringing about.

Consequently the question arises as to which is the action in the sense of being the subject of the moral predicates, "right" and "wrong". Whenever the two successions do not conflict, but merely differ by way of addition, there is for practical purposes no problem; and since the ordinary moral agent does not discriminate, the moral philosopher cannot do so either. But where there is a conflict the case is different. Where, for instance, the agent believes he is bringing about the succession a, b, c, d... (act A), and what actually ensues is a, b, e, f, or e, f, g, h... (act B), the ordinary moral consciousness does discriminate—it is forced by the facts to do so—between what it calls the agent's intention and what actually happens, between, that is to say, what the man thought he was doing and what in the event he found he had done. Moreover, where act A would have been right, act B would have been wrong or neutral, and where at the same time the agent wills act A because it is his duty, but finds act B coming about, the ordinary moral consciousness none the less holds that the man has done his duty. It does not believe for a moment that anyone can fail to do his duty while acting as his conscience, his sense of right and wrong, dictates; and it puts this point by saying that it is always right for a man to do what he thinks right.

Now this is really a very odd proposition. What it says is that it is right for a man to do what he thinks right, and it is implied that this is so whether in his thinking the man is thinking truly or falsely. But this, of course, is a self-contradiction, unless indeed the word "right" is being used in two different senses. It certainly means "obligatory", but it is difficult to see what other ethical significance it can have. In any case, as we have seen, it is clear that what the ordinary moral consciousness means can be equally well stated in the form, A man ought always to do what he thinks he ought to do. And, moreover, in saying this it is saying something significant, and not just falling into self-contradiction.

What is intended seems to be that mental error cannot turn morality into immorality, cannot at all affect the rightness or wrongness of what is done. If the agent follows his sense of duty he has done his duty, and nothing can alter that. Even if it is act B which ensues instead of act A which was willed as right, the voice of duty has been respected and its claim met. The agent has done what was right for him to do; and from this it follows that what is right, that is, the action, is the willed succession of states of affairs, and not the actual succession which ensues. But this truth may be obscured by the fact that in acting we frequently gain fresh light on the situation and may therefore alter our opinion regarding our duty; but, none the less, given our earlier view of the situation, what we thought right was then our duty.

Thus the dictum that it is right for a man to do what he thinks right leads us to a more precise definition of action, and also rules out all theories which take an action as the actual succession of states of affairs. For from what has already been said it follows that in acting according to conscience an agent *knows* he is doing his duty—he does not have to wait and see whether he has managed to do it or not.

When, however, it is said that in acting the agent *knows* that he is doing his duty, that does not mean either that there is no doubt in the man's mind, or that he may not be in error about some factor in the situation. On the contrary, the dictum we have been considering, when properly understood, implies that such doubt and error may, and often do, exist. But it implies, too, that the doubt, for example, if it is there, is not ethical doubt; it is not the kind of doubt postulated or implied by most forms of utilitarianism, and all other theories which take as the subject of the predicates "right" and "wrong" the actual succession of states of affairs. The agent does not in fact doubt the rightness of what he is doing; he knows in acting that he is fulfilling his obligations.

Yet he may be, and indeed people often are, doubtful on another question altogether; and, further, it is a question which arises along with, and in fact is covered by, the question, What is it my duty to do? This other question concerns the nature of the situation with which the agent is faced, and on this point there may very well be doubt. The agent may doubt whether the situation is of such and such a kind or not, but, of course, strictly, that is not a doubt about his duty—it is not ethical doubt. The agent knows that if the situation is of type A then act x is his duty, if B then y. He has to make up his mind between A and B, and having done it he must do what he then takes to be his duty. If, having decided that the situation is of type A, and having done x, he finds that the situation after all was of type B, he may say, "I should have done act y", but by that he does not mean that in doing x he acted against his sense of duty. Whether at all he means to impute blame depends entirely on whether he is to be blamed for concluding that the situation was of type A, whether, for example, he was over-hasty or careless in coming to that conclusion. There is always an obligation to be as thorough in one's estimation of the situation as time and circumstances will allow. Having decided in favour of A rather than B, however, no blame whatsoever attaches to the agent in respect of doing x. But since that is so, clearly what is judged to be right is not the actual succession of states of affairs, which may on the contrary be very far from right, but the succession of states of affairs willed by the agent.

There is, however, a type of ethical doubt which may be present; and this possibility may appear at first sight to conflict with what has already been said; but on closer examination it will be found that, although the doubt is truly ethical, it is doubt not about the rightness of an act, but about the goodness of a relevant state of affairs. Thus a man may doubt whether a certain state of affairs which he can produce is better than another which he can also produce, but having decided and acted according to his sense of duty, the man is held by the ordinary moral consciousness to have done his duty independently of whether his decision on the point of goodness was in fact right or wrong. Suppose, for example, that an agent decides that state A which he can produce is better than state B which he can also produce, and suppose that he wills that succession of states of affairs which includes A as its most relevant state, or, as we should ordinarily put it, suppose that he does the act which brings about A, and suppose, then, that having done that, he comes to the conclusion that while A as it has turned out is just as good as he had anticipated, B would, after all, have been better than he had anticipated for it, and better also than A—if all that is the case, has the agent still done his duty? Once again, I think, the ordinary moral consciousness will not blame him; it will say rather that he has acted according to his sense of duty and has done what it was right for him to do.

This means, however, that we must modify still further our definition of an act. What we have been doing is to consider several typical moral situations in which the ordinary consciousness gives the verdict that the agent did what was right just because he did what he thought was right; and we have now to define more accurately the act, the "thing" which was right in all those situations. We have already seen that since for duty it is in the last analysis irrelevant whether what is willed actually ensues or not, the act must be the willing of a certain succession of states of affairs, and not the actual succession which follows. But now a further modification requires to be made because of those situations in which the agent, having done what he took to be his duty (act A), decides later that he should have acted otherwise (act B), not because he alters his opinion about act A, but entirely because of a better insight into act B. None the less, in doing act A the agent is judged to have done his duty; and since that is so, the act which is judged to be right and dutiful must be, not just the willing of a succession of states of affairs having characteristics a, b, c, d . . . (act A), but the willing of a succession of states of affairs having these characteristics in preference to another succession of states of affairs having the characteristics which the agent first of all took to belong to act B. In willing what he takes to be right, the agent turns away from what he takes to be wrong; and the definition of action which we have just given takes this fact into account. By defining "act" in this way, and, as it seems from the argument, only by thus defining it, can an ethical theory be consistent with the dictum that it is always right for us to do what we think right.

There is indeed one objection to the crucial point in the argument at which the transition was made from the act as the actual succession to the act as the succession willed. The objection is that in so defining an act we depart from reality and introduce an element of irresponsibility. "Very well," the objector says in effect, "if you're right, it doesn't really matter whether I do this or not; so long as I will it I have done my duty." Strictly speaking, however, such an attitude is a practical impossibility. One just cannot will a thing unless one believes that one is going to bring it about. One cannot possibly will that one's house will suddenly be filled with gold, unless indeed one believes that such things have come within one's power. It is, of course, quite possible to desire without the corresponding belief, but to desire something and to will it are two very different things. Already, however, these considerations are relevant to an examination of the other important dictum of the ordinary moral consciousness, namely, " 'I ought' always implies 'I can' ".

Besides the proposition that it is right for a man to do what he thinks right, the ordinary moral consciousness gives vent to another which is also general, and therefore of great importance for moral theory. It says that "I ought" always implies "I can". An act is not obligatory upon me unless I can do it. But how can I know that I can do it? Ought I to try and see? This would mean that whenever I regarded an act, say act X, as my duty provided only that it was within my power to do it, I have a primary moral obligation to try to do it. We must say then, it seems, that if, having tried, I succeed, the act was really my duty; whereas if, having tried, I fail, the act was not my duty. In both cases, however, it was my duty to try; while in the first case it was also my duty to do the act, and in the second it was not my duty to do it.

Suppose, for example, that a man, C, returns home on leave from the army and finds an elderly neighbour, D, worried to death about his son; suppose further that D's son is also in the army and closely associated with C, who when starting on his leave left the boy in excellent health. If D's anxiety is known to be on the score of his son's safety and C is aware of that fact, then no doubt C has a duty to relieve that anxiety by telling D of his son's safety. But if we suppose further that D is a thorough-going pacifist and does not know what his son is doing, the situation is greatly altered. It is not clear now that D is anxious about his son's safety; equally well he may be worrying lest his son has joined the army. In the latter case it would not be C's duty to tell the father of the son's where-abouts. C's difficulty, however, is to know which is the case. What is the cause of D's obvious anxiety? If C could relieve D's anxiety by telling him of his son's safety, then he would consider himself under an obligation to do it. But can he? He doesn't know.

Ought he, then, to try? Hardly so—at any rate, not so long as there is so great a doubt; but let us suppose that it is his duty. Either he succeeds in relieving D's anxiety or he does not. In the former case, by doing what on this hypothesis was his duty, he does something else which by accident turns out to have been his duty also. If, however, he fails, he has then done one duty, and in doing it has done something which was not his duty, and perhaps been prevented from doing something else which was after all his duty (for example, from keeping a promise not important enough to prevent him relieving D's anxiety, but one he would have considered it more right to keep than to spend his time sending an elderly neighbour into a black rage against his patriotic son). The ordinary moral con-sciousness, however, rejects the situations envisaged as practical impossibilities, and ethical theory can only take that fact as a *reductio ad absurdum* of the hypothesis.

Further, the hypothesis is no less absurd if we alter the situation so that we are thinking of a case in which the agent is doubtful whether he can do act X, which would be his duty if he could do it, but in which he is not faced by the danger of increasing, instead of relieving, anxiety. It will still be the case that if the agent tries and succeeds, he had done his duty by accident, that is, something else beyond his control contri-buted to bring it about that he had done his duty; whereas if he fails he will be in the strange, indeed impossible situation of not having done his duty, perhaps of having done some-thing wrong, perhaps also of having been prevented from doing something else which was his duty, and all this while acting conscientiously. That is indeed a *reductio ad absurdum*.

Of course we can say that in the case of the anxious father his anxiety ought to have been relieved by someone, if possible, but so long as it was not clear that C was the man, it was not C's duty to relieve it. Where there is doubt there is no duty; and yet about the future there can never be certainty. All moral situations, it would seem, differ only in degree from the one instanced.

We started off on this line of argument by recognising that "I ought" implies "I can". We now see that if it does not imply "I know I can", we are landed in the absurdity of supposing that whenever we do our duty it is to some extent by accident or good guesswork, while on the other hand we may, in acting conscientiously, find that we have done what was not our duty, or even what was wrong, and may perhaps have been prevented from doing what was our duty. But it is also true that we can never *know* we can.

In all this, however, we have been going on one assumption, namely, that an act, as the subject of the moral predicates, "right" and "wrong", must be taken, not as the willing of a succession of states of affairs, but as the actual succession which ensues. Reasons have already been given for adopting the alternative definition of an act as the willing of a succession, and if this definition can help us to clear a way out of the present difficulties it will then be a definition logically presupposed, not only by the dictum that it's right to do what I think right, but also by the other dictum that "I ought" implies "I can".

On examination, this conclusion appears to be justified. It has already been argued that if the word "act" is taken to stand for the actual succession of states of affairs which follows upon a volition, then "I ought" implies not only that I can, but also that I know I can; and it has been pointed out that this condition of obligatoriness cannot possibly be fulfilled. The agent can never *know* that the actual succession is within his power. Whether it is or not depends on factors in the world outside the agent, and he can never be certain that he has accurately allowed for the influence of all of them. Even when he is most confident he may still be mistaken. On the other hand, whether an agent can *will* a given succession of states of affairs depends, not on external factors, but on a number of mental ones which can be summarily described as the attitude of the agent.

In particular, the agent just cannot will anything unless he believes that he can do it, unless he thinks that he can do it. In so thinking of course he may be in error, but none the less the thinking so is essential. The agent cannot will any succession of states of affairs unless he believes, or thinks, or takes for granted, that it is within his power to bring that succession about. The attitude of the agent is here all-important, and the point is that it cannot be one of doubt. A volition presupposes a non-ethical judgment about what the agent can do, whether it be arrived at instantly or after deliberation; and in willing the agent assumes that his judgment is true. It may of course be false, and in that case the actual succession will not correspond with the willed succession, but the assumption that his judgment is true is a necessary condition of his making the volition.

If, then, the act is defined as the willed succession, the dictum that "I ought" implies "I can" means that "I ought" implies that I can will the given succession, and that amounts to this, that "I ought" implies that I believe that the succession is within my power. If that is the agent's belief, then, although he may be mistaken, he can at any rate make the appropriate volition, that is to say, he can perform the act as the willed succession, and consequently he can say unconditionally whether it is his duty or not. There is no need first of all to try to perform the act and then to wait and see—if the agent believes he can perform it, then he *knows* whether it is obligatory.

In this way our earlier difficulties can be surmounted, and the second dictum of the ordinary moral consciousness is seen to uphold that definition of an act which a consideration of the first dictum led us to adopt.

It now remains to consider whether there is any other respect in which the definition of an act can be rendered more precise, and it is the purpose of the remainder of this chapter to show that there is. In particular, it will be argued that a distinction can be drawn in principle between an act and its results.

As a first step in this argument it will be necessary to consider in more detail the attitude of the agent in acting, to which reference has already been made; and it will perhaps enable us to get a clearer idea of this attitude if we contrast two different types of action, (a) action *simpliciter*, that is, action for no ulterior purpose or action which carries the reason for it within itself, and (b) that type of action in which the act is regarded as the means to an ulterior end. Such a comparison is likely to prove fruitful because this second kind of action involves, not only the attitude with which we are concerned, but also the attitude of the agent to the end; and that attitude is quite a different one.

In both kinds of action the willing is preceded by a non-ethical judgment, and the difference in attitude can be described in terms of the different relations obtaining between the judgments and their respective volitions. In the case of action *simpliciter* the judgment takes the form, Act X is within my power. In the other type of action there is a similar judgment about the means, Act Y, the means, is within my power; and so far as this judgment is concerned the two types of action do not fall part. There is, however, in addition, a judgment about the end, or, more strictly, about the relation between the means and the end—Act Y will realise the end, state of affairs Z. This judgment clearly bears some relation to the appropriate volition, but the question is whether this relation is the same as that between volition X and the judgment that act X is within my power. Or, in other words, is the agent's attitude to end Z the same as his attitude to act X (or, for that matter, to act Y)?

The answer is that the relation between the judgment and the volition in the one case is quite different from the corresponding relation in the other. For when an agent acts *simpliciter* (act X), and not in order to realise an ulterior end, he acts on the assumption that his non-ethical judgment is true, and that judgment, whether in fact it be true or false, is itself a fact on the basis of which the action is done. When, however, the agent acts (act Y) in order to realise an ulterior end, the judgment that act Y will realise this end is not relevant simply as a fact; on the contrary, its truth or falsity is the very thing that is in question and the act is a testing of it. In the one case the important thing about the judgment in relation to the volition is that the agent arrived at it; while, in the other, the important thing is whether in arriving at it he had hit on the truth or fallen into error.

This distinction may be further described with reference

to the situation with which the agent is faced. Here we must distinguish, however, between the objective situation, or the situation as it really is, and, on the other hand, the subjective situation, that is, the real situation as the agent sees and estimates it. It is clear that these will always differ in that the former will always be fuller than the latter. It is also clear that sometimes they will be different because the agent's estimate is mistaken. Moreover, it is equally certain that the situation with regard to which the agent acts is always the subjective situation. The agent cannot possibly act with reference to those aspects of the objective situation which distinguish it from the other.

Now the subjective situation consists of judgments (for example, "A short distance away there lives a very worried old man"), and for the most part these are made with a practical intent. Some, therefore, take the form, I can perform act X; and all of them, whether they take this form or not, are judgments upon the basis of which as facts the subsequent action is performed.

There are, however, other judgments made by the agent which do not go to make up the subjective situation with which he is faced, but are instead his response to it. He may say, for example, "Act X is my duty", or he may say, "Act Y will bring about state Z which I desire"; and these judgments, so far from constituting the subjective situation, provide instead the connecting links between that situation and the volition which is the final practical response to it.

In other words, the judgments which go to make up the situation are relevant to the volition as facts, and are its causal conditions. The other judgments give the reason for the volition, and are its cognitive counterparts. Whether the action is to justify itself to the agent depends on whether these judgments are in fact true or false.

Can we then draw a line in principle between those states of affairs which are constitutive of an act and those others which are resultant? If we can do this our definition of an act can be rendered more precise. Frequently it has been held that any line drawn between an act and its results must be purely arbitrary, and if we confine our attention to acts in the sense of actual successions of states of affairs this may well be true. We have, however, found reasons for defining an act, not as the actual succession, but as the willing of a succession. Can we then distinguish in principle between those states of affairs which are willed, and those later ones for which the word "results" would be appropriate? The answer is that we have already done so. The volition, as we have seen, can include in its content only those states of affairs with regard to which the agent can act on the assumption that he is bringing them about. The agent judges these possible for him, and his volition is based upon that judgment as upon a fact.

Those states of affairs, on the other hand, which follow an act of volition, and are therefore resultant, fall into one or another of three classes; (i) states of which the agent did not think, and about which therefore he made no judgment; (ii) states of which he did think, but which did not provide the reason for his acting; and about these he may or may not have made a judgment, but, if he did, his volition bears no essential relation to it, that is, it would have been made even if no judgment had been formed; and (iii) states of affairs of which the agent thought, and which provided the reason for his volition, the act itself being means to these as end. Here a judgment was formed, and the volition bears to it an essential relation, but the relation is not that which exists between a situation and the volition which is a response to it. On the contrary, the judgment is equally part of the response, and in the volition the truth or falsity of the judgment is put to the test.

What, then, is an act? An act is the willing of a succession of states of affairs, having certain characteristics, and terminating in the last state of affairs which the agent takes for granted he is bringing about; it is the willing of that succession-in-preference-to-the-other-successions-the-agent-took-to-be-within-his-power—the phrase "takes for granted" being here used to mean, not that the agent's judgment that the states are within his power is made on insufficient grounds (though strictly that is always true), but that the volition is based on the judgment as upon a fact, and the judgment itself is part of the situation in response to which the volition is made.

CHAPTER IX

ACT AND MOTIVE

As a result of the foregoing analysis, the area to which the predicates, right and wrong, are applicable has been delimited in two different directions: (i) as between what actually happens and what, on the other hand, the agent intends; and (ii) so far as consequences are concerned. The latter delimitation is not unconnected with the former, for, if what is right is what the agent intends, and not what actually happens, the content of what is right can hardly include the actual consequences of what happens. No more can it include the consequences which the agent anticipates, for, as we have seen in our consideration of the agent's attitude in acting, these cannot strictly be described as *intended* consequences, but rather as *expected* consequences. In other words, in the attitude of the agent we have found the source of a real, and not just of an arbitrary, distinction between an act and its consequences, a real distinction, that is to say, between what we do and what follows thereafter; and, of course, the predicates, right and wrong, apply to the former and not to the latter.

It may be fitting, however, at this point to note that nothing that has so far been said in this analysis is intended to decide the utilitarian issue one way or the other. At present the problem is to define what it is that is right, not to explain what it is that makes it right. So far as we have yet seen in our general task of reconstruction it might well be the character of an act's consequences which makes the act itself right. Even if that were the case, however, it would be beside the present point, which is concerned simply to discover what the act itself is which is right.

Moreover, this present task which we have set ourselves has not yet been completed, for although we have delimited in two directions the area to which the predicates, right and wrong, are ordinarily applied, although in other words we have delimited this area in the middle and at the end, as it were, we have not yet dealt with its beginning. And the question there is a crucial one, namely, Does the act which is right or wrong include or exclude the agent's motive? This question *is* crucial because the unity of the moral field, the cohesion of rightness and goodness, may well depend upon the answer to it.

Now if act and motive are to be separated in such a way that the act is not to be regarded as including the motive, it will, clearly, be easier to maintain this position if the act is taken, not as the series of states of affairs willed or intended, by the agent, but as the series which actually occurs. The reason is that what actually occurs, though caused by the agent and his motives, is only partly so caused and is dependent causally also upon other streams of events which do not emanate from the agent, for once an agent's intentions infiltrate into the objective world they come under the influence of, and in their turn influence, other causal series of events. Moreover, since all that is so, the temporal connection between the agent's motives and what actually occurs may well appear very largely accidental. On the other hand, it is quite clear that these considerations can *never* apply to the agent's motives in relation to the series of states of affairs willed or intended. Indeed, on the contrary, if the motive changes, then, although externally the act may appear the same, yet the act on its internal side, that is, the states of affairs willed, do change also. This alteration in the states of affairs willed, or in the intention, if we may so denote them, may consist in the introduction of new states of affairs, perhaps (or perhaps not) to the exclusion of others which were formerly there; or it may simply involve a change of emphasis, that is, a change in the ordering and subordination of the earlier states of affairs one to another. In other words, the motive constantly colours the act, and a different motive leads to a different act. If I pay my debts from the sense of duty my intention is one thing, whereas if I pay them purely and simply to escape the unpleasant consequences of not paying them my intention is something else, though the external act in the one case may be indistinguishable from the external act in the other.

Does, then, the act include the motive or not? In answering this we must take account of Professor L. A. Reid's argument in his book, *Creative Morality*, first published in 1936. There Professor Reid describes the separation of motive and act (whether by "act" we mean what actually occurs or the agent's intention) as a "false abstraction".[1] "An act or an action", he

---

[1] *Creative Morality*, p. 78.

says, "apart from its motive cannot be morally appraised at all, and when we do take the morally appraisable act or action with its motive we find that the motive or motives affect the quality of the action through and through."[2] All this, of course, is in harmony with what we have already said; and Professor Reid's point that whether an act is taken as the setting of oneself to do something (Professor Prichard) or as the actual doing of something (Sir David Ross),[3] the separation of act and motive is a false abstraction depends upon the recognition of several truths.

The first is that the actual series of events apart from the agent's intention has no moral significance whatsoever. "It is impossible", says Professor Reid, "to conceive of any 'act' in Ross's sense fulfilling any obligation, since the very idea of obligation involves the consciousness of a moral agent who is obliged."[4] But, secondly, even if the act is taken as the agent's intention, it is impossible to separate act and motive, for intention and motive are just different aspects of the same thing. This is what he says: "I believe that if we say, what is true, that there is no conscious action or part of an action without intention and no conscious action (or part of one) without motive, that the difference between motive and intention is simply a difference of emphasis upon the more internal, or upon the more externally focussed, aspects of the mind's state. A motive must have an object, but when we think of motive we are thinking rather of what drives us towards the object, than of the object itself. Intention must be driven, and the very idea of intention certainly contains . . . a dynamic element, but what is emphasized is the interest in the objective situation, what I have called the scheme of action. When in crime we speak of the intention, we certainly imply the activity of a striving mind, but we describe it normally in terms of its content in objective terms. When, on the other hand, we speak of the motive, we think of jealousy or avarice or cruelty, and these, though they in their turn must have objects, are matters where more emphasis is laid on the subjective than on the objective. We divide into two aspects, for the sake of understanding it, what is in fact one continuous whole; for intention is the fulfilment, the completion, the working out of motive, and

[2]*Creative Morality*, p. 80.
[3] *Creative Morality* was published after *Duty and Ignorance of Fact* and before *Foundations of Ethics*. Cf. *Creative Morality*, pp. 74–9.
[4] *Creative Morality*, p. 79.

motive without any intention, possible or actual, would be a contradiction in terms. We have to remember that action or conation is the real unit, and that we must distinguish that in us which strives, as the motive-aspect, and that *towards* which we strive, as the intentional aspect. It would not be accurate to say that every intention *is* a motive; it would be more accurate to say that every intention *has* a motive: every intention to a scheme of action is driven by something in us. And every motive has an intention, is a driving to a scheme of action possible or actual."[5] Further, Professor Reid deals with the common suggestion that the motive is the dominating intention, and holds instead that, strictly speaking, "'the' motive is that in us which drives us to a certain intention which dominates the lesser intentions in the whole willed scheme".[6] In other words, there is sense in talking of *the* motive, but the usage is misleading, for it blurs the real distinction between motive and intention as quite different aspects of the same thing. On the other hand, the reality of the distinction must not obscure the fact that the two are different aspects of *one thing*, namely, the act.

All this is clear; and, indeed, once it is seen that what is right is not the actual succession of states of affairs which happens to ensue, but the succession willed by the agent, it seems impossible to exclude the motive any longer. And yet, as we have already seen, both Prichard and Ross (in his later book) do continue to exclude it even when the act is taken, not as the external series of events, but as the setting of oneself to bring about something. Now this is really a very odd view of the matter, for if the act in this sense is completely separate from the motive we can presumably inquire what relationship holds between them since it can hardly be maintained that motive and act are quite unrelated. We are not explicitly told what this relationship is, but it does seem that the most plausible answer would be that the motive is the cause of, and prior to, the event which Prichard has described as the setting of oneself to do something and which alone, at the same time, he has designated the subject of the predicates, right and wrong. But *is* the motive prior to the act? What is prior is only a potential motive, and possibly only one amongst others; whereas, when it passes beyond mere potentiality, it continues into, and is contemporaneous with, the setting of oneself to do

[5] *Creative Morality*, pp. 71–2.   [6] *Ibid.*, p. 74.

something. Indeed, is it not just another aspect of the same thing? Thus the act is not one psychical event which is preceded by another, the motive. In truth it is not as a psychical event at all that the act is an act, the bearer of the moral qualities, right and wrong; for, clearly, it is not as *the setting of oneself to do* something, but as the setting of oneself to do *x*, that the act is morally significant.

The truth is that, while the arguments which support the subjective view of the act and tell against the objective view of it do delimit the area to which the predicates, right and wrong, are applicable, they do not delimit it in the way that Prichard and Ross appear to suppose. On their view, it would seem that we start the argument with a series of events, psychical, bodily, and external, bearing simple and irreversible temporal relations one to another, and that as the argument proceeds we find that the predicates we are considering apply either to one event in this simple and irreversible succession, or to a smaller part of this series, a part consisting of a few events which bear the same simple and irreversible temporal relations one to another. That this is the view taken is suggested by the argument which Prichard uses (and Ross quotes with approval) to shorten the series, namely, the argument that since we may have become paralysed, bodily and external events can be ruled out.

Yet in truth, when we look back on our analysis of this matter, it does seem that the area has been delimited, not by shortening a temporal series, but rather by enabling us to decide between two planes to only one of which does the simple and irreversible succession of events belong. If we are right in arguing that what is right or wrong is the subjective, and not the objective act, then the event or events, which is the act, is the act and is morally significant, not as this event or these events in their particular place in the series, but as being the willing of a series of events. It is not the series of events in simple and irreversible temporal relations one to another, *nor any part of such a series*, that is judged morally right or wrong, but rather the *willing* of such a series. No doubt the willing itself, regarded from one point of view, is just an event in such a series, for the human will is causally efficient. But it is more than that, and it is precisely as more than that that it is morally significant. Doubtless, as we have said, the willing is one event with its own particular place in a temporal series, but it transcends the limitations which ordinarily attach to an event in a simple and irreversible temporal succession, and it is present to each and all of the subsequent events, not as efficient cause, but as the agent's intention. It broods over the succession of events as the Spirit of God is said to brood over the created world; and the motive sustains the whole act. Thus we may say that in moving from the actual series of events to the intention of the agent as the subject of the moral predicates, right and wrong, we have not simply shortened a series, but have moved to a different plane altogether. Moreover, like the unity of thought, the unity of an act is more closely knit than the unity of a succession of events. Thinking takes time, but the thought of the premisses of an argument is not simply prior to, but is carried over into, the thought of the conclusion; and corresponding to this logical unity there is in action what may be called a purposive unity, which likewise is more closely knit than the unity of a succession of events and at the very least is a different kind of unity. Of course if it is held, as Prichard seems to hold, that what is right is a single event in the series, namely, the setting of oneself to do something, then it may be argued that the unity of an event is also different and more closely knit than the unity of a series of events. But enough has already been said to indicate that in fixing the subject of the moral predicates, right and wrong, as the subjective, and not the objective act, we have not simply shortened a series, nor concentrated attention upon a single event in the series, but have moved to a different plane altogether.

It may, perhaps, serve to make the theory to which our argument and analysis are pointing more distinct if at this point reference is made to the position of Professor L. A. Reid. As we have seen, Reid's objection to Prichard's view is that it involves a false abstraction of act from motive. He follows with approval Prichard's delimitation of what is right to the setting of ourselves to do something, but he objects strongly to the consideration of this apart from motive. "This", he says, "deprived of its context, means nothing at all; it is as empty of psychological and moral significance as the creaking of a door in an empty house."[7] And with this we have already found reason to agree. On the other hand, Reid accepts with certain qualifications Prichard's shortening of the series of events by leaving out the actual series which ensues upon the agent's

[7] *Creative Morality*, p. 76.

volition, and he also seems to regard the right act as a psychical event as such. "Mr. Prichard", he says, "has put us in his debt by showing clearly that the action for which we are really and fully responsible is a much narrower and more specific thing than is commonly thought. He points out, for example (what is obvious once realised), that I cannot even be said to determine with certainty whether or not I shall move my limbs, because some physiological disturbance might make it impossible." [8] Our contention has been, however, that the arguments do not prove this, do not prove that the act is "a much narrower and more specific thing than is commonly thought". It is just as broad and full as before, but it lies on a different plane than at first sight we might suppose. No doubt, since last I acted in a particular direction, I may, unknown to myself, have become the victim of a physiological disturbance, but even so my act, my intention, is just as extensive as it would have been in happier circumstances, although admittedly I shall in all probability realise quickly that the situation has changed and shall perform some other act or intention.

Reid's theory, however, stops short of this. Indeed, in one respect it is further from it than is the new intuitionist position, and it was this respect that was intended by our earlier remark that Reid accepted *with certain qualifications* Prichard's shortening of the series of events by leaving out of account the actual events which ensue upon the agent's volition. For although Reid accepts this delimitation so far as the concepts of duty and ought are concerned, he does not accept it unreservedly with regard to the conception of right. "'Right'", he tells us, "stands as a bridge (with abutments on either side) between *morality*, the praise- or blame-worthy, and the *objects* of morality, which are indispensable to morality and always relevant to it, and which yet lie *outside* morality's sphere." [9] Consequently, "right" is "an ambiguous and difficult notion. But we must retain the term, and we must recognise its real transitiveness". What does this mean? It means that "ought" and "duty" apply to the setting of oneself from a certain motive to do something, and they do apply whether this setting of oneself to do something is effective in actually producing what was intended or not. "Right", on the other hand, does not necessarily apply in such circumstances. Indeed, it only applies if *both* of two conditions or sets of conditions are realised: (i)

[8] *Creative Morality*, p. 75.   [9] *Ibid.*, pp. 55–6.

H

the conditions necessary to render an act dutiful; and (ii) the condition that the dutiful act is also effective in actually producing the best possible results in the circumstances. A right act is a dutiful act, but it is more for it is also the act which actually produces the most good. The view which Reid adopts "implies that right is not identical with duty, that in doing his duty a man does not necessarily achieve the fully or completely right. To fail in duty is wrong; without doing his duty a man cannot act rightly, but to act rightly though it implies dutifulness, implies more".[10] And this "something more" is of course the actual production of the best possible results. This means that, as Reid himself puts it, "rightness is only in part a moral notion and contains irreducibly objective and often uncontrollable factors, as well as subjective and controllable ones".[11]

So far as we have yet expounded the view, however, it leaves one minor point in ambiguity. It is admitted that the act which is obligatory or dutiful is the setting of oneself to do something from a certain motive, but it is not clear whether it is this dutiful act which may itself be right if its results are of a certain kind. This is not clear because it might well be the dutiful act plus certain results which is right; and indeed it appears that this is what Professor Reid intends, for he refers to "the awkwardness of distinguishing between the dutifulness of an intention and the rightness of an action"[12]—a phrase which seems to imply a distinction, not only between dutifulness and rightness, but also between intentions and actions—and later he reminds us "that 'actions' (or, more strictly, the external aspects of actions) are to be thought of as the fulfilment or physical actualisation of intention".[13]

As against all this, the position to which our argument has led us draws a distinction neither between rightness and dutifulness, nor between the subjects to which these predicates apply. Indeed, Professor Reid's conception of action as distinct from that of intention is a confused notion combining elements drawn from different spheres. Similarly, his notion of rightness is also mixed, being, as he admits, partly moral and partly amoral. It combines two quite diverse elements, an element of morality and an element of what may be called efficient causation. Consequently, we seem entitled to conclude

[10] *Creative Morality*, p. 58.   [12] *Ibid.*, p. 81.
[11] *Ibid.*, p. 78.   [13] *Ibid.*, p. 81.

that ethics has no concern with this complex notion of rightness, but only with its moral component. Professor Reid says, however, that although the other element, that of efficient causation, may not be morally significant, it "always has a moral *relevance*".[14] But the fact that something has moral relevance does not bring it within the domain of ethics. Indeed, almost anything under the sun may be morally relevant. If, for example, I have borrowed a red umbrella, then for the time being that red umbrella is morally relevant; and similarly if I have promised a black spaniel to a friend black spaniels have instantly acquired a moral relevance. Consequently, *if* rightness ever has the complex significance which Professor Reid assigns to it, then, although it may be morally relevant, none the less it is only an element of rightness which falls within the domain of ethics.

We are not here concerned to argue that rightness *never* does have this complex significance we have been considering. Our earlier argument, however, does seem to justify the assertion that whether or not the term ever has this significance, it is frequently used as the equivalent of oughtness and dutifulness. There are contexts in which for the word "right" we may substitute "obligatory" or "dutiful" without any loss of meaning. And even if on occasion the word is used to signify in addition an element of efficient causation, it does seem clear that ethics has no concern with rightness in so far as it does include this amoral component. No doubt, whether the term "right" is ever used to signify this fact or not, human conduct can be considered from a point of view which is concerned with its efficiency as a cause. But that is only one aspect of human conduct and there are many others. It may be considered, for example, as conforming or not with a certain standard of funniness; but of course ethics is not interested in that aspect as such. Similarly, it is not interested in the rightness of human action if by rightness we mean amongst other things its efficiency as a cause. Ethics *is* concerned with that aspect of conduct which we denominate moral; and Reid admits that the concept of rightness as he understands it is not entirely a moral notion.

The only consideration which would justify ethics in attending to rightness as Reid has defined it would be the contention that although rightness is only partly a moral notion, the word

[14] *Creative Morality*, p. 82.

stands for an organic unity which is more than the simple sum of its parts. But in fact it is nowhere apparent that this is so. Professor Reid indeed describes it as a bridge "with abutments on either side"; but actually it looks rather like two abutments without the bridge. Rightness includes oughtness and effectiveness, and there is nothing else contained in it.

We have already said that we are not concerned to deny that *sometimes* the word "right" may stand for this complex notion. Yet Reid holds that it *always* stands for oughtness and effectiveness together; and, therefore, if we can discover his reasons for this assertion, and if we find that they do not justify it, there will be no reason to suppose that the word ever does bear this unusual sense. Why, then, does Reid define the term in this way? He tells us himself in an important passage. "The proposition at issue", he says, "is not that right *means* productive of most good, but that it *includes* it. It immediately follows from this that even if future results do condition the rightness or wrongness of an action, they are not a sufficient condition. No one is suggesting that right and wrong are *merely* a matter of chance or even of probability, that right action is *merely* 'fortunate' action. On the other hand, I think we are bound to admit that the idea of right contains in it an obstinate and ineradicable element of objectivity. Moral actions are carried out in a world of events which go their way independently of human knowledge. The aim of moral intentions is to change and manipulate, and to change and manipulate 'for the best', those real events whose course is only partially known, partially controllable and partially predictable. What is aimed at is, among other things, the best result. We may not be certain how to attain the best results, but we do aim at them, they are our target or our standard, and without this moral life would lose its objectivity and its reality."[15] Now this means that the term "right" has been defined in a way which is partly amoral for a reason which is, one must admit, a moral reason, namely, to do justice to the objectivity and reality of the moral life. But this reason does not support the definition which is based upon it.

For one thing, the moral life could continue unaltered and without loss if the word "right" were ruled out of the moral vocabulary, and we were left only with such words as "obligatory" and "dutiful". And, in the second place, the reason for this is that the objectivity and reality of the moral life does not mean that what is right is partly or completely included in the world of objective events, but rather that what is right is necessarily conditioned by, and constantly bears a reference to, the world of objective events. This is an important point, that the world of objective events provides the occasion, but not the very stuff, of morality. Does what is right consist partly or entirely of events in the objective world? To this question we have already given a negative answer in contending that what is right is the willing of a series of events from a certain motive, and that although this willing is doubtless a psychical event or a series of such events, it is not as such that it is right or wrong—the psychical event is only one term in a series, whereas the intention is equally present to different parts of the series.

But in concentrating upon intentions as the subjects of the moral predicates, have we not deprived the moral life of its objectivity and its reality? In other words, may not a critic say in effect, "Very well, then, if you're right, it does not really matter whether I do this or not; so long as I will it or intend it I have done my duty"? This, however, is a question which we have already answered.[16] As we have already said, the attitude described is a practical impossibility. We cannot will anything unless we believe that we are bringing it about. Here, of course, we must avoid confusion with that other sense of the word "intention", in which it stands for what may be called floating or unadopted intentions, and indicates not that we are doing something, but simply that we are proposing to do it. So long, however, as we are thinking of volitions, it is clear that we cannot will anything unless we believe that we can bring it about in the objective world as it confronts us at the time. Consequently, a volition is necessarily occasioned by the objective world, although as a volition, that is to say, as the subject of moral predicates it does not fall itself within that world.

It might seem that Professor Reid's position could be defended on the ground that drawing a distinction between right and duty it makes possible a consistent interpretation of the dictum of the ordinary moral consciousness that a man ought to do what he *thinks* right. And no doubt it does make this possible. "The content of my duty will, on its cognitive side, be the content of my *opinion* of the optimific, my *opinion* of the right."[17] It follows from our earlier argument, however, that this dictum does not require this interpretation (since another

---

[16] Cf. p. 212 above.   [17] *Creative Morality*, p. 57 (italics mine).

interpretation is also possible[18]), and that in fact it does not imply a distinction between right on the one hand and dutiful or obligatory on the other (since the same point can be made by saying that I ought to do whatever I take to be my duty).

It would appear, then, that a conclusive case cannot be made out for including in the notion of rightness an element of efficient causation, and that if moral rightness ever is a component in a broader notion of rightness, which is only partly moral, that fact cannot concern the moral philosopher as such. As moral terms "right", "dutiful" and "obligatory" are all synonymous; and what is right is the willing from a certain motive of a certain series of events in preference to certain other series. Nor can it be argued that this account of the subject of the moral predicates deprives the moral life of its objectivity and reality, for to argue thus is to mistake the rôle played by the objective world of events in the moral life itself. This objective world is not the substance of morality, but it is (so far as we can see) the indispensable condition and occasion of it. A hat or an umbrella or so many coins as such or even so many coins considered as the exchange equivalent of so many eggs and so on—these things are not morally significant in themselves. They are only, as we have said, morally relevant. They are only the means—yet the only means that we can imagine—whereby a moral being can express himself. They are the occasion, let us repeat, but not the substance of morality.

Now the relevance of all these considerations to the question of act and motive, to the question, that is, whether an act as the subject of the moral predicates, right and wrong, does or does not include a motive, is that if the act is to be conceived in the manner indicated by our argument, then it seems impossible to separate act and motive. If the act, the real subject of these predicates, is rightly regarded as something which transcends the temporal succession of objective events,[19] then the separation of act and motive must seem a false abstraction, for the separation is possible only if the act is regarded as a series of events which does not include the motive which is regarded as another and prior event. As Professor Reid has plainly argued, the motive and the intention are different aspects of the same thing.

[18] Cf. p. 209 above.
[19] It does not transcend the temporal succession of act A, act B, act C, and so on; but the agent's character does transcend *this* succession.

We cannot leave the matter there, however, without giving some consideration to the arguments adduced, mainly by the new intuitionism, to prove that motives *cannot* be included in acts if acts are taken as the proper subject of the predicates, right and wrong. Of these arguments there are three main lines which they may follow.

The first of these starts from the two points that "I ought" implies "I can", whereas motives are not within our control. The conclusion is that motives cannot be included in the content of our obligations. Now, quite clearly, it is true that at any given time, in any given situation, there are certain motives which I cannot bring into play, and if "I ought" implies "I can" then it follows that my obligation, whatever it may be, is not to act from any of these motives. Moreover, if anything is certain in ethics it is that "I ought" does imply "I can". On the other hand, it is also clear that my obligation is not to act from no motive at all. Indeed, I cannot possibly act without some motive of one kind or another, and of course once again "I ought" implies that I can.

Here, however, the second of the three lines of argument crosses the present one, for, the new intuitionism asserts, it is quite clear that a right act can be done from a bad motive, and the implication is that the motive, since it may be bad, cannot be included in the content of an obligation. This contention, however, presupposes the discrete view of action as a series of events, a view which we have seen fit to discard; and the truth is, as we have seen, that motives colour actions, and that if the motive changes so also do the act and that aspect of the act which distinguishes itself from the motive as the intention. The motive, then, colours the intention; both motive and intention are aspects of the same thing and are inseparably associated together, and consequently the motive must be included in the conception of what it is that is right. On the other hand, it does seem that the new intuitionist account of this matter contains one important element of truth which may be confused with the contention that motives are not included in the area to which the predicates, "right" and "dutiful", apply, but which is really distinguishable from it. This truth is that although what is right includes a motive appropriate to the intention, the aspect of the act which renders it dutiful is not the motive-aspect but the intention-aspect.

This point may, of course, be disputed. Reid, for example,

declares, "it is your duty to act from the best motive possible now, and to construct a general disposition of the best motives you can for the future".[20] And yet it does seem clear that in any given situation we have to choose, not between motives, but between courses of action, intentions, and from the point of view of practice we have to decide, not which motive is best, but rather which course of action is right with regard to the situation which confronts us, which course of action is obligatory upon us in that situation. My duty now is *not* to act from the best possible motive. It is a fairly safe generalisation that if we are constantly concerned with our motives we shall quickly find ourselves, or at least be found, neglecting even the most obvious duties. Indeed, it is not at all clear that we can say of good motives that one is better than another. Some motives we can declare good, and others bad, but there seem to be others still which may be either good or bad. Love of others, for example, is generally supposed to be good, a desire to inflict pain is bad, but the love of self and of one's own family may be good or bad. Indeed, even the love of others may be bad. The truth seems to be that while there may be a few motives which are perversions of human nature, and always and absolutely bad, there are no motives which are absolutely good. They are good only as occupying their proper place and acting in due measure in a good character. It is the character which is one and good. The separate motives are abstractions from it. But this is a matter which will demand a more detailed examination later on. Meanwhile the point remains that in practice the true moral life is concerned with the intention-aspect of acts, and not with their motive-aspect; and any account of morality which portrays moral choice as a choice of motives does not ring true to the moral consciousness.

Yet it is hardly true that motives are of no practical concern in the moral life. If the moral life cannot be lived by means of an exclusive attention to the inner life of motive, it is certain that it is impoverished by a complete disregard of that inner life. If it is not our duty now to act from the best possible motive, it may be our duty "to construct a general disposition of the best motives we can for the future". In particular it may be a duty to guard against vicious tendencies and besetting sins, to get rid of certain weaknesses here and to strengthen our character there. Such things seem fairly included in any

[20] *Creative Morality*, p. 63.

list of the matters with which the moral life is concerned. But,
it must be noticed, the corresponding acts are dutiful, when
they are dutiful, not because of the present motives from which
they are done, but because of the intention which here happens
to be the weakening or strengthening of certain other motives.
This duty of self-improvement is therefore like other duties,
and if it sometimes seems to conflict with these that is not in
principle different from a conflict within the latter. Further,
since character and motives colour acts, it is not unlikely that
the duty of self-improvement will coincide, rather than conflict,
with other duties. At any rate, even in the case of the duty of
self-improvement, it is clear that in the moral life we are
concerned with the intention-aspect of acts rather than with
their motive-aspects. None the less, motive and intention,
though distinguishable, are really inseparable, and motives
are therefore included in the content of what it is that is right.

So much, then, for the first line of argument by which the
new intuitionism seeks to prove that motives cannot be included
in the content of what is right. We have already referred to the
second line of argument, but may now consider it in its
own strength. It is based on the assertion, which purports to
be a report of the facts of the moral consciousness, that a right
act can be done from an entirely bad motive. We have already
questioned this point, and have indeed argued that on the
contrary motives colour their acts, and that therefore, if the
act, or rather the intention-aspect of the act, is right, the
motive-aspect is not inappropriate. Yet it is unlikely that the
assertion would have been made, and made so emphatically
without some apparent reason. And the truth seems to be, not
that a right act can be done from an entirely bad motive, but
that a right act is often done, perhaps always so far as we can
tell, from mixed motives. The appropriate motive is frequently
impure, is buttressed up and supported by other motives which
happen, in the given situation, to move in the same direction.
It is said, for example, that a debtor can do his duty, can pay
his debt, say, of twenty pounds, from an entirely bad motive,
for example, from a fear of unpleasant consequences to himself.
But let us see what precisely this means. If his motive is entirely
bad, if his only motive, for example, is a fear of unpleasant
consequences to himself, then the sum of twenty pounds has no
significance for him whatsoever as the sum *due*. He will simply
seek to escape as lightly as he can, he will pay the smallest sum

which will obviate the unpleasant consequences, and whatever he does his act will have a closer kinship to an act of bribery than to the due payment of a debt. It may be (although of course it may not) that externally his act will appear the same as if his motive were other than it is, but who can say that without any thought of duty, without the slightest trace of dutiful impulse, whether habitual or not, without the faintest notion of present duty, the man has yet done what is right? And if it is still held that he has, how can it be consistently denied that one, in every respect a man, a member of human society, yet totally lacking in the endowment of a moral consciousness, might yet contrive by fortunate accident, not only to do his duty once and again, but even to discharge all his moral obligations from the beginning of life to the end? No doubt it may be difficult, in fact it is difficult for an observer to say whether either of these men has acted rightly or not, but if the observer could have insight into the agent's state of mind, could picture the entirely selfish interest hovering over the external events, he would, we can safely say, have no hesitation in denying that a duty had been performed, and would rebut any self-righteous claims subsequently made by the agent. Of course, in the instance of the debt, the creditor may have received his twenty pounds, and received it from the proper source, but that simply means that we may receive that to which we have a moral right without the performance of a duty by anyone. In this case the creditor might have received his due in several ways without the performance of a duty. He might have received it, if, being a strong personality, he had contrived to hypnotise the debtor; or again the debtor might have sent a letter of abuse in an envelope in which he had earlier placed twenty pounds now long since forgotten. The satisfaction of a right is not in itself sufficient proof of the fulfilment of a duty.

On the other hand, to say that a right act is never done from an entirely bad motive is not to say that a right act is always done from a perfectly good one. On the contrary, it is often done from mixed motives. Frequently the pure motive is supported and strengthened by other motives, and for the moral man it is not an uncommon experience to kill two birds with the one stone. Indeed, the metaphor is instructive, for in a case of mixed motives it is really two acts that are done in one, a right act and possibly a neutral one (certainly not a wrong one, for it does not conflict with the right); and duty does not demand that the lesser motive should not be in play, but rather, as we have seen, that we do such and such. Moreover, two points are to be borne in mind. The first is that to act from mixed motives, to do two acts in one is an entirely different thing from acting from an entirely bad motive, that is, doing one act in place of the right one. Secondly, it must not be supposed that we can constantly act rightly from mixed motives, for there are other right acts which make very little appeal to inappropriate motives.

We turn now to the third line of argument by which intuitionism seeks to exclude motives from the content of what is right. One of the most important motives from a moral point of view, it says, is the sense of duty; but if motives are included in the content of what is right, the statement that it is my duty to do act A from a sense of duty must in the end mean that it is my duty to do act A from a sense that it is my duty to do act A from a sense . . . and so on *ad infinitum*.

Now Professor Reid tries to get round this argument by holding that we have two senses of duty, a sense, for example, that X is my duty, and a sense that we ought to do X from a sense of duty. They are distinguished by their objects, in the one case an action, and in the other "a cognitional-conational state of mind". [21] Yet this will hardly do, for if we are held to have two senses of duty what guarantee have we that they will not lead in different directions? Professor Reid, however, can escape this point, but only because he is dealing with this particular motive, a sense of duty; and in general the critical point remains that if in deciding what to do we are to attend both to the motive-aspect of acts and to their intention-aspect, there is the possibility that we shall be led in different directions at the same time. But let us see how this can be avoided in the case of the sense of duty. It may be said that if in any situation I have a sense of duty that I ought to do act A, in all situations I have a sense of duty that I ought to follow my other sense of duty wherever it may lead, whether to act A in this situation, act B in that, and so on. And this does seem to be Professor Reid's meaning. "Of any moral being at all who *is* a moral being," he says, "it can be morally required at any time that he should summon the motive of duty into activity. . . . But probably not more than this can *always* be required of all moral human beings." [22] In other words, I have a sense of duty, concerned directly with actions, which may tell me, for example, to do act A in situation S; and I have another sense of duty, concerned with motives, which tells me always to follow the former sense of duty. But if these two senses of duty cannot conflict, they are yet redundant. The fact is that we do not seem to have this other general sense of duty. And indeed, further, if the first sense of duty does not itself carry full authority, but requires the second to commend it, should not the second have a third to commend *it*, and the third a fourth, and so on. Once again the infinite regress is upon us. I have a sense that I ought to do act A; I have a sense that I ought to follow this sense; I have another that I ought to follow this one . . . and so on to infinity. Both fact and theory combine to support the contention that, after all, there is only one sense of duty.

None the less there is a certain amount of truth in Professor Reid's argument. It is that every moral situation has a double aspect, and this secondary aspect consists of the fact that whatever I do my act will help to mould my character. Human actions have a boomerang effect. And on occasion (we have already noted that it is occasionally and not constantly that this happens) this fact may give rise to a duty, the duty of self-improvement, of weakening this motive or of strengthening that, and this may lead of course to an apparent conflict of duties or the duty may coincide, as is more likely, with some other externally directed duty. But the point of immediate importance is not the comparative rarity of the event, but its precise nature. The thesis is that although there are *some* duties which are concerned with character and motives, these motives are relevant, not as the motives of the dutiful acts (they are not that), but as included in the intention.

Consequently, even what is true in Professor Reid's account of this matter does not meet Sir David Ross's objection.

Can, then, motives be included in what is right without falling into an infinite regress in the case of a particular motive, namely, the sense of obligation? The answer is that they can because an act is judged right, not because of its motive-aspect, but simply and solely because of its intention-aspect. Strictly speaking, it is the intention that is judged right (and so *in a sense* motives are not included in the content of obligations),

[22] *Creative Morality*, p. 65.

but the intention is something which cannot exist by itself but must carry with it its own proper and appropriate motive by which it is coloured.

But as the point is crucial let us look at this matter more closely. And there are several things which we must constantly bear in mind regarding it, namely, that no act can be done without any motive whatsoever, that a right act cannot be done from an entirely bad motive, that on the contrary the motive constantly colours the act, and that in fact motive and intention are distinguishable but inseparable aspects of the same thing. Now, bearing these points in mind, we can, it seems, distinguish three different cases.

(i) In the first place, there may be, prior to the raising of the question of duty, an urge to do what in fact is the right act, due to a motive other than the sense of duty. Benevolence, for example, may incline me towards the act before I judge the act right; and then when the question of duty is raised, my sense of duty looks, as it were, over the shoulders of the existing motive and judges the intention right. But though it is the intention which is judged right, the intention is nothing apart from the motive.

(ii) In the second place, there may be, curiously enough, prior to the raising of the question of duty, an urge to do what is in fact the right act, due to a motive which is like, is indeed derived from, the sense of obligation, but is not to be identified with it. It may happen, for example, that often when I raise the question of duty the dutiful act turns out to be the payment of a debt, and in the course of time there may arise an inclination to pay debts, which is dutiful and derived from the sense of duty, but is not identifiable with it. It might be described as a sense of *prima facie* duty. And here again what happens when the question of duty is fully raised is that the moral consciousness looks at the intention to which the inclination points and judges it right or wrong. But of course the intention is again nothing without the motive which picks it out of the situation and defines it. Both these cases have this in common that the dutiful act turns out to be one to which there was an inclination apart from, and prior to, the proper raising of the question of duty.

(iii) In the third place, however, it is possible that the moral consciousness, once the question of duty has been raised, will indicate as the right act one to which there was no prior inclination. Here again it is clear that it is the intention that is judged right, but it is still true that an intention without a motive is *nothing*. In this case, however, although there is no prior motive, the recognition of the intention as right gives rise itself to a motive, namely, what is properly meant by the sense of duty as a motive.

In all three cases, it is seen, it is in virtue of the intention, and not at all in virtue of the motive, that an act is judged right; but on the other hand an intention without a motive is nothing, and if the motive is changed so also is the intention. Thus in a sense motives are not, in another sense they *are*, included in the content of obligation. They are distinguishable from what is judged right, but not separable from it. Indeed, on the contrary, they are part and parcel of it. Now since in a sense motives are not included in the content of obligation, since in other words they are distinguishable from intentions which are the proper subject of right and wrong, there is no question of an infinite regress. On the other hand, since motive and intention are not separable, since indeed the motive colours the intention, and consequently the moral goodness of the motive and the rightness of the intention are not after all two entirely different questions, it follows that moral goodness and rightness do not fall so hopelessly apart as would appear from the contentions of the new intuitionism.

CHAPTER X

THE MORAL SITUATION

So FAR, IN what may be called our analysis of the conditions of morality, we have been concerned mainly with actions. But besides actions and the agents who perform them, there is the moral situation in which the action is done by the agent, and this too deserves some consideration. Indeed, already we have been compelled to attend to this in some degree, for we have already drawn a distinction between the objective and the subjective situations, and we have seen that it is the latter that is relevant to morality. The subjective and the objective situations are always different. The latter is always fuller than the other, and often the two are at variance in certain respects. Moreover, as we have argued, it can only be with regard to the subjective situation that the agents acts, for he cannot possibly act with regard to those aspects of the objective situation which distinguish it from the subjective.

Now so far as the subjective situation covers the same ground as the objective situation, the account we are being compelled to give of this particular condition of morality seems simple and straightforward enough. Even if within this area the subjective situation is at variance with the objective in several respects, that fact presents little or no difficulty. No matter how much it may conflict with the facts as they really are, the subjective situation, after all, is simply the objective situation *as the agent sees it*; and, since he sees it in the way he does, he cannot be expected to act with regard to the situation, not as he sees it, but as in fact it really is. It seems certain that it is the agent's duty to deal with the situation as it appears to him, and it seems nonsense to suggest that his duty may be to deal with the situation, as if it possessed characters contrary to those he takes it to possess. No doubt, since, generally speaking, the moral situation is that an agent is confronted by facts which may belie his opinion of them, every agent has always a duty to entertain as accurate an opinion of the facts as he possibly can; but, whether he fulfils this duty or not, there also can be no doubt that in any given particular situation his duty must be, or rather must involve, dealing with the situation as he sees it.

The case, however, is not so simple when we pass from those aspects of the subjective situation in which it covers the same ground as the objective (though possibly conflicting with it in several respects within that area), to those aspects of the subjective situation in which it falls short of, and fails to cover, the same ground as the objective situation. As we saw when we first drew the distinction, the objective situation is always fuller than the subjective. That is to say, there are always aspects of the objective situation about which the agent is not mistaken but of which he is completely unaware. At any given time, for example, it may be the case, but at the same time I may never dream, that by sending money to a particular address in a distant town I may be able to meet a very severe human need. Moreover, it is clear that I cannot have a duty in respect of those aspects of the objective situation of which I am completely unaware. If, for instance, I am completely ignorant of the circumstances in the distant town it is certainly not my duty to send money to some address there. Yet the matter is not quite so simple as all that.

It will be remembered that when first we drew the distinction between subjective and objective situations we noted that the former consists of judgments made by the agent. Further, it was seen that there are at least two different kinds of judgment which go to make up the subjective situation, the one merely descriptive of the situation, and the other indicating actions which the agent considers he can perform in this situation. Now, no doubt there is a sense in which the situation consists of the former set of judgments, while the latter is not included in it but is based upon it (indeed our use of the word "situation" in the preceding sentence already implies this). It seems clear, however, that the total practical situation consists of both sets of judgment, but that within this situation a distinction may be drawn between the set of judgments which deal with what are taken to be actual facts and the set of judgments which deal with potential actions. And for the sake of convenience we may be allowed to name the former the theoretical judgments and the latter the practical judgments.

Now, so far as the theoretical judgments are concerned, it seems true to say that if there is any part of the objective situation not covered by this part of the subjective situation, an agent can have no duty with regard to such facts. This, indeed, is the case of which an examination has already been given. The needy person in a distant town was not represented in the theoretical part of the subjective situation and, therefore, I was under no obligation to act with regard to such a person.

A similar conclusion is not so evident, however, when we pass from the theoretical part to the practical part of the subjective situation. By way of illustration we may take the Biblical instance of the man who fell amongst thieves and was left injured by the wayside. Upon anyone who knew nothing of this occurrence there was of course no duty to render assistance; and that is the case with which we have already dealt. But we are told that a Levite passed by, and we are to suppose that he did notice the injured man, and that he was roughly aware of his condition. Consequently the existence of the man's need was covered by the theoretical part of the subjective situation. But from this point the further description of the case can follow one or other of two different routes. On the one hand, it may be supposed that the Levite realised on seeing the man's condition that he might himself render assistance and that indeed it was his duty to do so. If this were so we can only say that the Levite failed to do his duty. But on the other hand (and this is the possibility which concerns us at the moment), it may have been the case that, although he was aware of the man's condition, the Levite did not dream for a moment that he might render assistance. It may never have occurred to him owing to a lack of interest, that is to say, to a lack of motive. Such a case is a practical possibility. It happens frequently that we are roughly aware of the facts, but it just does not strike us that we can do anything about them. The formal description of cases like that is that while the objective elements are covered by the theoretical side of the subjective situation, they do not enter into the practical side; and the question arises whether the facts must be covered by the practical as well as by the theoretical side of the subjective situation before they can give rise to an obligation. We have already seen that unless they are covered by the theoretical side the facts cannot impose a duty; and the present problem is to determine whether to that end they must also be covered by what we have called the practical side of the subjective situation. And in terms of our illustration the question amounts to this, If it just did not occur to the Levite that he might assist the man who had been injured by robbers, did the Levite fail to do his duty?

On examination it would seem that we must give a negative answer to this question, in other words, that we cannot give a different answer in this case from that which was given in the other case where the facts were not covered by the theoretical side of the subjective situation. If the Levite did not realise that he could render a certain service it seems hardly plausible to say that none the less he ought to have rendered it. Indeed, we ordinarily draw a distinction between failure to do one's duty and not realising that we might have done something else, as when we excuse a person on the ground that he just did not think. Moreover, the actions which we realise we can do are selected by motives, and if in addition to these actions there are some that in some sense we might have done but did not think of doing, the explanation can only be that we had no motive to do them, or, at any rate, that at the moment we were not under the influence of the appropriate motive. But if we had not a presently active motive to do them, then in another perfectly good sense we could not do them, for, on the level of specifically human conduct, we cannot do anything without a motive. If that is admitted it follows from the principle that "I ought" implies "I can" that the acts in question were not morally obligatory.

Now it is important to notice on what precise ground the Levite is thus excused. It is on the ground that it did not occur to him that he might render some assistance, and it is not on the ground that he did not raise the question of duty at all. For one thing, that would be no excuse whatsoever—what exactly our duty is may depend on our view of the situation, but the fact of duty does not depend upon our recognition of it. In the second place, it is quite possible that in the given case the Levite did raise the question of duty. It may be that he would very much have preferred to remain at home that day, but that having promised to attend a conference he may have considered it his duty to be there, and he may in fact have been on his way thither when he passed the injured man. The excuse is that whether he raised the question of duty or not it did not strike him that he could if he cared render assistance to the man. To excuse him on this ground is in perfect harmony with the dictum that a man ought always to do what he thinks right; but it is clear that this dictum cannot justify any attempt to excuse him on the ground that he did not raise the question of duty at all.

None the less it seems certain that, although since it did not strike the Levite that he could assist the injured man it cannot be held that he failed to do his duty in not assisting him, he did fail to do some duty. However he may be excused, we think that his insensitiveness is blameworthy. But the question arises, How can our theory take account of this fact if it is right, as it seems to be, in maintaining that it can never be a man's duty to perform an action which he did not realize he could perform? The answer is that, although with regard to the objective situation as he saw it, that is, with regard to the subjective situation in the sense already defined, the Levite may well have done his duty, he may none the less have failed to do his duty with regard to the secondary aspect of that or other situations, that is, with regard to the effect of his actions upon his own character. It may then be said with consistency that perhaps on this occasion, and certainly on other earlier occasions, the man ought to have acted in such a way as to cultivate and strengthen the benevolent motive.

With regard to a duty in respect of the secondary aspect of the subjective situation, however, it may be asked how this duty is affected by the possibility of different opinions concerning this aspect. In other words, is it the case here also that a man ought to do what he thinks right? Now when we dealt with this question in connection with a man's duty in respect, not of the secondary, but of the primary aspect of the situation, we saw that there were two main possibilities, namely, that he might be in error in his ethical thinking or again in his non-ethical thinking; and we found reason to believe that in either case his duty is a duty with regard to the subjective situation constituted by his thinking, whether it be mistaken or not. Moreover, in the present connection there seem to be the same main possibilities, namely, that the man may be in error in his ethical thinking or again in his non-ethical thinking. In the former case he may entertain a somewhat false ideal of human character; but, given that he does really entertain it sincerely, it must be allowed that his duty is to act according to his lights. It cannot be his duty to act according to someone else's lights. Does a similar conclusion hold then with regard to the other main possibility of error, namely, in the agent's non-ethical thinking, that is, in this connection, in his thinking about the state of his own character? Here, however, there is a difficulty, for it does not appear that there is in this case the same possibility of *genuine and sincere* error. The agent knows these facts from the inside as he could never know the facts of the objective world. No doubt if he could fall into genuine error in this department of the moral life his duties here also would be duties with regard to the subjective situation. But it is the possibility of the event of genuine error here that is itself in question. This, of course, is not to say that men always entertain perfectly true opinions about the facts of their own character. On the contrary, they very frequently have false opinions on this matter; but very frequently, if not always, that is due, not to genuine and sincere error, but to wishful or wilful thinking, that is, to self-deception. Does then the characterisation of erroneous thinking as wishful or wilful make any difference to the part this thinking plays in the moral life? Surely it does, for wishful or wilful thinking is thinking that is morally wrong. Consequently, so far as our mistaken thinking is wishful or wilful, it does not contribute to the subjective situation with regard to which our duties are duties; and, clearly, this holds, not only in the case of the secondary aspect of the situation, which is our present subject, but also in the case of the primary aspect with which we have already dealt. The subjective situation, that is to say, is the objective situation as the agent sees it *in so far as his seeing it thus is genuine and sincere and not wishful or wilful.*

Yet, while it must be recognised that there is not the same possibility of genuine and sincere error in our non-ethical thinking about the state of our own characters as there is in our non-ethical thinking about the objective world, it can hardly be maintained that there is *no* possibility of such error at all. Although, on the one hand, we see our characters from the inside, it is the case, on the other hand, that in dealing with character we are dealing with spiritual facts which it is peculiarly difficult to grasp clearly and distinctly, and that, in general, the ordinary man is unable to disentangle and analyse these facts and arrive at precisely true opinions concerning them without considerable training or the guidance of someone who has received such training. In this matter, too, even the expert may be deceived, for the spiritual equipment of men is an exceedingly complicated structure as the science of psychology has discovered. We have already noticed that perhaps the most frequent case of human action is that in which the agent's motives are mixed, and that in itself gives rise to a vast possibility of error in our non-ethical thinking about our own characters.

The recognition of all this, however, must not be taken as diminishing the emphasis already laid upon the possibility of wishful or wilful thinking especially in regard to our own spiritual achievement. Such thinking is a potent factor which falls to be recognised in any analysis of the moral life; but, we have been saying, its recognition must not blind the analyst to the possibility of error which is genuine and sincere. Further, in so far as a man's error in thinking about his own character *is* genuine and sincere, it seems clear that his duties in this matter are duties in respect of the subjective, not the objective, situation.

Here, however, we must pause to gather together the threads of an argument that is apparently full of complications.

We have seen that a duty is a duty with regard to the subjective situation, that is, with regard to the objective situation as the agent sees it; but we have also seen that it is so only in so far as the agent's thinking about the objective situation is not wilful. Further, we have seen that this subjective situation has a secondary aspect which consists of the agent's opinion of the effect that any action will have upon his own character. These, however (although for the sake of careful analysis we have distinguished them), are not two different situations with which at the same time the agent may be confronted and in which he may have different duties. They are distinguishable aspects of the same situation, and although they may give rise to an apparent conflict of duties this apparent conflict is in principle no different from apparent conflicts to which the primary aspect of the situation may by itself give rise. Moreover, we have argued, although duties in respect of the secondary aspect are concerned with motives, they are concerned with motives only as part of the intention, and it is always in virtue of the intentional aspect of an act that it is either right or wrong. On the other hand, although motive and intention are distinguishable, they are inseparable. The motive colours the intention, and so indirectly affects the rightness of the act; and it is impossible that a right act should be done from an entirely bad motive. We recall also the definition

of an act as the willing of a series of states of affairs terminating in a certain state of affairs and as the willing of this
series in preference to all other series which the agent took for
granted he could bring about in the same situation. Thus the
situation, the act, and the relationship between act and motive
have so far been defined; and in any given situation we may
have a duty which consists of an act as we have defined it, and
which is a duty with regard to the total situation (that is,
including primary and secondary aspects) as it also has been
defined.

Over and above all this, however, and besides our particular
duty in any given situation, our argument has implied that we
have a duty in general to be careful and accurate in our
apprehension of situations (both primary and secondary
aspects), and in particular to avoid wishful or wilful thinking.
Indeed, careless thinking is just a special kind of wilful thinking;
and, as we have seen, wilful thinking does not contribute to the
subjective situation with regard to which men have duties, but
is itself morally wrong, that is, is a breach of duty. Now two
different accounts may be given of this "duty in general". It
may, on the one hand, be taken as an additional duty, additional, that is to say, to our particular duties which vary
from situation to situation; whereas, on the other hand, it may
be regarded as a distinguishable aspect of every duty. In the
former case it may be argued that the "duty in general" is
really a separate duty and occupies a different portion of time
from that occupied by the other particular duties. Thus, for
example, I have a duty now first of all to apprehend my total
situation accurately and without the intrusion of wilful thinking; and then secondly, having done that or not as the case
may be, I may have another duty to act in a particular way
with regard to the total situation as I see it. If I fail to do the
first duty, that is the "duty in general", that fact does not
prevent my having or my doing a particular duty. This, of
course, is inconsistent with what we have already said to the
effect that wilful thinking does not contribute to the subjective
situation. None the less it is a possible account of the matter,
and something may be said in favour of it. It may be argued,
for example, that there is no difference in principle between
this account and the account which is normally given of
another kind of situation, namely, that in which, for instance,
a bank clerk has made a private use of some of the bank's

money. The clerk failed to do his duty in making that use of the money; but having so failed he is now confronted, it is said, by a different situation to which his failure contributes and in which it is his duty to refund the money and perhaps also to take his punishment. But the two cases are not exactly parallel. In the latter case the subsequent right action consists of undoing as much as possible the earlier wrong one, whereas in the other case it does not consist of any such thing. Indeed, to make the cases parallel in this respect we should have to suppose that the bank clerk, having appropriated the bank's money, began to argue thus with himself, "I have taken this money by a breach of duty, but whether rightly or wrongly it is now in my possession, and I have to consider what right use to make of it, and I think that my duty is to give part at least to that needy family who live across the road." Further, let us now suppose that the bank clerk performs this action. Has he then done what is right or not? The answer is that his action has some of the characteristics of a right action, that if circumstances were otherwise it might well be right, but that in fact as things are it is quite definitely wrong. If we did not know the earlier history of the bank clerk we might well commend his generosity, and yet his action is undoubtedly wrong. The moral is that moral situations in the lifetime of a single individual cannot be entirely isolated one from another. They are held together by the self-identity of a single agent, and his present situation is coloured by his history. Thus it would appear, not only that the original parallel between the wishful thinker and the faithless banker is inexact, but also that we cannot isolate his wishful thinking from the situation which presents itself on the basis of it. His morally wrong thinking penetrates what we are apt to call the later situation, and any action he does within it is vitiated from the beginning, unless indeed, like the bank clerk in the original instance, he first seeks to undo the wrong that has been done. But this means that every particular duty includes, or has as an aspect of it, the duty to look reality straight in the face.

So far we have been dealing with the moral situation in its formal aspect; and it is now necessary to turn attention to the content of the moral situation, and to inquire whether any universal judgment may be made regarding it. In particular we must ask whether the moral situation is necessarily a social situation or not.

It has frequently been said that man, besides being a moral being, is essentially a social being, and the question naturally arises whether there is any connection between these two attributes. At the outset it can be fairly assumed that man does possess the latter attribute as well as the former. Indeed it is now almost a truism that man *is* a social being, and that apart from the society of his fellows he cannot exist. Like many other truisms, however, this assertion can be understood in several different senses, and not all of these are necessarily, or obviously, true. It may simply mean, for example, that it would be impracticable for a solitary human being to exist, owing to the particular manner in which men come into being, and also on account of the various ways in which by mutual assistance they sustain their existence. But some or all of these facts may be accidental, and clearly, to say that solitary man is practically impossible is not in the least to say that he is logically inconceivable. His non-existence may be due, not to the intrinsic nature of man as man, but to the nature of the world which does exist and of which man finds himself an inhabitant. Of course it depends on what we mean by "man", and if his nature is taken to include, not just a material body, but into the bargain a particular kind of animal one, then no doubt the reference to his fellows is already present.

When, however, it is said that man is a social being, it is generally intended to point, not to something which man has in common with the beasts of the field, but rather to something which tends to raise him above their level, and it is usually felt that man is being described in his spiritual capacity, and not simply as a bodily being. It is as a rational being that man is also a social being.

It may be, however, that whereas all his rational activities, viewed as a whole and considered in their relation one to another, could not be performed except in the context of society, yet some of them, taken in separation from the rest, might be pursued by solitary man. The search for truth, for instance, in science and philosophy looks as if it could be undertaken by a single man living by himself completely isolated from all other human beings. Certainly his discoveries would benefit no one but himself, the truth would die with him, but the task would still be capable of performance. No doubt scientific results have social implications, but only because society is already there. No doubt the pursuit of truth is immeasurably assisted by the fact that men do live in society, but, after all, assistance is not creation. No doubt, also, society has in fact and in history made man what he is, a being able to distinguish between truth and error, but what is in question is not the way by which man has arrived, but the manner in which he may continue to be himself. And, so far as the discovery of truth is concerned, it does not appear altogether impossible for a man, in perfect isolation from his fellows, to exercise his human faculties in this direction.

Nor is the case greatly altered when we turn from the search and discovery of truth to the appreciation and creation of beauty. Greatly impoverished in this respect as a life entirely outside of society would undoubtedly be, it would hardly be completely devoid of aesthetic experience. Here, as in the case of science and philosophy, the activity seems possible in solitude, although society has made, and has still to make, a vast contribution both to the facility with which the appropriate activity is performed, and to the magnitude of the results achieved.

Does this, then, hold still when we pass from truth and beauty to goodness and morality? At any rate, the case is not so simple. On the one hand, the activities already considered are often held to possess a moral value, and truth and beauty are said themselves to be good. On the other hand, one aspect of morality, at least, is essentially social. So much so, indeed, that Kant believed that he could express the whole moral law in the formula, "So act as to treat humanity, whether in thine own person or in that of any other, in every case as an end withal, and never as a means only." And when Kant said this he did not mean that *some* moral rules have a social significance; he meant rather that morality in its whole extent is social, and when he formulated the moral law in purely formal fashion and without reference even to humanity, he still could not abstract from a plurality of moral beings. "Act only on that maxim," he said, "whereby thou canst at the same time will that it should become a universal law"; and, of course, a law which is for one man only, a law, that is, which is made and obeyed by a single individual and by him alone, is a travesty of law. Morality for Kant is through and through a social activity.

There is, indeed, a branch of ethics which might well be called social ethics, and which consists in the application of the moral law to certain types of corporate action within society, and even to certain types of social action whether co-operative or not. Thus there is an ethics of government and an ethics of business, and so on, and these together might be called social ethics. But suitable as the title may be in many respects, it is also liable to mislead because it carries with it the suggestion that there is another type of ethics which is not social. This special branch of ethics, however, does not owe its separate existence to the fact that it and it alone deals with the mutual relationships of men, but rather to the fact that it is concerned with specially complex social situations. To these it applies the moral law, and it can do so only because the moral law has to do already of itself with society in general. Society is given with morality, and if the former is taken away duty also disappears.

That, at any rate, seems to be what Kant would have said, for it is implied even in his most formal statement of the demand that duty makes upon us. Morality itself and not just a branch of it is thoroughly social. On the other hand, as we have seen, it seems that solitary man would not have escaped entirely from the realm of moral values. In deciding to spend his time eating and drinking, or seeking after truth, or creating things of beauty, he would appear to have earned by his choice one moral epithet or another. The conclusion emerges that it is pre-eminently as a moral being that man is also a social being; but it is recognised, too, that there is an element of paradox in this contention, since, while from one point of view morality is intrinsically social, from another it seems possible in solitude.

This complication, however, need not detain us, for even if it is held that moral distinctions would still apply to the solitary life in that the choice of beauty or truth as an end would be morally good, it does seem clear that the moral distinctions (if any) which do apply are "morally good or bad" and in general "good or bad", but not "right or wrong". Now in our argument hitherto we have been chiefly concerned with the latter distinction. Indeed, our analysis has been an attempt to discover what judgments about the act, the situation and the agent are logically presupposed by our use of this distinction between what is right and what is wrong. Consequently we may be allowed, in the meantime at any rate, to continue the discussion under this limitation, as if the whole of morality were covered by the distinction between right and wrong, while recognising that at a later stage in the discussion we may have to take account of the possibility that other moral distinctions have a wider application. Meanwhile we shall proceed as if morality were confined to the area to which "right" and "wrong" do undoubtedly apply, and we shall ask whether the moral situation in this sense is necessarily a social situation. So far, in dealing with this question, we have shown that the affirmative theory represents in general a defensible point of view and may fairly be attributed to Kant himself. None the less we must consider this matter critically and in greater detail, and inquire whether it is really the case that man, as a being subject to the claims of duty, is necessarily a social being.

The answer appears to be in the affirmative. Morality in the sense of duty is thoroughly social, and every duty implies a right, that is, a moral right and not necessarily a legal right nor even a right known to the person who possesses it. When, for example, I am under an obligation to fulfil a promise, there is someone else, the promisee, who has a right to the fulfilment. Even where no undertaking has been made, when, for instance, I find myself in a position substantially to help someone in a difficulty who has hitherto been quite unknown to me, I consider myself under an obligation to do so, and the other person in his turn has a moral right to the service. Here, however, we must carefully distinguish three things. First of all, there are legal rights, and while we need not attempt an adequate definition of these we can point to one essential characteristic, namely, that the person or body against whom the right is possessed is fixed and settled by law and may therefore be known to the person in whom the right resides. Secondly, there are other rights regarding which it can be said that although they are moral and not legal the person possessing the right possesses it against someone known to himself. Thus, if I promise something to A, A in turn has a right to it and knows or can know that he has this right against me; and, in general, this holds of all rights arising out of someone else's past acts. In addition, however, there are other moral but non-legal rights which do not have this characteristic, which are, that is to say, rights against an unknown x. There are many cases in which it is extremely difficult for anyone else to know what the agent's duty really is (consider, for example, the earlier illustration of the generous bank-clerk), and consequently it is clear that many moral rights are of the third type which we have just distinguished. Indeed, it may be argued that it is always impossible for anyone else to know what the agent's duty actually is, and that, therefore, all moral but non-legal rights are of this third class. Thus the second class would be emptied, or at least reduced in status to a class of what may be called, by an adaptation of Sir David Ross's terminology, *prima facie* moral rights. At any rate, whether there is a second class or not, it seems clear that there are moral rights which are rights against an unknown x. Thus the fact that, when I am under a moral obligation to perform some service for A, A himself does not always think so, may be due, either to the fact that he does not know that I, more than anyone else, am in a position to assist him, or to the fact that he does not know that he has a greater moral claim upon my help than all others who may simultaneously have some claim upon me. Or, of course, it may be due to some combination of these two factors. Moreover, in rendering a service to someone, and in thus doing my duty, I may be satisfying a moral right which the recipient has, not against me, but against society in general.

There are, however, two classes of duty which do not appear at first sight to involve a right possessed by another person altogether. The first of these is the class of duties to oneself. A social worker, for example, has a duty, and a corresponding right to find time for his meals and a certain amount of recreation. The right in this case is vested in the agent himself. Does it follow that here at any rate is a class of duty which is not necessarily social? Not at all. In solitude a man would doubtless have to arrange for food and recreation, but the task could hardly be called a duty, and there would be no meaning in saying that the agent had a right to the time so spent. The social worker, on the other hand, has himself a right simply because others have rights and claims on his time and attention; and he has a duty to himself because he is under many obligations to other people as well. The terms "right" and "duty" have a meaning only as regulative of social relations, and apart from society they cease to be significant.

Then there is another class of duty which is not obviously of a social texture. As we have already seen, the pursuit of such things as truth and beauty may be itself good, but not dutiful; and it is possible in solitude. On the other hand, if a man is endowed with gifts which would enable him to seek after any of these things with some measure of success, it may well be his duty to devote a certain amount of his time to these ends. But since the pursuit of these is possible in isolation from his fellows, his duty to follow them would appear to be a non-social duty. On closer examination, however, this inference cannot be upheld.

First of all, we should notice that the duty, if there is one, is not to discover truth or to create beautiful things—that may not be possible for the agent—but to set himself to do these things, or, in other words, to use his talents in an effort to achieve these ends. In the second place, if, because of his gifts and training, a man does have a duty thus to set himself to discover truth, it is a duty only on account of the fact that other people have similar duties to devote themselves to other ends. His duty is of the form, "It's up to me rather than you". As in the case of the social worker the competition of rights was a necessary condition of his having a duty to himself, so here the comparison of abilities is quite essential to there being an obligation of the kind we are considering. In isolation from his fellows a man may choose to spend himself in seeking after truth, and a life so lived in such conditions might, so far as we have yet seen, be good; but even if the man were by talents perfectly fitted for that occupation, his choice of it would be neither right nor wrong. It *might* be good, but *not* dutiful. Duty would only arise when the man is in relation to other people with various capacities for one thing or another; and then he would have other duties as well, and would constantly have to strike a balance or make a choice between different competing claims.

Thus the realm of duty is entirely social, and we conclude, therefore, that the moral situation in the sense in which we are at present using the phrase, that is, as a situation in which I may have some duty to perform, is of necessity a social situation.

In this argument there is one loose end which requires to be tidied up somewhat before the discussion is allowed to continue. For we have made free use of the terminology of rights, and have seen (a) that *some* moral but non-legal rights are rights, not against a particular individual or group of individuals, nor yet against society in general, but against an unknown *x*, and (b) that *all* rights may be of this kind. Indeed, if due weight is given to the proposition that every moral right to A implies a duty on someone's part to confer A, and also to the proposition that it is every man's duty to do what he himself thinks right, it becomes a pointed question how, or under what conditions, rights may be more determinate than they are if possessed simply against an unknown *x*, for though I may think that I have a right to A against X, X on his part may consider it his duty to perform some act quite other than that of conferring A upon me. In fact the situation is even more difficult, for it is quite possible and perfectly conceivable that whereas I consider myself to have a right to A, no single person nor any group of persons nor society in general considers it a duty to confer A upon me. But what manner of right is this which I have against an unknown *x*, who, besides being unknown, is as a matter of fact non-existent? The explanation is that a right, even a moral right, is not a purely moral concept. Thus Muirhead quotes T. E. Holland's definition of a right in general as "one man's capacity of influencing the acts of another, by means, not of his own strength, but of opinion or the force of society",[1] and remarks with approval that this definition, whatever its defects, "emphasizes the important fact that for the existence of a right in the full sense of the word recognition is necessary". A sentence or so later he does indeed complain of the definition that "it contains an implicit denial not only that, besides the rights actually recognized by society, whether by its law or by its public opinion, there are rights founded on the requirements of human nature itself—things that are rights simply because they are 'right'—but also that there is any essential relation at all between the adjectival and the substantival meaning of the word".[2] Now in suggesting that a right is not a purely moral concept, we are not concerned to deny that there is such an essential relation between rights and "being right", that is, between rights and duties, nor are we directly concerned to support one theory of the *ground* of rights rather than another. What *is* intended is that rights, if they do presuppose duties, presuppose, in addition to duties, a general recognition of these duties—just as the rules of propriety, the conception of which is not a purely moral

[1] *Rights*, E.R.E., vol. 10, pp. 770–1.
[2] *Ibid.*, p. 771a.

conception, presuppose a general practice. Duties, unlike rights, do not presuppose a *general* recognition. If I consider it my duty to perform act A then it is my duty so to act even if in doing so I am resisting the prevailing moral convictions of the surrounding society. But my right to A depends upon general recognition.

It may not always appear that this is so. It frequently happens that attempts are made to gain recognition for claims which are called rights but which, as the statement of the case implies, are not generally recognised. It will be found, however, that such attempts proceed by reference, explicit or implicit, to what *is* generally recognised; and it is held that the "right" which is for the moment excluded from the general recognition is so excluded, either through a restricted apprehension of what is recognised, or through a faulty application of it to particular situations. In the former case, for example, if it is generally recognised that all builders have a right to a fair living wage, the joiner may well defend his corresponding "right" on the ground that the existing general recognition is an unreasonably restricted apprehension of the principle that all workmen ought to have a fair living wage. And in the other case, if it is generally recognised that all workmen ought to have a fair living wage, and if it is generally supposed that £3 per week is such a wage, a "right" to £5 may be defended on the ground that the existing practice represents a faulty application of a sound principle.

It will be noticed that it is difficult to state this case without using language which implies that there are rights prior to a general recognition. The truth is, however, as Muirhead says, that the general recognition is necessary for the existence of rights in the full sense of the word. Prior to the recognition there are what may be called moral *claims*, the concept of which is a purely moral concept; but, although from a moral point of view the general recognition adds nothing, it is essential if the claims are to become rights. Thus the concept of rights is not a purely moral concept, and what our recent argument has really shown is that duties, along with moral *claims*, belong essentially to a social system.

This means that right acts are done in a social context, within, that is to say, a system of personal relationships; and modern intuitionism seems to have grasped this aspect of the truth when it declares that "the essential defect of the 'ideal

utilitarian' theory is that it ignores, or at least does not do full
justice to, the highly personal character of duty".[3] It is held
that ideal utilitarianism "seems to simplify unduly our relations to our fellows. It says, in effect, that the only morally
significant relation in which my neighbours stand to me is that
of being possible beneficiaries by my action".[4] The weakness
of the utilitarian theory, however, is not just that it over-
simplifies personal relationships (by reducing them in effect to
one personal relation, namely, that which obtains between
benefactor and beneficiary), but also that it tacitly mis-
represents these relationships. The picture of society which
utilitarianism seems to imply is one in which for each centre of
consciousness and action all other such centres are objects and
not subjects, specially significant objects, no doubt, from a
moral point of view, but still objects. This attitude or implication can be traced back to Mill's atomic view of society
according to which each is to count as one and none as more
than one. Such a view seems to start from one centre of consciousness and action and to reach the idea of society by a
process of simple addition of other such centres which may
become the objects of attention and action on the part of the
first centre. This, however, is not just an over-simplification of
personal relations in the sense that it reduces the diversity of
these relations to one single relationship; it is rather a misapprehension of the nature of personal relations, of the nature
of society, in which, ideally or morally, persons are related as
subject to subject and not just as subject to object. On the
other hand, it is part of the strength of the new intuitionism
that, whether explicitly or implicitly, it seems to recognise this
fact, especially when it regards the judgment of duty as
arising, not from a calculation of an action's effects upon
objects, but rather from a comparison of claims emanating
from subjects. In this way intuitionism is consistent with a line
of thought which has been developed in modern times,
especially in Germany, and which looks back to the work of
Martin Buber as its inspiration. In his book *I and Thou* Buber
distinguishes between the twofold attitude of man "in accordance with the twofold nature of the primary words which he
speaks". These primary words are "I-Thou" and "I-It", and,
therefore, they "do not signify things but they intimate

[3] Ross, *The Right and the Good*, p. 22.
[4] *Ibid.*, p. 19.

relations". [5] This means that a man is faced with two different worlds, a world of persons and a world of things, a world of "Thou" and a world of "It", and the "Thou" is not just a specially significant "It". Rather it belongs to a different realm, and the man's attitude to it and the relationship in which he stands to it are completely different from those which obtain in the case of "It". At bottom the distinction appears to rest upon the difference between a world of objects on the one hand, and, on the other, a world of subjects, a society, a realm of ends.

We have seen that acts as the bearers of the moral qualities, right and wrong, fall within a system of personal relations, a world of subjects, and have persons, therefore, not only as their *termini a quo*, but also as their *termini ad quem*. Further, like persons, acts are somehow "above" time, though related in a peculiar way to events in time. Acts are in some way supra-temporal responses to a social and personal situation, a situation in which the relevant factors are persons, that is, subjects. Every action is a reaction, and it is this that ideal utilitarianism fails to grasp.

On the other hand, it must not be supposed that the relation in which acts stand to events in time is without importance. On the contrary, it is this relation which ensures the objectivity of the moral life. The world of objects and of series of objective events in time is necessary as the occasion and as the means of expression for actions in the realm of personal relations. As Ward has put it, "nature not only provides the scenery and properties of history but the actors themselves seem to have sprung from its soil, to owe their position largely to its co-operation, and to come into touch with each other solely through its means". [6] And again, with reference to Lotze and Berkeley, he says, "the entire physical world, 'the whole choir of heaven and furniture of earth', is but the medium, divinely constituted and sustained—as it were the language and the instrumentality—whereby finite spirits communicate and interact". [7] It must be borne in mind, however, that unlike Berkeley, Lotze and Ward, we are not here concerned with the metaphysical status of the realm of objects, nor with the precise account that must be given of the interaction between subject

[5] *I and Thou* (Eng. tr. by R. G. Smith), p. 3.
[6] *Realm of Ends, Pluralism and Theism*, p. 3.
[7] *Ibid.*, p. 217.

I

and object and between subject and subject. Our task has been to discover the logical presuppositions of our moral experience and moral judgments, and we have found that in a perfectly ordinary sense objective events are the *occasion* of moral actions, and not their "parts". The act belongs to the realm of personal relationship, is not to be identified with a series of objective events, and finds its place rather in the realm of subjects or of ends.

CHAPTER XI

THE CRITERION OF RIGHTNESS

WE HAVE NOW completed our preliminary analysis of the conditions logically presupposed by our moral experience and in particular by our moral judgments that certain acts are right and others wrong. We have indicated the essential context of actions which may bear one or other of these moral predicates, and we have considered the nature of right action, both with regard to the meaning of "right" and with regard to the nature of actions which may be right or wrong. The results which we have reached in this analysis may be briefly summarised in the following fashion.

(i) The idea of right is simple, unanalysable and indefinable, and is the idea of a peculiar relation obtaining between an agent, an act and a situation.

(ii) Acts which may be right do not consist of a series of objective events in time. They are, indeed, peculiarly related to such series, but in themselves, like judgments, they are supra-temporal. They have no doubt a place in time, but they have no temporal extension, that is, have no parts which are temporally related one to another. They have, however, two distinguishable but inseparable aspects, motive and intention, and these are so related one to another that it is not true that the same intention may proceed from one or other of several different motives. What is true is that, where motive and intention change, the series of objective events to which the act is related need not change.

(iii) These acts take place in a social context, and the situation is the subjective situation, that is, the objective situation as the agent sees it, provided that his thinking about the situation is genuine and sincere and not wilful.

Having, therefore, completed this part of our inquiry, we must now turn to the consideration of the criterion of rightness, that is, to the consideration of what it is that renders some acts right.

At the outset we may notice that, from the history of ethical thought and from our review of the principal ethical theories, there seem to be three main answers to this question, namely, that it is some characteristic of the motive which makes the act right, that it is some characteristic of the act itself which makes it right, and that it is some characteristic of the consequences of the act which renders it right; and it may well be profitable for us to follow this division of the subject in our examination of this question.

In the first place, then, there is the suggestion that it is some characteristic of the motive that renders an act right; and in principle there would seem to be two more precise possibilities falling under this head. For (a) it might be held that the characteristic of the motive which renders an act right is a moral quality (other of course than rightness itself), and (b) it might be held that the characteristic in question is a non-moral quality.

Within the former of these sub-divisions it is clear that the only plausible, if not possible, suggestion is that it is the moral goodness of the motive which renders the act right; and it might be argued that in defence of this theory the authority of Kant may be invoked. Certainly Kant maintained that the rightness of acts does not depend on the goodness of their results, and that in fact results are not really unconditionally good. Before the time of Kant it was fairly generally assumed that the word "right" simply means "productive of good results", and it was certainly left to Kant to insist, not only that when we call an act right or dutiful we do not *mean* that it has or will have good results, but even that *in fact* acts are right whether they have good results or not. Up to this point Kant's position is tolerably clear, but in its further development it unfortunately becomes somewhat ambiguous, and to the end it remains uncertain whether Kant departed from traditional ethics because he disagreed with its implied view concerning "right", or instead because he differed from it with regard to "good". For he did hold that the good ends at which right acts were traditionally held to aim were good only in a very suspect sense. In fact they were not unconditionally good, but only relatively so, with reference to someone who happened to desire them; and there was nothing unconditionally good save the good will, and a good will was one which spent itself in doing its duty. But was the will good because it issued in acts which were right, or were the acts right because they proceeded from a will which was good?

Apart, however, from the question of the authority of Kant, we must inquire what can be said for or against the suggestion that it is the moral goodness of the motive which renders an act right. Now on examination it would appear that this theory as so far defined lacks precision, for it is quite possible that in any given situation there may be two possible acts the motives to both of which are both morally good. None the less one of the acts may be right and the other wrong. Can it be said then that that act is right the motive of which is morally better than the motive of any other act possible in the same situation? The difficulty is, however, to give any real meaning to the phrase "morally better". No doubt it could be fittingly applied to a pure or unmixed motive as compared with an impure motive, or, more loosely, to a good motive as compared with a bad one. This latter usage does, however, seem a loose usage, for what is really meant is that the one motive is morally good whereas the other is morally bad. Moreover, the application of the phrase "morally better" to cases in which a pure motive is contrasted with an impure one is not in principle different from, indeed is only a more complicated instance of, the other looser usage to which we have just referred. For to say that mixed motive B is less morally good than pure motive A is not to imply that there are degrees of moral goodness, but is rather to assert that B has at least two "parts", B' and B'', and that of these B' is morally good whereas B'' is morally bad or indifferent. In any case, even if these applications of the phrase "morally better" were permitted, neither would meet the case, which is also quite possible, in which two acts may be done by the agent and in which, although only one act is right and dutiful, the motives to both acts are both morally good and both unmixed. And it does seem impossible to say that pure benevolence, for example, is morally better than filial affection or any other morally good motive. The reason is that although an act is judged right in respect of a situation and a motive is also judged morally good in respect of what may be called a situation, the two situations are not comparable. They are, in fact, unlike in one important respect, namely, that in the case of what is right the situation has room for only one act, while in the case of what is morally good the situation, which consists of a man's character, has room for *all* morally good motives. When we say that a motive is morally good we seem to mean at least this, that there is a place for it in the character of a man who is morally good. Of course, we do compare men's *characters* in respect of moral goodness, and we say that one is better than another; but here again we mean, as it appears on reflection, either that the character of the one is morally good while the character of the other is morally bad, or that one is morally good while the other is mixed, or that the goodness of one is less mixed than the goodness of the other. When we examine this matter closely and carefully, we find, it is suggested, that the degrees of moral goodness which a comparative use of the phrase "morally good" undoubtedly implies are more than a little elusive, and we conclude that the comparative use of the phrase may represent a difference in the degree of pointedness with which we judge that certain things are morally good and others morally bad (as when we say euphemistically that A is morally better than B, meaning that A is morally good and B is morally bad), or it may represent a difference in the degree of purity of those things which are judged morally good or bad (as when we say that A is morally better than B, meaning that A is a less mixed motive than B), but that there are no degrees of moral goodness which alone would justify a strict employment of the comparison we are considering. But if, in any given situation, we cannot compare the motives in respect of their moral goodness, the theory cannot be upheld that it is the moral goodness of the motive which renders an act right.

A second argument which issues in the same conclusion is that the sense of duty is a morally good motive, if not pre-eminently so, and that it presupposes an independent recognition that an act is right. And in fact, as we have already seen, it is to the intention, and not to the motive, that we attend when we judge that a certain act is right.[1]

We turn, then, to the suggestion that it is some non-moral quality of the motive which renders an act right; but this theory need not detain us, for it is ruled out by the last argument that

[1] Cf. ch. ix above.
  These arguments also hold against Field's theory that the ultimate bearers of the fundamental moral quality (goodness) are, not motives, but states of mind which include motives (cf. Field, "Kant's First Moral Principle", *Mind*, January 1932, pp. 32–6). Moreover, if we go beyond motives to states of minds it seems impossible to draw the line short of a complete state of mind at any one moment; but if that is either good or bad and so renders the ensuing act either right or wrong, then before I act, before I choose what I am going to do, the moral quality of my act is already determined. The point is, not that given a complete state of mind only one act can possibly ensue, but rather that given a state of mind the moral quality of the ensuing act is fixed, whether its non-moral qualities are determined or not.

in fact it is to the intention, and not to the motive, that we attend when we judge that an act is right. Indeed, we cannot *distinctively* describe any motive, except in terms, not perhaps of the precise intention with which in any given situation it is associated, but of a general form of that intention of which the latter is but an instance. Benevolence, for example, is a desire to do good, not to this particular person in this particular case, but to others in general; and the motive cannot be described except in terms of this general intention, this *type* of the intention to which it gives rise in particular cases. Now even if it be allowed that an act is right on account of the character of this general intention, it is still in virtue of a quality of the intention, and not of the motive, that the act is judged right and dutiful. But, secondly, it is in fact the case that the act is right, not as benevolence, for example, in general, but as this particular instance of benevolence. In other words, it is not the general intention but the precise intention that renders an act right.

Indeed, when it is borne in mind, as in this argument, that motive and intention are but two distinguishable aspects of the same thing, it becomes a question, not whether it is any quality of the motive, moral or non-moral, which determines the rightness of the act, but rather how such a theory can be plausibly suggested and maintained; and the answer appears to be that the theory in any plausible form presupposes a view of action which we have seen fit to reject, namely, that the act itself is a series of events in time and its motive another but earlier event.

We pass now to another of the three main possible answers to the question what it is that renders right acts right; and this time we are to consider the utilitarian theory that it is the character of the consequences that renders an act right. Once more there are two sub-divisions of the matter, for the characteristic of the consequences in question may be either a moral or a non-moral quality. But, again, the former is the more important historically, and, moreover, some at least of the arguments which tell against this view will be found fatal also to the other possibility that it is a non-moral quality of the consequences which renders an act right.

We have already given some consideration to the utilitarian type of ethical theory, and we have traced the process by which it has shaken itself free from some of its earlier peculiarities, in particular from the doctrine of psychological egoism and from the hedonistic doctrine that pleasure is the only thing good. In its developed form, we saw, it holds that an act is right if its consequences are good, or, rather, better than the consequences of any alternative act possible for the agent in the same situation. In describing this process as a development we were careful to point out that the assumption must not be made that the later forms were nearer the truth than the earlier. We were concerned with the nature of utilitarian doctrine, and not with the question of its truth. None the less the description of the process as a development was justified, for (a) the doctrine of psychological egoism was not a moral doctrine at all, although it might have serious implications for morality, and (b) even if pleasure is the only thing good, the statement that an act is right if it produces more pleasure than any of its alternatives is really an elliptical form of the more complex statement that an act is right if its consequences are better than those of any of its alternatives and that pleasure is the only thing good. In other words, the process was a development because it separated off more precisely the area we define as *moral* experience, and within that area it made explicit what previously was only implicit in the tenets of the theory. This means that the general form of utilitarian theory has become clear, namely, that an act is right if its consequences are better than those of any alternative act possible in the same situation; and, consequently, if the theory so stated falls before criticism, there will be no need to enter into the controversy between hedonistic and non-hedonistic utilitarianism, whereas if the general theory survives a critical consideration of that question is a task which could hardly be escaped.

There is, however, one preliminary point to be noted. We have already seen that right is a simple and indefinable notion, whereas in *Principia Ethica*, where the general form of utilitarian theory is most clearly to be found, Professor Moore *defines* "right" as meaning "productive of the best possible result". This definition, of course, offers a target for criticism, but, it is to be noticed, the definition does not belong of necessity to the general form of utilitarian doctrine. The theory could be restated in such a form that productivity of good results appeared, not as a definition, but as the criterion of rightness; and indeed Professor Moore does himself make this alteration in his later but smaller book, *Ethics*. We cannot therefore lay any weight whatsoever on this aspect of the matter, if we are to deal with the general and essential form of utilitarian doctrine.

Now we have already noted one implication of utilitarianism. It is that if the rightness of an act depends on the goodness of its consequences, or rather upon the fact that its consequences are better than those of any other act possible for the agent in the same situation, it follows that the agent can never *know* whether he has done his duty or not. Beforehand he cannot be sure, for if the crucial factor is the goodness of the consequences then all consequences may be relevant and later unforeseen consequences may easily upset the agent's calculations. This is still true even after the act has been done for the series of consequences may go on indefinitely. But, more important than that, the agent may be in error about the nearer consequences, and he can never be sure, before or after, whether he has made a mistake or not. This is so because, although in acting he may verify his opinion about the immediate consequences of the act he chooses to perform, he cannot verify his opinion about the immediate consequences of the acts he does not perform. Moreover, since morality always involves a choice, it must always be the case that the agent does not *know* that he has done his duty, even if it is allowed that distant consequences may legitimately be discounted.

This of course is simply an implication, and not a criticism, of utilitarianism in general; but the question does arise whether this implication is consistent with the findings of the ordinary moral consciousness and with *their* implications. One such finding is contained in the dictum that a man ought to do what he thinks right, and, if our earlier argument is to be trusted, this means that mental error can never be the sole or sufficient cause of wrong-doing. There is indeed another interpretation of the dictum which proceeds by distinguishing in meaning between "ought" and "right", or, when the dictum declares that it is right for a man to do what he thinks right, by treating "right" in this proposition as an ambiguous term. This, however, is not the place to discuss the merits of this suggestion. We have already considered the matter, and have found reason to suppose that "right" in this dictum, and indeed wherever it is used with a completely moral significance, is not ambiguous. If this is so, it follows, as we have seen, that wrong-doing can never be due to mental error or miscalculation. A man can never fail to do his duty while acting in a completely conscientious fashion. But this flatly contradicts the implication of utilitarianism, and since our guide in ethics is the ordinary moral consciousness and not any particular theory, the utilitarian position must be ruled out of court.

We have just noticed that utilitarianism may try to escape the force of this argument by offering a different interpretation of the dictum we have stressed, and by holding that the term "right" is ambiguous and that in one of its senses it bears a different meaning from the term "ought". At an earlier stage in the argument we gave reasons for denying the validity of this interpretation; but now we must notice that, even if this interpretation were allowed to pass without question, the utilitarian would not have come to the end of his difficulties. He would doubtless say that an act is right if its consequences are actually better than the consequences of any alternative act possible in the same situation, but that what the agent ought to do is the act which in his opinion will probably have the better consequences. In this, however, there are two factors which may differ in degree, for there may be different degrees of probability, and also, according to the utilitarian, different degrees of goodness. The agent will then have to weigh a degree of probability in the balance over against a degree of goodness; and this looks like an impossible task. It is something like the old hedonistic calculus appearing in a new guise.

Now it would appear that utilitarians have not been entirely unaware of these difficulties, for although some have held to the position with which we have been dealing, others have tried to re-state the matter in a more defensible form. More than that, they have seemed to succeed in finding such a form in a certain modification of the general utilitarian doctrine, to the effect that an act is right if its probable consequences are better than the probable consequences of any other act possible for the agent in the same situation. Thus we find Laird declaring that "it is always the duty of a moral agent to do what is *probably best*—that is to say, to choose the action which in itself and in its probable consequences seems better than any other action in itself and in its probable consequences". [2] This, of course, refers to duty, and some moralists draw a distinction between duty and right or between two meanings of "right". Laird, however, does not allow this, and puts the matter thus: "The main distinctions in this affair are very neatly described by Mr. Russell when he distinguishes between the most

[2] *Study in Moral Theory*, p. 71.

fortunate, the wisest, and the right action (*Philosophical Essays*, pp. 22–6). (Mr. Russell says "subjectively" right, but the qualification, I think, is a mistake.) The most fortunate act, in this language, is that which together with its consequences achieves the best result. It is the act whose fate is the best. The wisest act is that which is based upon the best available information, and upon the most reasonable conjecture possible at any time concerning its probable fate. The right act for any agent is the wisest act which the agent with his measure of wisdom, and with his opportunities for reflexion, can attain."[3] This means that the act which to the agent will probably have the best consequences is, according to Professor Moore the obligatory act, according to Mr. Russell the subjectively right act, and according to Laird the dutiful or obligatory act and that which is right without qualification.

In the first place, however, this modification of the utilitarian position does not escape the last criticism which we offered, for on this new theory the agent may well be faced with the task of weighing a difference in the degree of probability against a difference in the degree of goodness, a task which is similar to that which arose out of the old hedonistic calculus and which is equally impossible.

Further, in the second place, it is the intention of this theory, not to hold that it is a quality of act A which makes act A right, but to maintain that it is a quality (the goodness) of x, which is related to act A, that makes act A the right act. Is it the case, however, that on the modified theory x *is* related to act A? There seem to be two possibilities. On the one hand, it may be held that act A is related to its consequences but that these are only probably good; while, on the other hand, the assertion may be that act A is related to probable consequences that are good, that is, that act A is only probably related to good consequences. But a probable relation is not a relation, and probable goodness is not goodness. Probabilities do not belong to the reality about which we are judging, but express a relationship between our judgments and the evidence we have for making them. Since this is so, it seems impossible that a probable judgment should ever give rise to anything other than a probable judgment; it seems impossible, that is to say, that we should be able to pass from the realm which consists of the relation between our judgments and the evidence for them, to the realm which consists of

[3] *Study in Moral Theory*, p. 74.

the reality about which we are judging. If this is so the statement that act A will probably have good consequences or that the consequences of act A will probably be good can be the ground only of a statement to the effect, not that act A is right, but that act A is *probably* right; and that of course brings us back to the form of utilitarianism which has regard to the *actual* consequences of an act.

As against all this, it may be said that while in general it is doubtless true that a probable judgment can give rise only to another probable judgment, there is one exception, namely, that it is right for a man to do what he thinks will probably have the best possible results. And on the face of it this contention seems plausible enough; but on examination it appears that part at least of this plausibility derives from the plausibility of the original theory from which the theory we are considering is a departure. In other words, so far as this new form of utilitarianism relies on its apparent plausibility rather than on its ability to meet criticism successfully, it is really trying to run with the hares while hunting with the hounds. In this way. It is plausible, let us admit, to assert a necessary connection between right action and the best possible results. Utilitarianism in its original form asserts one such connection, that it is the goodness of the results which makes the act right; and so utilitarianism inherits the initial plausibility. But, as we have seen, there are difficulties in maintaining this utilitarian position; and so the plausibility of the theory is diminished. Then comes the modified form of utilitarianism which seeks to get round these difficulties by having regard, not to actual consequences, but to probable consequences; and so for it the earlier plausibility is restored— until it is seen that the new theory does *not* assert a necessary connection between a right act and the best possible results, but only a probable connection. Thus it largely derives its plausibility from the plausibility of a theory of which it is a modification, and from which it has departed in *the* most important respect. Consequently, if utilitarianism is to stand, it must stand in its original form, asserting a connection between right actions and their actual (not just their probable) results.

Before we proceed further with the discussion of this subject, it may be well at this point to notice one type of argument which is common in considerations of the tenability of utilitarianism. It may be called the "test-case" type of argument, and it consists of putting a supposed moral situation in which one or other of two acts may be right, and of arguing that if one act is right utilitarianism must be true, whereas if the other is right utilitarianism is false. Now this type of argument has a long and honourable history in ethical thought and discussion, and can trace itself back to the work of Socrates, many of whose arguments were to the effect that if a certain account of morality implied that in a given situation a certain act was right, then, if it were generally agreed that in such a situation the act in question *was* right, the theory was so far substantiated, while, if it were generally agreed that the act in question was *not* right, the theory was conclusively disproved and instantly to be discarded. Clearly, however, there is one factor which conditions the effectiveness of this type of argument, namely, a general agreement as to what in the given situation is the right thing to do. Where this condition is unfulfilled the argument can prove nothing in general terms. The most it can do is to convert one individual here, another there—on either side. Further, it can be understood that as progress is made in ethical science, all the main rival theories are more and more found to be in harmony with what it is *generally agreed* that men ought to do in different kinds of situation, and that consequently, so far as the discussion appeals to particular cases, the weight of the argument falls increasingly upon those particular cases regarding which there is *not* general agreement. But these are the very cases which are least able to bear the weight of controversy. Moreover, so far as the use of the argument by utilitarians is concerned, its force depends largely upon the assumption that to deny the utilitarian theory is to deny a necessary connection between right actions and good results. But this assumption is manifestly false. Utilitarianism does not have a monopoly of the belief that there is a necessary connection between right actions and good results. It does assert such a connection in one particular form, in that it is *because* the results are good that the act is right. But the belief in the necessary connection can be retained in another form, in the faith, for example (which goes beyond morality although it may in itself fall short of religion), that right acts will necessarily in the long run have the best possible results. And this contention is quite compatible with a denial of the utilitarian doctrine. The question at issue, when utilitarianism is under discussion, is not whether in fact right acts have the best possible results, not even whether right acts have of necessity the best possible results, but whether they are right *because* they have the best possible results.

We turn now to a consideration of a more general character, namely, the way in which utilitarianism describes what in general it is we do when we perform a right action, or the way in which utilitarianism implies that this ought to be described. In this connection it is immaterial whether we take utilitarianism as having regard to actual consequences or as having regard to probable consequences. For the sake of brevity we shall refer to the earlier form, but on the silent understanding that what is said applies equally to the modified form suggested by Laird. How then does utilitarianism imply that the moral life, the life of duty, is to be described? Generally speaking, it consists of doing that act which will have the best possible consequences. Now this involves that any situation may be morally significant, and that in every situation we ought to consider the consequences of each possible act in order to discover which is our duty. More than that, it seems unlikely that in any situation all possible acts will have exactly similar consequences so far as their goodness or badness is concerned; and the implication of utilitarianism is, therefore, that it is unlikely that any situation will be morally insignificant; whereas in fact we ordinarily believe that many situations are morally insignificant and that the acts we do in them are morally neutral. In other words, we ordinarily believe that duty in general has an intrusive quality. The truth is that the moral life is like a superstructure built upon a foundation of natural life, and that not every part of this natural life bears the weight of moral meaning and significance. If life is taken as a whole it is only here and there that duty and morality *intrude*; and many practical situations are morally insignificant.

The general view of right action presupposed by utilitarian doctrine also implies that duty is not necessarily a social phenomenon. Even if it is laid down that only states of consciousness can be good, it is clear that solitary man on this view would still be subject to the law of duty. On the utilitarian theory the social aspect of morality, when it has such an aspect, is accidental, and morality itself would still be possible if there were only one man left in the universe. Now solitary man is a subject, but he is a subject confronted by nothing but objects; and, since solitary man is also on this theory a moral agent, the presumption is that even social man in so far as he is a moral agent is a subject confronted by objects, and that other men are for him, *qua* moral agent, merely objects of his dutiful intentions. But, as we have seen, morality is a social phenomenon, and duties occur within a system of personal relationships, that is, among subjects.

Allied to this consideration there is another, that if solitary man is also a moral agent, and if, as seems reasonable, natural and purely objective events and entities do not suggest moral distinctions, our idea of duty must be something of an innate idea and in acting on it a man is simply being true to his own private nature; whereas in truth our knowledge of moral distinctions seems to arise in the context of our social intercourse and experience, and our obedience to the voice of duty appears, not as a following of the bent of our own nature (though also not necessarily as a running counter to that bent), but as the satisfaction of the claims of something larger than ourselves.

There remains one general line of comment and criticism of the utilitarian position. It is that whether the criterion of rightness is found in the goodness either of the actual or of the probable consequences, the act which is right is regarded as the cause, actually or potentially, of these consequences. It follows, therefore, that utilitarianism implies a view of right action which takes the action as one event or, more likely, as a series of events within a larger series of events in time. But, if we are to trust our earlier analysis of the logical presuppositions of those ordinary moral judgments which employ the predicates "right" and "wrong", then this view of an act, which, as we have just seen, utilitarianism necessarily implies, is a false view. An act is not a series of objective events in time, nor any part, however short, of such a series. Rather it is an entity which is certainly related to a series of objective events, but is distinguishable from them and is not related to them as their cause but rather as their moral meaning. Consequently, so considered, that is, as an act, a moral phenomenon, it has no consequences; and it follows therefore that utilitarianism errs from the beginning by applying the predicates "right" and "wrong" to that which cannot bear them.

We have now considered and found wanting the suggestion that it is some quality (moral or otherwise) of the motive which renders acts right, and also the suggestion that it is some quality (moral or otherwise) of the consequences which renders

an act right. There remains only the third possibility that the
criterion of rightness is to be found in some quality of the act
itself. This would seem at first sight to be the position upheld
by the new intuitionism; but that cannot be allowed without
qualification. It will be remembered that the new intuitionism
does indeed maintain that an act is right because it has the
quality of being the keeping of a promise or the payment of a
debt or the making of reparation for an injury done, and so on;
but in addition to these obligations it is held "that if we are
ever under no special obligation such as that of fidelity to a
promisee or of gratitude to a benefactor, we ought to do what
will produce most good".[4] Again, Sir David Ross tells us that
he himself finds "no difficulty in recognising, in the tendency
which an act has to amend the situation in the best possible
way, i.e. to produce the maximum good, something in virtue
of which that act tends to be fitting to the situation";[5] and
later he speaks of that principle of duty "which bids us set
ourselves to produce the greatest good".[6] Now all this reads
as if the special obligations of intuitionism were superimposed
upon a general utilitarian scheme,[7] and this of course fails to
do justice to what we have called the intrusive quality of duty.
Indeed, all the objections we found against utilitarianism must
apply also to this part of the new intuitionism. There is indeed
one passage in which Sir David Ross seems to be trying to
modify the utilitarian part of his doctrine, for he argues that
just as in the case of promise-keeping "my act is not only the
packing and posting of a book but the fulfilling of a promise,
and just as it is in the latter capacity and not in the former that
it is my duty, so an act whereby I augment the general good is
not only, let us say, the writing of a begging letter on behalf of
a hospital, but the producing (or ensuring) of whatever good
ensues therefrom, and it is in the latter capacity and not in the
former that it is right, if it *is* right. That which is right is
right not because it is an act, one thing, which will produce
another thing, an increase of the general welfare, but because
it is itself the producing of an increase in the general welfare".[8]
But this contention loses its plausibility whenever there are
many intermediate stages between my initiation of change and

[4] Ross, *The Right and the Good*, p. 39.
[5] *Foundations of Ethics*, p. 81.
[6] *Ibid.*, p. 175.
[7] Cf. Ross, *Foundations of Ethics*, pp. 79–84.
[8] *The Right and the Good*, p. 47.

the increase in the general welfare; and this is more than a mere possibility since our duty is described as the duty of producing as much good as possible, and since therefore all consequences, late or early, are entirely relevant. In any case this modification is later abandoned when it is held that our duty is to *set ourselves* to produce as much good as we can. This "setting of ourselves" is, as we saw, an event or, at best, a very short series of events within a longer temporal succession; consequently the act is thought to be justified by its results, actual or anticipated; and that of course is utilitarianism and subject therefore to the objections we have already advanced.

Yet there do seem to be certain facts to which the new intuitionists try to do justice by introducing this element of utilitarianism into their theory. For besides what Sir David Ross calls special obligations, there are other duties such as those of beneficence, self-improvement, and the proportionment of happiness to virtue (justice); and these, it is held, "come under the general principle that we should produce as much good as possible". [9] But it is surely the case that if these duties come under any general principle at all it is not the principle "that we should produce as much good as possible", but rather that we should produce this or that determinate good. It is this latter principle that alone does justice to the intrusive character of duty, and to the fact that we do not discover our duty by a calculation and comparison of consequences. It would seem, therefore, that we must reject the new intuitionism as it stands as not involving as radical a rejection of utilitarianism as the facts of the moral consciousness would warrant.

In addition to this line of criticism there is another which takes its start from the fact that the new intuitionism, whether regarding the act as the doing of something or as the setting of oneself to do it, takes as the subject of the predicates "right" and "wrong" something which is either an event or a short series of events in a temporal succession of events; and that intuitionism does do this is most clearly seen in its clear-cut separation of act from motive. Moreover, this view of action is not one which can be upheld.

On the other hand, this view of action which we are holding to be mistaken is not involved in each and every exposition of intuitionism, is not necessarily involved in intuitionism in

[9] *The Right and the Good*, p. 27.

general, but happens to be present in the particular exposition of the theory with which we have been concerned. Indeed, if intuitionism finds the criterion of rightness in the qualities of acts, it may be that the view of action we have found reason to adopt will lead us to an intuitionist position, for, certainly, it precludes us from accepting any form of utilitarianism, and further, although sentimentalism may be somewhat nearer the truth, we have seen none the less that it is in virtue of their intentional aspects that acts are judged right or wrong.

Indeed, it does seem that we must accept the intuitionist account of this matter subject to two modifications: (i) that the act, the subject of the predicate "right", must be regarded in the way to which our argument has led us; and (ii) that the general duty of beneficence, self-improvement and justice should be thought of, not as a duty to produce as much good as possible, but as a duty to produce a certain determinate good. For, clearly, (a) we do have duties to pay debts, to keep promises, to tell the truth, and so on; and (b) these are recognised as duties quite apart from any attempt to estimate the relative amounts of goodness involved. No doubt it can be shown that these duties involve important "goods", but this argument, if it is used to indicate the ground upon which these different acts are regarded as duties, has something of the character of a rationalisation, giving a theoretical justification which is not the real justification. The argument is in fact dangerous, for, although it may be that all right acts produce more good than their alternatives, that does not necessarily prove that they are right *because* of this interesting fact about them. Moreover, the argument itself loses force and is weakened if the consideration of the *consequences* of acts is rigorously excluded; and yet, as we saw in our examination of utilitarianism, the consideration of consequences must be excluded if our theory is to be in harmony with the conclusions which we have already reached. Further, if the argument is to be trusted, it follows that the various criteria of rightness, the different characteristics which render right acts right, cannot be reduced to the single characteristic of being the cause of something good. Nor is it necessary that moral theory should reduce the various criteria of rightness to a single characteristic. Sir David Ross has pointed this out forcibly in an important passage. "The view which admits only one intuition", he says, "—that only the production of maximum good is right—

gratifies our natural wish to reach unity and simplicity in our moral theory. We have a natural wish to reach a single principle from which the rightness or wrongness of all actions can be deduced. But it is more important that a theory be true than that it be simple; and I have tried to show that a system which admits only this one intuition is false to what we all really think about what makes acts right or wrong. After all, there is no more justification for expecting a single ground of rightness than for expecting a single ground of goodness, and agathistic or generalised Utilitarianism recognises a variety of goods without succeeding in finding, or even feeling any need to find, a single ground of the goodness of them all. It is, to my mind, a mistake in principle to think that there is any presumption in favour of the truth of a monistic against a pluralistic theory in morals, or, for that matter, in metaphysics either. When we are faced with two or more ostensible grounds of rightness, it is proper to examine them to find whether they have a single character in common; but if we cannot find one we have no reason to assume that our failure is due to the weakness of our thought and not to the nature of the facts."[10]

None the less, Ross does not exclude from the task of the moralist, rather he explicitly includes in it, the *search* for a single principle, for if there is no presumption in favour of monism there is certainly none in favour of pluralism. Now we have already considered the most common suggestion of a single comprehensive principle of rightness, namely, that an act is right only if it is productive of more good than its alternatives. We have, however, found this suggestion wanting because the argument in defence of it loses its plausibility whenever the consideration of consequences is excluded; and we have at an earlier stage found good reason to exclude such considerations.

There is, however, another suggestion of a single principle, and it is a suggestion which has behind it the authority of Kant. Indeed, the suggestion is made in three different forms, one that has regard to the form of the moral principle, namely, that we are to act only on that maxim whereby we can at the same time will that it should become a universal law; another that has regard to the content, namely, that we are to act so as to treat humanity, whether in our own person or in that of another, in every case as an end withal, never as a means only;

[10] *Foundations of Ethics*, pp. 82 ff.

and a third which Kant describes as a complete characterisation, namely, that all maxims ought by their own legislation to
harmonize with a possible kingdom of ends.[11]

Now in a consideration of this proposal a preliminary question
arises regarding the precise meaning which Kant attached to
the word "maxim". What, in this context, is a maxim? It is
clear that it is not a motive. It has more to do with intention
than with motive, for Kant seems to have in mind something
like a principle of action; and yet the maxim cannot be simply
identified with the intention, for, strictly speaking, an intention
cannot become a universal law. The maxim is rather the
intention before it has properly become an intention, that is, as
considered by, and held before, the mind of the agent, and as
expressed in the form of a judgment, perhaps in the form of an
imperative judgment such as "Do x,y,z". Further, the intention
includes not only what is chosen, but also the alternatives to that
choice and the circumstances in which it is chosen; and so in
like manner the maxim will also take account of these factors. It
will then be the suggestion that the agent should do x,y,z, in
preference to p,q,r, in circumstances a,b,c.

When we turn from this preliminary point we find that of the
three different formulations by means of which Kant expounds
his ethical principle the first and the second represent two
different principles while the third formulation attempts simply
to combine these other two. In the first place there is the
criterion of rightness contained in the suggestion that an act
is right if, and only if, its maxim can without contradiction be
willed as a universal law; while, in the second place, it is held
that an act is right if by it persons are treated as ends and not
as means only. Further, it would seem that of these two principles it is the former which Kant regards as offering the
"strict method"[12] of determining what is right; and we may
therefore fittingly begin with a consideration of this principle.

At the outset it must be admitted that rules of rightness are
universal, that is to say, that if act A is right for X then, all
other things being equal, act A would also be right for Y and for
Z. It may be, however, and in fact it is the case, that this universality is an implication of rightness rather than a criterion of
rightness. It has often been pointed out that when Kant himself
came to apply the principle as a criterion of rightness, he was

---

[11] *Grundlegung*, Abbott's E. T., pp. 54–5.
[12] *Ibid.*, p. 55.

able to reach plausible conclusions only because he unwittingly introduced other principles altogether. Thus when he deals with the rightness of repaying debts and, in general, of keeping promises,[13] he does inquire regarding the result of a universal breach of these rules, but this result upholds the rules, not because it reveals a contradiction, but because it clearly involves a state of affairs which no normal person would desire. Nor should this fact surprise us. For although doubtless if a maxim is to be the maxim of a right action, it must be such that it can be expressed without logical contradiction in a universal law, it does not follow, it is not true, that all such maxims are the maxims of right actions. When we ask, What is the right act here? it is certain that the act in question falls within the class of all acts which can be done by all without contradiction; but what we want to know is not just what acts are there which it is logically possible for all to do, but rather which of these it is right for all to do. Thus, we conclude, universality is an implication of rightness, but is by no means a sufficient criterion of rightness. And it only remains to notice that even Kant's unconscious introduction of the idea of what is desirable does not yield clear conclusions. For it might be argued that I ought *not* to pay my debts, since, if everyone did likewise, it would spell the end of a credit-system, and would involve a state of society in which men might give or refuse to give, but in which they would not lend without security. It is an open question which of the two social systems is the more to be desired; but it is certain that, whichever it may be, my duty now is to pay my debts.

None the less, Kant's argument has a certain plausibility, and the explanation is a curious one. It is that whereas, according to Kant, this formal principle is the "strict method" while the others are useful for gaining an *entrance* for the moral law, in fact this formal principle is not strict, does not offer a sufficient and conclusive criterion of rightness, but does help to gain an entrance for the moral law. In fact, expressed in other ways, it has considerable practical importance. "How would you like it, or what would happen, if everyone else were to do that?" we sometimes say; and "Do unto others as ye would that they should do unto you" is obviously a moral appeal and not a moral theory.

Does then Kant's other principle provide the ground upon

[13] *Grundlegung*, p. 40.

which acts are judged right, namely, that in these acts we treat humanity, whether in our own person or in that of another, as an end and not as a means only? Now it may be agreed that in all right action we treat one person or another as an end and not just as a means. On the other hand, in many right actions we subordinate to the interests or needs of one person the interests or needs of another, and fail to treat the latter as an end. This means that in many cases, in cases of an apparent conflict of duty, Kant's principle affords no clear criterion of what is right, for in such cases, whichever of the conflicting duties we adopt, we both observe this principle and fail to observe it. We cannot say that we observe it more by following one course of action rather than another, for there are no degrees of "treatment as an end" and no degrees of "treatment as a means". But if Kant's principle had expressed the underlying ground of rightness, one would have expected that in its light apparent conflicts of duty would have been revealed as *merely* apparent, and that it would have offered a clear criterion in such cases. In fact, however, what the principle offers us is not the underlying ground of all right actions, but a philosophical generalisation or theory based upon our prior recognition that certain kinds of act are right; and the principle does not express the necessary and universal characteristic of acts which are right under actual conditions, but gives an account, based upon the recognition of these right acts, of the general type of behaviour in ideal conditions. It is possible, indeed it is probable, that this principle of Kant's would have a place in a complete moral theory, but not, we conclude, as the actual criterion of rightness, but as a general principle of conduct to which the principles of rightness point as an ideal.

We are compelled, therefore, to return to the intuitionist theory of morals which recognises a diversity of principles of rightness, such as that it is right to keep promises and pay debts, that it is right to tell the truth, and so on. It must not be supposed, however, that this theory is itself without difficulty. On the contrary, there is a stubborn difficulty in all cases of an apparent conflict of duties; and this problem, it can be seen, confronts every theory which recognises a plurality of principles of rightness, for wherever there is such a plurality there is always inevitably the possibility that an occasion will arise on which they are in conflict. Kant admitted a single criterion of rightness which gave rise to several more particular principles of duty; but because his single principle referred to a quality which did not admit of degrees he too had to deal with cases of conflict between particular principles of duty. Indeed, our criticism of Kant turned upon this fact that his single principle of duty did not do what a single principle ought to do, namely, to decide in cases of apparent conflict; and in fact Kant was unable to decide such cases without introducing another principle altogether, that which distinguishes duties of perfect obligation which admit of no exception and duties of imperfect obligation which may on occasion have to be set aside.

Now this solution of Kant's to the problem of apparent conflicts is perhaps the simplest solution that can be given; and yet when it is more closely examined we find that it does not meet the case. In the first place, it would be difficult to discover even one duty which is always a duty without exception; while, in the second place, even if such duties of perfect obligation were to be found, the distinction between duties of perfect, and duties of imperfect obligation can decide only in cases of a conflict between a duty of perfect obligation and a duty of imperfect obligation, and does not help in the least to decide when there is a conflict between two or more duties of perfect obligation, or again between two or more duties of imperfect obligation.

Besides this solution, however, there is another which has played a large part historically, and which says in effect that there is no problem since our duty is always to do that act which has the best consequences. This of course is the utilitarian solution, and it is certainly true that if there is a single criterion of duty which refers to a quality, such as goodness, which admits, or is held to admit of degrees, then there can be no problem. On the other hand, this account of the matter falls to the ground with the general theory of utilitarianism of which it is a part.

The problem, however, is a real problem for the new intuitionism, and the solution offered is a novel one. In dealing with this subject Ross refers to the utilitarian view and then adds that "a different account may be given of the matter, an account which will, I believe, show itself to be the true one. It may be said that besides the duty of fulfilling promises I have and recognize a duty of relieving distress, and that when I think it right to do the latter at the cost of not doing the former, it is not because I think I shall produce more good thereby but because I think it the duty which is in the circumstances more of a duty. This account surely corresponds much more closely with what we really think in such a situation. If, so far as I can see, I could bring equal amounts of good into being by fulfilling my promise and by helping someone to whom I had made no promise, I should not hesitate to regard the former as my duty. Yet on the view that what is right is right because it is productive of the most good I should not so regard it ".[14] The vital point here is that where I decide, for example, that act A is right I so judge "because I think it the duty which is in the circumstances *more of a duty*". Here we have the factor which varies in degree, not goodness, but rightness. This is a strange assertion and one which has to counter the criticism that an act is either a duty or not a duty, and it is never more or less of a duty.

But before we can proceed with our discussion of this point we have to take account of a complication, for to the passage already quoted Ross adds a footnote to the effect that the duties in question "are not strictly speaking duties, but things that tend to be our duty, or *prima facie* duties".[15] It is plain, however, that the intuitionists themselves are uneasy about this phrase "*prima facie* duty". Ross declares that "it says at the same time too much and too little".[16] On the one hand, it suggests that what we are speaking of is a certain kind of duty, whereas in fact it is not any kind of duty at all. On the other hand, it suggests also that what we are speaking of is only the appearance and not the reality of a situation, whereas it is instead an "objective fact". A *prima facie* duty then is a conditional duty,[17] something which tends to be a duty, which would be a duty if the relevant characteristic were the only morally significant factor in the situation. And it is these *prima facie* duties which vary in degree, which are subject to the qualifications "more" and "less". Our actual duties are duties without qualification. "We are bound to do that act whose *prima facie* obligatoriness in those respects in which it is *prima facie* obligatory most outweighs its *prima facie* disobligatoriness in those respects in which it is *prima facie*

---

[14] *The Right and the Good*, p. 18.
[15] *Ibid.*, p. 18 note.
[16] *Foundations of Ethics*, p. 84; cf. *The Right and the Good*, pp. 19–20.
[17] Cf. Ross, *The Right and the Good*, p. 19.

disobligatory".[18] This *prima facie* obligatoriness varies in degree, but obligatoriness *sans phrase* does not.

Ross gives an analogy from nature to this variation in degree and this tendency to be right. An object, he says,[19] may tend to move towards another object in accordance with the law of gravitation, but its actual course will be the result, not of this attraction only, but of all the forces to which it is subject. At the same time Ross notes that whereas the word "tendency" here denotes a causal relation, it cannot denote a causal relation when used to explain the meaning of "*prima facie* rightness". To this we must add that the analogy is subject to a further limitation, for while in the case of natural forces the resultant course is a compromise, in the case of conflicting *prima facie* duties the outcome is not a compromise but a choice. Consequently we shall do well to attend to Ross's warning that it may be better not to use the word tendency in a moral context. More accurately, *prima facie* rightness means conditional rightness.

Once we free ourselves, however, from the influence of a misleading analogy from nature, it becomes more difficult to see how *prima facie* or conditional rightness can vary in degree. If when I say in any situation that I have a *prima facie* duty to keep my promise I mean that if promise-keeping were the only morally significant action in the situation it would be my duty to keep my promise, then there seems nothing present which can be subject to variations in degree. If the condition holds then the act in question is my duty, and is so simply, and is not less or more of a duty. If the condition does not hold then the act may be a duty or it may not, but in either case it can hardly be more or less of a duty. Either it is my duty or it is not. Nor can the variation in degree belong to the *conditional* aspect of the fact, for either the duty is conditional or it is unconditional, and there is no sense in saying that it is more or less conditional. Further, if it is impossible to attach the variation in degree either to the conditional aspect of the fact or to that other aspect denoted by the word "obligation", it is equally impossible to attach it to the fact taken as a whole. How can a conditional duty be more or less of a conditional duty, without being either "more or less conditional" or "more or less of a duty"? If neither of these alternatives is possible, it follows

[18] Ross, *Foundations of Ethics*, p. 85.
[19] *The Right and the Good*, pp. 28-9.

that a conditional duty is simply a conditional duty, and is not more or less of a conditional duty. The truth is that the suggestion that *prima facie* obligatoriness varies in degree loses all its plausibility when the association with ideas of natural tendency is broken.

Yet if our argument has proved anything it has proved that the moral pluralism of the new intuitionism is more in harmony with the facts of the ordinary moral consciousness than any theory, such as utilitarianism, which recognises a single criterion of rightness. On the other hand, it is precisely on account of its pluralistic outlook that intuitionism is confronted by the difficulty with which we are dealing. For it is pluralism as such which gives rise to apparent conflicts of duty, and it is to meet such cases that a distinction is drawn between rightness and *prima facie* rightness. When, however, *prima facie* rightness is interpreted in terms of tendencies we find that the argument proceeds by means of a natural analogy which, when considered strictly, is seen to be inapplicable to the moral sphere. Moreover, when *prima facie* rightness is defined as conditional rightness it is found again that no progress can be made, for the qualification "more or less" does not hold of conditional rightness and consequently a comparison and choice between the conflicting *prima facie* duties is impossible. Indeed the conditional character of *prima facie* duties is important only in situations where there are several such duties and where therefore there is a conflict; but of course in such situations we are faced with two conditional duties in circumstances in which neither of the two conditions is fulfilled. If promise-keeping is the only morally significant action then I have a duty to keep my promise; if helping those in need is the only morally significant action then I have a duty to help them: but these qualifications are important only when I may have *both* *prima facie* duties, and then, *ex hypothesi*, neither condition is fulfilled for neither action is the only morally significant action in the situation. Consequently, the conception of conditional rightness does not solve our problem of apparent conflicts of duty.

The new intuitionists, however, have still another way of describing the fact. Professor Prichard has suggested the word "claim" as suitably covering what is in mind; but, as Ross holds, it suffers from the defect that it describes the matter "from the point of view of the person to be affected by the action ", and not from the point of view of the agent. What is wanted, then, is a word which indicates moral claims but from the side of the agent who may have to meet the claims; and Mr. Carritt has the suggestion that the word "responsibility" meets the case, a suggestion which Sir David Ross "gladly accepts".[20] Now either responsibilities are distinct from duties, in which case the new intuitionism has arrived at a single criterion of duty, namely, that we should always fulfil the greatest responsibility; or else responsibilities are defined in terms of duties, and then the problem is on our hands once again. Of these two possible interpretations the latter seems to be the true one. Moral agents do have responsibilities, a father, for example, has a responsibility for his child, but that simply means that he has certain duties towards his child which can be regarded either as so many responsibilities or as one responsibility, that is, a class of duties which can be grouped together on the ground that they are all owed by the same parent to the same child.

Thus none of the possible interpretations of *prima facie* rightness helps satisfactorily to solve the problem created by apparent conflicts of duty; and they do fail because among the different duties there seems to be no common principle, other than rightness, which can be subject to variations of degree and which could provide, therefore, a basis of comparison. We seem driven, therefore, to suppose either that duty itself varies in degree or else that conflicts of duty may be real conflicts and not just apparent. Neither proposition, however, is free from difficulty. If duties vary in degree then it may be my duty not to do what is, however, a duty, and this, of course, is nonsense. On the other hand, if the conflict is real and not just apparent, it means that at any time I may be morally obliged to do two things both of which I cannot do, and although this is not obviously nonsense it does conflict with the dictum that "I ought" implies "I can".

But it is necessary to be more exact. When in such cases the agent is confronted with a conflict of duties, A and B, it is not correct to say that he has a duty to do both A and B. There are no doubt cases in which it is our duty to do not just one thing but two. If, for example, a child is ill, it is the parents' duty to send for the doctor, but it is also the parents' duty to give the child some attention themselves. But, of course, there

[20] Cf. Carritt, *Morals and Politics*, p. 185; *Foundations of Ethics*, p. 85.

is no real conflict here. The double duty is clear enough, although there may well be some doubt as to the most effective ordering and expression of this double duty. The case we are considering, however, is not like that, for in it there is a real conflict of mutually exclusive duties. It may well be admitted that such cases are more rare than is often supposed, and that many alleged cases of conflict are really cases of double duties in which the ordering and method of fulfilment demand some careful consideration. Where, however, there is a genuine conflict of mutually exclusive duties, it is clear that our duty is *not* "to do both act A and act B", and that it is only if it were that that this account of the matter would be out of harmony with the dictum that "I ought" implies "I can". Our duty is not "to do both A and B"; rather, we have a duty to do act A and we have *another* duty to do act B. Of course we cannot do both, but then we do not have a duty to do both. We have instead two different and conflicting duties; and the necessary choice is not a dutiful choice, not a choice which seeks to decide which act is our duty (for, *ex hypothesi*, both *are* duties), but a choice between two duties, a choice, therefore, which cannot possibly be made on any principle of rightness (so long as "right" and "dutiful" are taken as synonyms, and we have already argued that in a full moral connotation they *are* synonyms).

This does not necessarily mean, however, that the choice is a completely amoral choice. It is possible that the choice can be made on a principle which is a moral principle, but which is not a principle of rightness; and it is to the investigation of this possibility that we must now turn.

THE RIGHT AND THE GOOD

I T WILL BE remembered that our discussion up to this point
has taken place within certain limitations, within the limitation that we have been concerned only with that aspect of
morality which, so far as we could see, was essentially social, that
is to say, with that aspect of morality which was covered by the
term "duty". Our discussion, however, has led us to a point at
which we are now required to dispense with that limitation.
When we were considering the social aspect of morality we
came to the conclusion that while the entire sphere of duty was
essentially social, there might be another part of morality
which was not social, or at least not essentially so. Thus we
found that the choice of what is good might itself be good,
though it would not necessarily be dutiful and it might be
possible in solitude. If this were so, then, in harmony with the
suggestion with which our last chapter closed, it might be held
that the choice between conflicting duties, though it cannot
itself be dutiful, might none the less be good. Similarly, it
might be held that the choice, for example, of one profession
rather than another, which is amongst other things the choice
of one set of duties rather than another, may be good without
being dutiful. But here we must be careful, for the word
"choice" is ambiguous. It may mean what is chosen or it may
mean the choosing of it; that is, it may refer either to the
objective or to the subjective aspect of the fact. Now when we
talk of a dutiful choice we are using the word in the former of
these two senses. When we say, for example, that A made a
dutiful choice, we mean that he chose to do that thing which
it was his duty to do. But when we talk of a good choice we
may be thinking either of the choosing or of what is chosen.
Now so far our investigation has been concerned with duty, and
therefore with what is chosen, with the objective aspect of
choice. But we have seemed driven to the conclusion that we
cannot give a completely coherent account of this subject
without going beyond it, and taking into consideration moral
choices which are not dutiful but are good. It is not yet clear

whether this extension will or will not enable us to give a coherent account of dutiful choice; but at any rate we are to investigate the possibility. At the outset of that investigation, however, we find that the phrase "good choice" is ambiguous, and that there are therefore two lines along which the argument might develop, namely, in terms of good choosing or in terms of things chosen which are good. The truth is, however, that a little consideration reveals that the former of these two conceptions is of little assistance in the present connection. The reason is that it is only in a subsidiary and secondary fashion, as we shall see later, that the goodness of choosing A (apart from the goodness of A, if A is good) can be a reason or ground for the choice of A. Consequently, in the course of the argument which follows we shall use the phrase "a good choice" to denote the choice of something good, whether or not the choosing is also good, unless a contrary warning is explicitly given.

The suggestion is, then, that there are two different kinds of moral choice, a good choice and a dutiful choice; but with these two moral principles moral theory cannot remain content, for even if the introduction of the idea of a good choice helps to solve the problem occasioned by a conflict of duties, there is still the possibility of a conflict between the two moral principles themselves. Therefore, there inevitably arises for ethics the problem of resolving this sheer plurality of principle into a single coherent whole; for unless morality in general is self-consistent it ceases to be significant, and indeed ceases to be what we all mean by morality.

It can, of course, be argued that within moral philosophy there is no solution to this problem; but (a) this possibility does not save the moral philosopher from the necessity of seeking an ethical solution; and (b) even if no ethical solution is found it is still possible that there may be a solution beyond the limits of ethics. Thus we find Professor de Burgh stating at the very outset of his book *From Morality to Religion* that "moral experience presents a problem which philosophy is unable to solve, and which points to religion for its solution". "This problem," he continues, "is that of the dualism of ethical principles, according as conduct is motivated by the thought of obligation or by desire of a rational good."[1] It may be, then, that to our present problem there is no purely

[1] *From Morality to Religion*, p. 1.

ethical solution; but at any rate we cannot make that assumption, and we are compelled at least to look for a solution.

Now it will be remembered that in Bradley's ethical theory the roots of this problem were also present, for he clearly recognised two sections of moral living, one which comprised "my station and its duties" and the other consisting of ideal non-social morality. In addition to these, indeed, there was what Bradley called ideal social morality; but of this we need not here take account, for it simply combines certain of the salient characteristics of the other two. Like "my station and its duties" it is thoroughly social; like ideal non-social morality it is equally ideal. The problem therefore arises in its most acute form when we realise the possibility of a conflict between "my station and its duties" on the one hand and ideal non-social morality on the other. But so far as Bradley's explicit theory is concerned the matter did not appear as a problem, acute or otherwise. For one thing he held that such a conflict is no different in principle from one between different duties both or all of which fall within "my station and its duties", and is therefore a matter for moral art rather than ethical science. Moreover, for theory, the two principles were held together under the conception of self-realisation. We saw, however, when dealing with Bradley, that it is questionable whether the term "self-realisation" is used in the same sense when applied first to "my station and its duties" and then to ideal non-social morality. The conception of self-realisation changes as the transition is made, the idea of the self to be realised is different in the one case from that in the other, and the two are mutually incompatible. Moreover, as we also saw, the conflict between the two sections of morality is not a conflict between two apparent duties which can be resolved by an appeal to the common principle of duty, but is instead a conflict of principle.

Now such a conflict can be resolved only by an appeal to a more fundamental principle common to the principles which are, or may be, found in opposition. Where, however, is such a principle to be found? It may indeed be argued that the choice of what is dutiful and the choice of what is good have one thing in common, namely, moral goodness. This possibility we are in fact compelled to admit—both choices may be morally good. And it is this possibility that justifies Bradley in holding the two kinds of choice together under the idea of self-realisation, for both choices are expressions of the good will. The good will, as we saw, is the morally good will, and a distinction can be drawn only in degree, in degree of perfection and of universality; that is to say, the good will can be distinguished from the morally good will, only because although A's will and B's may be morally good, the good will is perfect, and, moreover, is identifiable neither with A's nor with B's but is such that the distinction between A and B does not enter into the matter. Such differences, however, do not support a radical distinction between the goodness of the good will and moral goodness.

Can then this moral goodness which is common to the choice of what is dutiful and the choice of what is good furnish a ground on which a conflict between these two moral principles of choice may be resolved? In the first place, it must be noticed that whatever answer is given to this question it can hardly be maintained that moral goodness is a more fundamental principle than either that of duty or that of goodness. An act may be morally good because it is dutiful, but not necessarily dutiful because it is morally good. Further, moral goodness is not other than goodness, but is rather one special form of goodness which attaches to moral agents and their actions. In the second place, however, it would be very difficult to maintain that, whereas moral goodness is the ground neither of the dutifulness of certain acts nor of the goodness of certain ends, it is none the less the ground upon which a conflict between these two principles is to be morally resolved. With such a solution moral theory cannot rest content, unless some good reason can be discovered why in such particular cases, in cases, that is to say, of *conflict* between the two moral principles, dutifulness of action and goodness of end, and in no other cases, the criterion should be moral goodness, the moral goodness of the prospective action. As it is, the suggestion that in such cases moral goodness should decide bears the character of an invocation of a *deus ex machina*. Moreover, if the decisive factor is to be found in goodness of any kind, there is in principle no reason why it should be found exclusively in moral goodness. No doubt in practice moral goodness might be on occasion decisive as supplementing one or other of two equally balanced non-moral goods, and so as rendering possible a choice between them; but the principle which covers such cases is, clearly, not moral goodness, but goodness in general. Thus when the suggestion that the decisive factor is to be found in moral goodness is examined, it is soon lost in the more general contention that the decisive ground is goodness.

Before we pass to a consideration of this more general contention, however, it will be well to examine quite a different possibility, the possibility that *no* conflict is possible between the two principles of moral choice, the obligatoriness of actions and the goodness of ends. Thus, it might be argued that while these two principles share the total field of human behaviour, none the less they neither overlap nor conflict one with another. In other words, conflict may be avoided by dividing the area to which the principles are applied. On this view, the whole field of human behaviour falls into two parts, one of which is judged either right or wrong and the other either good or bad. Such a theory, however, need not detain us long, for it can hardly be worked out consistently with the facts. In its most plausible form it would probably say that "good" and "bad" are relevant to decisions, such as the choice of a vocation, which involve taking the long view; whereas the voice of duty is decisive in matters of purely immediate concern. Yet the two principles cannot be held apart in this way. For one thing the difference between long-range and short-range choices is a matter only of degree, and there are many border-line cases which do not clearly belong to one class rather than the other. Moreover, questions of right and wrong enter even into long-range decisions (for example, in the case of a man whose wife has been suddenly rendered a permanent invalid). On the other hand, the difference between a good end and a bad end is not entirely irrelevant to any moral situation with which we may be faced. The two moral principles persistently refuse to be separated and imprisoned in different compartments of human conduct.

The possibility, however, that a conflict of moral principles is impossible may be worked out in a different direction altogether, in a direction suggested by a passage from Professor de Burgh, not by assigning the different principles to different sections of human conduct, but by attributing them to different people.[2] But against this suggestion similar objections hold. It cannot, of course, be maintained that the difference between one person and another is merely one of degree, but it is true that

[2] *From Morality to Religion*, pp. 69 ff.

K

the proposition that some people are habitually moved by the thought of duty while others respond to the thought of what is good, can be defended only *up to a point*. No doubt it contains a certain amount of truth, but the fact seems to be that although the thought of duty or the thought of what is good may be combined in very different proportions in different lives, yet both are present or potential in all human life. And indeed it was not Professor de Burgh's intention to deny this. "The two types of conduct that have been distinguished", he says,[3] ". . . viz., moral action, where *praxis* is for *praxis'* sake, and action for good, where *praxis* reaches its consummation in *theoria*—are rather abstract moments in practical experience than self-contained and isolable courses of action. A single act may indeed exhibit one motive to the exclusion of the other, nay, more, as we have seen, one or other may be predominant over a whole life; but in no man is either motive entirely absent. No philosopher will discount the importance of analysing the concrete into its component factors before rectifying the abstraction—which, after all, is a matter of degree—by showing how the factors co-operate in actual experience. When once the distinction has been grasped, it is easy to see how they come to be associated, and 'by just exchange' to effect a mutual enrichment."

It is not quite clear, however, what is to be understood by "abstract moments in practical experience" as opposed to "self-contained and isolable courses of action". Indeed, there seem to be two possible interpretations, for the abstract moment may be an aspect of something which has at the same time other aspects, or it may be literally a moment, a section of something larger, which is yet part and parcel of the bigger entity. Moreover, Professor de Burgh proceeds to give two instances, and one of these is compatible with the one interpretation and the other with the other interpretation. On the one hand, the pursuit of what is good, he says, may be upheld, when desire and enthusiasm flag, by the thought of duty; while, on the other hand, the doing of one's duty is morally good and the moral goodness may become an extra motive on later occasions, although there is here a moral danger of self-complacency, and "normally moral goodness comes by the way", is a by-product of the performance of ordinary duties. But whatever be the precise interpretation, the general point is clear, that the thought

[3] *From Morality to Religion*, pp. 92-3.

of duty and the desire of what is good may powerfully reinforce one another, and in practice either may be predominant. If, however, the two may thus reinforce each other, it is also the case that they may be found in opposition; and this de Burgh also recognises. In speaking of artistic activity he declares that "such activity may at a given time even be morally blame-worthy, however good the object of desire. It may be the artist's duty to forgo his art in order to help a friend or to fight in the service of his country". [4]

We return, therefore, to the problem raised by the possibility of a conflict between the two moral principles; and we have already considered the suggested solution that in such cases the criterion is to be found in moral goodness, and we have seen that this solution is quickly lost in the more general solution that the criterion is goodness.

It will be noticed, however, that this solution does not conform to the type the possibility of which we set out to investigate. We came to the consideration of this problem, it will be remembered, through the awareness of another problem somewhat similar to this one and upon which it was hoped that the present discussion might throw some light. In the original case the problem was one which arose through the possibility of a conflict between two duties; and in the course of considering this question we seemed driven to the conclusion that the conflict, when it occurred, must be real and not apparent; that is, that both duties were really duties; and therefore to the further conclusion that the choice between them could not be a dutiful choice, for although it must be the choice of what was in fact a duty it could not be the choice of a duty as such. None the less it was possible that the choice might be a moral choice, in that it might be a good choice though not a dutiful choice. We saw, however, that even if this solution could be worked out in a satisfactory manner, it could only be at the expense of confronting ourselves with another problem occasioned by the possibility of a conflict between the moral principle of dutiful choices and the moral principle of good choices. We turned, therefore, to a consideration, first of all, of this new problem; and its solution seemed to require the discovery of a third moral principle more fundamental than the other two which might be found in conflict. In this context we examined the principle of moral goodness as possibly supplying the required fundamental

[4] *From Morality to Religion*, p. 38.

principle, only to find that it was not, after all, a third principle at all. Moreover, no other principle appeared to take its place, and we were compelled instead to consider, in its different forms, the suggestion that in reality no conflict was possible between the moral principle of dutiful choices and the moral principle of good choices. We found, however, that no solution to our problem can be reached in this direction; and we are now forced to examine the contention that goodness is a more fundamental principle than that of duty. Now, as we have said, this solution does not conform to the type the possibility of which we have been investigating. We are still dealing, it must be remembered, with the problem occasioned by the possibility of a conflict between the principle of dutiful choices and the principle of good choices; and we are dealing with this problem as a preliminary step towards solving another, occasioned by a conflict of duties. Further, we have been trying to solve our preliminary problem by seeking either a more fundamental moral principle which would serve as a criterion in cases of conflict, or some proof that a conflict is not possible; and having failed in both directions we are now turning to consider the contention that where the principle of duty and the principle of goodness are found in conflict the latter is to be taken as more fundamental. And, on reflection, this contention does seem to contain at least one grain of truth, namely, that there is no third moral principle in addition to obligatoriness and goodness.

At the outset, however, we must endeavour to give this suggested theory a more definite meaning. What can be intended when it is said that the principle of goodness is more fundamental than that of duty, and that where the two are in conflict it is the latter which must yield? Now, strictly speaking, the suggestion, taken in the context in which it has appeared, means that the principle of duty in general is less binding than that of good, and that therefore where the sense of obligation and the desire for what is good are found in conflict it is the latter which ought to prevail. But, it must be asked, what is meant by the word "ought" in this statement of the case? Is the word used in an economic sense, as indicating the true path of self-interest? Clearly not. Rather, the ground taken is higher ground, indeed moral ground, and it is meant that morally we ought to adopt the one course rather than the other. In other words, the theory which has set out to debase the principle of duty ends by reinstating it as universally binding. Moreover, on reflection, it is seen that once we understand the terms we are employing such an issue is inevitable. In any situation act A may be good and its alternative, act B, may be better; the consequences of the one may be good and the consequences of the other bad; but no matter what allocations of goodness may obtain, and even if there is an overwhelming preponderance of good on one side rather than the other, it is still possible to ask, "But which act *ought* I to perform?" and the answer to that, it is felt, concludes the matter. Formally, at any rate, then, the principle of duty is binding and supreme in every conceivable moral situation.

The truth of this, however, is often disguised by the temptation towards a theory of rigourism or asceticism in ethical thinking. It is easy to suppose that since a dutiful act is more prominent, is more easily recognised when it is done in face of contrary inclination and without the support of desire, this negative aspect is essential to the idea of duty. Thus even Kant is found declaring that "to be beneficent when we can is a duty; and, besides this, there are many minds so sympathetically constituted that, without any other motive of vanity or self-interest, they find a pleasure in spreading joy around them, and can take delight in the satisfaction of others so far as it is their own work. But I maintain that in such a case an action of this kind, however proper, however amiable it may be, has nevertheless no true moral worth, but is on a level with other inclinations, e.g. the inclination to honour, which, if it is happily directed to that which is in fact of public utility and accordant with duty, and consequently honourable, deserves praise and encouragement, but not esteem. For the maxim lacks the moral import, namely, that such actions be done *from duty*, not from inclination".[5]

Moreover, de Burgh is driven to the recognition of the two moral principles, action from a sense of duty and action from desire of a rational good, as two quite different ethical principles, simply because consciously or unconsciously he has adopted a rigouristic conception of duty. In a personal note he tells us that "a life worth living has always presented itself to me as a task to be faced rather than as an ideal end to be desired and enjoyed".[6] On the other hand, he recognises that "there

[5] *Grundlegung*, Abbott's E. T., p. 14.
[6] *From Morality to Religion*, p. 71.

are many—perhaps the greater number—who, as I have found in personal intercourse, are chiefly moved to act by a vivid and growing consciousness of ideal good, akin to something in their own nature, which compels them to seek the good spontaneously, without thought . . . of moral obligation".[7] Now the guiding principle behind this distinction is the presence or absence of direct desire. The two types of action are distinguished because in one case inclination points directly in the direction of the "moral" action, whereas in the other case it does not.

Yet, surely, this is an error. As Muirhead points out, "the defect of the ascetic theory is not that it lays emphasis on the negative aspect of morality, but that it treats that aspect as the final one".[8] This rigouristic conception of duty is the notion of a self-defeating principle, for if essentially duty resists desire it still requires desire for its own defiant existence. Moreover, it is the case that in fact, although duty may often be in the face of contrary desire, it is not essentially so. The formula of duty is not that I ought to do act A provided that I have no desire to do it or even provided that I have a desire not to do it, but that I ought to do it whether I want to or not.

Once all this is recognised it proves the inadequacy of a rigouristic conception of duty; and that in turn means that the chief obstacle has been removed which prevents a recognition of the comprehensive character of the principle of duty. The principle of duty applies then to the whole field of moral conduct; and in every conceivable practical situation it is possible for the agent to ask, "What ought I to do?" Not only so, but, clearly, the answer to that question is, from a moral point of view, formally final. That is to say, the answer may be rejected on moral grounds, but only in respect of its content and not at all in regard to its form. If it is said to me that in a given situation I ought to do act A, I may, of course, rebel on moral grounds, but my rejection is necessarily of the form, "I ought *not* to do act A, as you suggest, but I *ought* to do act B". Thus, formally, the principle of duty is quite fundamental, and covers the whole extent of the moral life.

This conclusion seems straightforward enough and almost

[7] *From Morality to Religion*, p. 72.
[8] *Elements of Ethics*, p. 129, para. 58.

elementary; and yet, as we have seen in the case of Professor de Burgh, for example, it is not generally accepted, and the failure to recognise the comprehensive character of the principle of duty seems to be due to an unduly narrow and rigouristic interpretation of duty. In the instance of Professor de Burgh, it will be remembered, the scope of duty was limited by the recognition of another moral principle which he described in terms of desire for a rational good. The scope of duty, however, is sometimes limited by the recognition of another moral principle, which shares the moral field with the principle of duty, which therefore restricts the applicability of the latter, which may or may not be identifiable with what de Burgh has called desire for a rational good, but which is described rather by Lord Lindsay (cf. *The Two Moralities*) as grace, and by Professor T. E. Jessop (cf. *Law and Love*) as love. In the case of the latter this failure to recognise the comprehensive character of the principle of duty is also in part due to a narrowly rigouristic interpretation of duty. "The moral life", he says, "conceived as unswerving obedience to duty involves in practice a state of tension under which, with a large number of people, health and even sanity may crack." [9] Again he says that "the ethic of duty, rigidly followed—and the whole point of this ethic is that it must be rigidly followed—leaves too much of actual, inevitable, *and desirable* living outside of it". [10] And, finally, in contrast to those who profess to follow the voice of duty he speaks of minds "unspoiled by moral rigour". [11]

There is, however, another unduly narrow interpretation of duty (apart from the rigouristic interpretation) which obscures the comprehensiveness of the principle of duty. It is that which identifies the moral principle of duty with what passes for it in any given society at any given time, that is, the interpretation which identifies the principle of duty with the recognition of it, the formulation of it, and even the practice of it, current at any particular point in history. This, as we have already argued, is an error. It is the error of confusing the principle of duty with the principle of propriety; and, clearly, the current practice of duty may fall short of its current formulation, that in turn may fall short of its current recognition, and the recognition of the principle may fall short of the reality which

---

[9] *Law and Love*, p. 39. [10] *Ibid.*, pp. 40-1.
[11] *Ibid.*, p. 43.

is recognised. We have already argued that Lord Lindsay's careful argument in *The Two Moralities* is vitiated by this confusion; and Professor Jessop appears to make the same mistake in *Law and Love*. To give but one instance, he says that "the morality of duty, for all its strenuousness, is in one respect an easy way out of the problems which experience sets us. It throws nearly all the stress on will and very little on intelligence. . . . We listen to a memory masquerading as conscience instead of looking at the facts".[12] Unquestionably, this holds against, and condemns, much of our current practice, and much of our current profession as well; but, surely, it does not hold against the ideal. It is unfair to blame the ideal for the failings of idealists.

Thus the failure to recognise the comprehensive character of the principle of duty has its roots in some interpretation of that principle which, in one way or another, is unduly narrow. But there is one positive argument which seeks to confine the principle of duty to something less than the entire area of moral living, and it is to be found both in Lord Lindsay's book and in Professor Jessop's. Indeed, were it not for the existence of this argument, it would be manifestly unfair both to Lord Lindsay and to Professor Jessop to object to their confinement of duty to a part only of the moral life, for, beyond question, there is something which passes with perhaps a majority of moral agents as the morality of duty and indeed as the whole of morality, something which is variously denominated "the morality of my station and its duties" by Lord Lindsay, "the morality of duty" by Professor Jessop, and "the principle of propriety" in the earlier argument of these pages, and something, further, the limits of which require to be defined as Lord Lindsay and Professor Jessop have done. The discussion, therefore, might well be one about the use of words, were it not for the positive argument to which reference has already been made.

This argument is to the effect that there is a section of the moral life having characteristics which prevent its subsumption under the principle of duty; and the argument has two sides. At an earlier stage in our discussion we came to the conclusion that "duty", "right" and "ought" all stand for the same thing; and we are now to consider an argument which seems to show that there is a sphere of moral living which

[12] *Law and Love*, p. 41.

repudiates the idea of duty by showing that there is a sphere which repudiates the idea of ought and also by showing that the same sphere repudiates the idea of right. Certainly, in his description of the morality of grace, Lord Lindsay does not forgo completely the right to use the word "duty". He allows that "perhaps we can say . . . that we have a duty to respond to the highest demands that we can hear", and he also allows that "it is not absurd to say that it is our duty to forgive those who have wronged us".[13] But what is left of the idea of duty if the idea of ought and the idea of right are explicitly repelled? The qualifications may be taken to indicate an attenuated form; but without the substance of ought and right it is not even a shadow of its former self.

In the first place, then, it is held that the moral sphere of grace repudiates the idea of ought. "It is not", says Lord Lindsay plainly, "what is expected of you. It cannot be said to be owed to any other person. We do not claim that others should do acts of grace to us nor expect other persons to claim as a right that we should do acts of grace to them. Dr. Bosanquet described ordinary morality as 'the world of claims and counter-claims'. The kind of conduct which this morality asks for is outside that world."[14] Now this passage really contains two distinguishable propositions which are treated either as identical or as implying one another, but which, according to our view, belong to two different contexts of thought. These propositions are (i) that the gracious act is not *owed*, is not obligatory; and (ii) that no one has a *right* to the performance of the gracious act. In the case of the former, the ruling idea (that of "owed") belongs to the realm of duty; but in the case of the latter, the ruling idea does not so belong. The conception of a right is not a purely moral conception. Though based upon duty, it bears an essential reference to the current apprehension and practice of duty. It is not duties and rights that are reciprocal, but duties and what we have called *claims*; and claims just *are*, without being either made or recognised. Moreover, as we have seen, so far from a claim necessarily residing in a person aware of its existence, it need not reside in a person at all, but may reside in society in general, or, perhaps more precisely, in the social situation. Consequently,

[13] *The Two Moralities*, p. 43; cf. the subtitle of this book, " Our Duty to God and to Society".
[14] *Ibid.*, p. 43.

although there may be, indeed although there are, many moral acts to which no one has a right, it does not follow on that account that they fall outwith the sphere of duty. On the contrary, if, as seems to be the case, they are owed, are obligatory, if, in other words, the agent ought to perform them, they fall within the sphere of duty.

In the second place, however, it is held that the moral sphere of grace or love repudiates the idea of right, or at least transcends it. "In the morality of my station and its duties," says Lord Lindsay, "the duties are of the station and are therefore more or less fixed and plainly defined. The morality of challenge assumes that we shall do more than a duty demanded of us, but it does not give us a scale of how much more; does not say, 'there is one definite right according to one morality and the addition of a certain percentage will give you what is right according to the standard of the morality of challenge'. It is not as though in the one morality you drove off from the ladies' tee and in the other from the medal tee. When the disciple asked, 'How oft shall I forgive my brother—unto seven times?' and was answered, 'Unto seventy times seven', that answer did not mean that on the four hundred and ninety-first offence he need not forgive. It meant that there was no limit. If the objection be made: 'Yes, but that does imply that there is always one right thing to do—namely, to forgive'; the answer is that 'forgiveness' is not a simple uniform action: it is giving back love to enmity and there is no measure of the way you behave to people you love. . . . . There may be one *right* thing to do in any given situation, but the right thing may be bare of grace or may take on innumerable forms of beauty. The morality of grace implies creativeness and initiative and imagination. In the morality of grace there may be many alternative actions which are equally 'right'."[15] In speaking of the morality of love, Professor Jessop makes a somewhat similar point, "that it blurs the distinction of right and wrong, at times ignores it, and always dethrones it from the highest place".[16] Again, on the same subject he declares, "it is full of considerate lies and sweet deceits, of charming impetuosities and gracious whims and magnificent improprieties. . . . It has no conscious rules of procedure, no principles of equitable exchange, no constitution drawn up with pedantic precision to define obligations and safeguard

[15] *The Two Moralities*, pp. 46 ff.   [16] *Law and Love*, p. 57.

rights, to set forth just how much others should do for us and just how little we should do for others".[17] Finally, the issue of the argument is this, that "the morality of duty and the morality of love are disparate".[18]

Now all this offers a very valuable corrective to tendencies in popular moral thought and practice which seem almost inevitable; but even from the point of view of practice, as Professor Daniel Lamont has pointed out,[19] the doctrine is dangerous. Moreover, setting out, as these two books do, to give an account of specifically Christian ethics, they can none the less be attacked on specifically Christian grounds. Thus Professor Lamont resists the contention that the morality of love and the morality of duty are disparate, "when it is so plain in the teaching of Jesus that the morality of love *fulfils* the morality of duty".[20] In the present context, however, we are interested in this teaching, neither from the point of view of practice nor from that of a specifically Christian ethic; our concern is rather with the implications of the doctrine in the field of general ethical theory, for if truth is one the teaching does have such implications.[21] In particular, it is implied that there is a section of the moral life which repudiates the idea of right, and therefore, as we have argued, the idea of duty. But is there such a section of the moral life?

The argument is then that beyond a certain level of moral living there may in any situation be several gracious acts but none that is *the* right act. Yet if any act is right it seems clear that it is *the* right act in the given situation, and not simply *a* right act. The question is, however, whether there is any section of moral living where the conception of right is really in this way inapplicable. It may perhaps clarify the discussion of this matter if we notice two different points which seem true and either of which may be confused with the contention that there may be several gracious acts in any one situation. First of all, it seems true that in any situation there may be several acts each of which exceeds, to different extents, "the righteousness of scribes and pharisees", the current recognition and practice of moral principles. Thus, if conventional morality insists that I go one mile with a weary and uncertain traveller,

[17] *Law and Love*, p. 185.
[18] *Ibid.*, p. 184.
[19] Review of Jessop, *Law and Love*, in *Evangelical Quarterly*, April 1941, pp. 148–50.
[20] *Ibid.*, p. 149.
[21] Cf. Waterhouse, "Ethics and Christian Ethics", *Philosophy*, April 1943, pp. 50–9.

I may go one and a half, or one and three-quarters or even two miles, and all three acts exceed what is required by the principles of propriety. But if the characteristics which differentiate the three acts one from another and from the conventional act are morally significant, it seems certain that morality, that is, ideal as opposed to conventional morality, demands that which exceeds to the greatest extent. Consequently, although I may exceed what is expected of me by doing any one of several acts, I still fall short of ideal morality in all but one of these.

The second point which may be confused, not only with the contention that there may be several gracious acts in one situation, but also with the point just distinguished from that contention, is in reality rather different. Lord Lindsay, it will be remembered, resists the suggestion that in a given type of situation our duty is always to do one thing, namely, to forgive, and he resists this suggestion on the ground that forgiveness is not one single uniform action. We may forgive in all sorts of different ways. On the other hand, it may be held, in all these cases what we ought to do is to forgive. No doubt we may do it in many different ways, but this variety does not affect the essential self-identity of the act of forgiving, just as we may return a book we have borrowed in several different ways and by several different routes, but what, in spite of the variety, we do, and what we ought to do is to return the borrowed book. More technically, and in harmony with our conclusions regarding the nature of action, there may in any act be intermediate states of affairs which are morally indifferent, and even in the morally significant states of affairs there may be aspects which are not morally significant, or whose only moral significance is derived from the really significant aspects and states of affairs. Further, since those aspects and states of affairs are morally indifferent, they may, within limits imposed by the situation, be replaced by others without altering the essential character of the act; and there is no reason why this should hold only of acts such as the returning of a borrowed book and not of acts such as the forgiving of an injury received. Indeed, they are both acts in the same sense, and our earlier account of the nature of action applies to the one as much as to the other. The difference between the two "kinds" of act seems to be that in the one case the significant state of affairs is more purely spiritual than in the other; but this is a difference of degree. There seems to be no essential difference between the two "kinds" of act; although, without laying too much stress on the point, we might hazard the opinion that (a) where the significant state of affairs is more purely spiritual there is a wider variety of intermediate states from which to choose, and (b), in spite of this, these intermediate stages in becoming actual acquire more freely, by the manner of their enactment, the moral significance of the act, they reflect more clearly the nature of the willed succession which is the act. Thus, I may forgive my neighbour so diversely that I may either give him a verbal message or invite him to a meal in my house; but if I really mean what I am about, the intermediate stages as they are enacted, which by themselves are completely devoid of moral significance, readily acquire some share of the graciousness of the act proper. The point, however, is this, that the act of forgiving, for example, is just as uniformly a single action as is the act of returning a borrowed book, and that to emphasise the graciousness of states of affairs which are both intermediate and actual is not only to stress what is merely incidental, but is indeed to stress what is not even part of the act (though related to it). [22] Further, if an act of forgiving, in one shape or another, is demanded by a situation, then in that situation that act, the essential act, is the right act. This does not mean, of course, that it presupposes a deliberate raising of the question of duty; often, on the contrary, the act is done instantly under the influence of a quickened insight which may not be able to give a detailed account of itself. Yet it is surely the case that, looking back, the agent must judge or must be able to judge, either that he did or that he failed to do, what he ought to have done, and that that verdict is the final one from a moral point of view.

[22] If in a footnote one may deal with this matter on specifically Christian grounds, it may be said that the general impression left by the life and deeds of Christ is not an impression of " considerate lies and sweet deceits, of charming impetuosities and gracious whims and magnificent improprieties". These, or some of them, may be there; but the essential impression is of One who went infallibly to the heart of any practical situation and met unfailingly its essential demands (cf. Luke, v, 18–20). In his review of Professor Jessop's book, Professor Lamont says, " The blurring of the marches between good and evil arises from an even more serious blurring. Professor Jessop blurs the marches between God and man. His theme is ethical, but his doctrinal position reveals itself occasionally as in the following words: ' When Jesus said that God is love He implied that God is perfectly human, and when He beckoned us to the life of love He meant that we can become imperfectly divine ' (p. 56). The best thing to do with such a statement is simply to deny it." This, of course, is outside our present province, but it is all of a piece with a more distinctively ethical point, namely, that the doctrine we have been considering seems guided by a false analogy with creativeness. Perhaps creativeness is involved, but moral action is essentially a reaction, a response.

If, then, the argument is to be trusted, and if the contrary arguments have been satisfactorily explained, it follows, not only that the principle of duty is formally final, but also that it covers the whole extent of the moral life, and that consequently our problem of a conflict between the principle of dutiful choices and the principle of good choices is found to be identical with our earlier problem of a conflict of duties.

CHAPTER XIII

THE GOOD AND THE CONTENT
OF DUTY

IN OUR LAST chapter the argument completed, as it were, a full circle, for the avenue we set out to explore, so far from offering us a way out of our difficulties, led us back to the point from which we started. At its outset we were concerned with the problem occasioned by a conflict of duties, and we were anxious to discover whether or not the choice between such conflicting duties might be moral, for example good, without being dutiful. We found, however, not only that, if a moral choice is possible between conflicting duties, if, that is to say, morality is self-consistent, it must be possible to make a dutiful choice in such circumstances, but also that the problem raised by a conflict between the sense of obligation and the desire of a rational good is simply a special case of the same problem.

Bradley was, then, right in his contention that the question raised by a conflict between "my station and its duties" on the one hand and ideal non-social morality, for example, on the other is in principle no different from that raised by a conflict of duties falling within "my station and its duties". Bradley also held, however, that such questions were a matter, not for moral science, but for moral art. Now if by that he meant that where two duties seem to collide only the ordinary moral consciousness can decide between them, then, no doubt, he was perfectly right. But that does not mean that such cases are not of the first interest and importance to ethical science, for the presumption of ethics is that in so deciding the ordinary moral consciousness is guided, whether intuitively or otherwise, by some principle; and consequently, under the continuing assumption that the moral judgment represents a rational and potentially self-consistent activity, ethical science is incomplete so long as it recognises a sheer plurality of moral principles. And that is precisely the position at which Bradley left off. For if, formally, the principle of duty prevails over the whole field of moral conduct, yet, materially, that is, from the point of view of duty's content, there is involved a plurality of moral principles, since "my station and its duties" is essentially social whereas, so far as we have yet seen, what Bradley calls ideal morality need not be so.

Moreover, so far as our own account of the latter is concerned, the same difficulty is present even within the area covered by Bradley's description "my station and its duties", for so far we have been unable to discover a single criterion underlying the various principles which lay it down that it is right to keep promises, right to tell the truth, right to promote a determinate good, and so on; and, as we have said, moral theory cannot rest content with this sheer plurality of principles. At a certain level of reflection such a statement of the case may of course be satisfactory enough; but when it is seen that in a given situation any two of the principles mentioned may be in conflict, and that, for example, it may on occasion be wrong to tell the truth or promote a determinate good, there is a clear necessity to carry the discussion a stage further and to discover *why* it is that a certain kind of act which is normally right may yet at times be wrong.

The obvious answer is that the different kinds of normally right acts have some characteristic in common, which, however, they share in different degrees, and which, indeed, may be possessed by the same kind of act to a different extent at different times. In theory this common characteristic may either be rightness itself or some other characteristic different from rightness. We have already seen, however, that, contrary to the supposition of the new intuitionists, it cannot be rightness, for rightness does not differ in degree and there is no sense at all in saying that one act is *more right* than another. It is true that to do them justice the new intuitionists do not say precisely what we have just alleged. They speak, not of rightness as differing in degree, but of *prima facie* rightness as subject to such variations; but we have already attempted without success to discover this character which is to be called, not rightness, but *prima facie* rightness, and which is sufficiently like rightness to share its name but is unlike it in this respect that it is subject to variations in degree.

The other possibility is that the common characteristic is to be found in something other than rightness, and the most common suggestion is that it is to be found in goodness or in some relation to goodness. Now this type of theory may take one or other of two forms. Clearly, it subordinates, from a material as opposed to a formal point of view, rightness to goodness, and regards the latter as in some sense the more fundamental notion of the two; but, it is to be noticed, the word "fundamental" is ambiguous and may mean one or other of two quite different things. When it is suggested that goodness is more fundamental than rightness it may be meant either that the very concept of rightness is derivative from that of goodness, or that although that is not the case none the less nothing is right for the moral consciousness unless it is, or bears a certain relation to, something which is good. In the former case, goodness is *logically* fundamental, while in the latter it is fundamental only *for the moral consciousness*. In the former case the connection is a logical one, while in the latter it is a moral one. On the one hand, rightness is said to be *derivative* from goodness, whereas, on the other, it is held to be *dependent* upon goodness. In other words, in the one case the matter is made to rest upon a logical proof, while in the other it rests upon a moral intuition. There are, then, two different meanings which can be attached to the present suggestion; and in fact it has been advanced in the history of ethical thought, now in one of these forms, now in the other.

In the first place, then, there is the more radical assertion of the more fundamental character of goodness, which holds, not just that for the moral consciousness nothing is right unless it is, or bears a relation to, something which is good, but that rightness itself is derived from the idea of goodness. This is the theory which rests its case upon a logical proof; and in principle it may take one or other of two forms according as the logical proof starts from the idea of right or from the idea of good. In the former case, the central point has been that "right" *means* "productive of a good result"; but this possibility need not here detain us since we have already seen that, whatever "right" may mean and whatever it is that makes acts right, "right" itself does *not* mean "productive of a good result".

From the other side, the principal argument is that to say that A is good logically implies that A ought to be,[1] and by this

---

[1] " In our view the idea of ' good ' or ' value ' is logically the primary conception, though psychologically the idea of ' right ' may often in modern men be more explicitly developed. That action is right which tends to bring about the good. There is no attempt here to get rid of the ultimate unanalysable ' ought '. The good is that which ' ought ' to be." (Rashdall, *Theory of Good and Evil*, 2nd ed., vol. i, p. 135).

L

third term, "ought-to-be-ness" or *seinsollen*, the transition is made to rightness, that is, to "ought-to-do-ness" or *thunsollen*. To this, however, as the new intuitionists have argued, there is one effective reply, namely, that so far from the idea of *thunsollen* being derived from the idea of goodness through the idea of *seinsollen* as a third term, the idea of *seinsollen* really represents an abstraction from the idea of *thunsollen*. In other words, the phrase "ought to be" has no meaning apart from the idea of "ought-to-do". When it is said that A ought to be it is meant that someone ought to bring A into existence. Where this hidden reference to a possible agent is completely absent the phrase "ought to be" is without meaning, unless indeed it represents, as it sometimes does, an inaccurate and misleading way of saying that something is good. This is seen more clearly when it is recognised that obligatoriness is not a quality of any thing, but is rather a relation between at least two things and indeed a relation between an act on the one side and an agent on the other. Moreover, it is to be noticed that even if it is allowed that in saying that A is good we are implying that A ought to be, this implication and the theory which upholds it do not make the transition to *thunsollen* as easy as is sometimes supposed. Indeed, the theory proves either too much or too little to succeed. According to this theory, as it is found in Nicolai Hartmann's *Ethik*, [2] if A is good then A ought to be, and if there is some human being who can realise A then the *seinsollen* is transformed into the *thunsollen*. But the trouble here is that this account of the matter simply fails to meet the difficulty with which we have been so much concerned, for although normally it may be my duty to promote a determinate good, it may on occasion be my duty not to do so. Yet, on the present theory, the "ought-to-do" follows with logical necessity; and the result may be that in any given situation I ought to perform each of several alternative courses of action. Thus the theory proves far too much. But if the *thunsollen* fails to follow in the case of one or more of these actions, why should it follow in the case of any other action? The theory now proves too little.

The matter may be put otherwise. If the proposition that A is good implies that A ought to be, then, presumably, the proposition that B is better than A implies that to a higher degree B ought to be. So much for the transition from good to *seinsollen*. But what happens in the transition from *seinsollen* to *thunsollen*?

---

[2] *Ethik*, Coit's E. T., vol. i, pp. 256-62.

Clearly, one or other of two things. Given the presence of an agent who can by different acts in the same situation realise both A and B, either it follows by logical necessity that the agent ought to produce A and to a greater extent ought to produce B, or else the *thunsollen* follows in neither case by logical necessity and the conclusion that the agent ought to produce, say, B is a matter not of logical proof but of moral intuition. The former alternative is the very mistake we have already refused to accept from the hands of the new intuitionists, and the latter is for the most part identifiable with the less radical theory that we must now turn to consider.

According to the less violent assertion of the connection between rightness and goodness, the ordinary moral consciousness recognises an obligation in any situation to perform that act which is, or is related to, the "best possible" in that situation. This statement of the position is, of course, designedly general, in order that it may comprehend all possible variations falling under the one principle; and indeed it errs in not being sufficiently general, for the phrase "best possible" may require more or less drastic modification. It is simply used in the present context to cover two things, that the theory asserts a connection between rightness and goodness and that the theory cannot rest content with that if it is to offer a solution to the problem occasioned by a conflict of apparent duties.

Now we have already dealt with moral theories which belong to this general type. Thus, we have considered sentimentalism, which holds essentially that that act is right which is morally best; and we have seen that whereas this means that that act is right which has the morally best motive, there is considerable difficulty in giving meaning to the phrase "morally good" whenever it assumes a comparative or superlative form, and that in any case in judging an act right we attend to its intentional aspect and not to its motive-aspect. Again, we have considered utilitarianism, which holds in its most defensible form that that act is right which is productive of the best possible consequences in the given situation; and for a variety of reasons we were compelled to reject this theory as a final account of morality. Indeed, we discovered, not only that it failed to give an accurate definition of the criterion of rightness in acts, but even that the view it presupposed of the acts which are right was itself inadequate. Finally, we have reviewed the ethics of idealism and have found that in the last resort idealism accepts the fundamental doctrine of sentimentalism that it is the will itself that is good. Thus, for one reason or another, we have rejected the main forms taken by this general type of ethical theory which we are considering. None the less we cannot lightly reject this general approach, and that for two reasons. In the first place, it does profess to report the verdict of the ordinary moral consciousness, which is of course the last court of appeal in ethics, and there does appear to be an almost ineradicable conviction that rightness and goodness *are* connected, a conviction, therefore, which must either be accepted or explained away. In the second place, it appears to offer the one hope of a rational and self-consistent account of morality, for the alternatives are disappointing. Rightness itself is out of the question, for it does not vary in degree; *prima facie* rightness, which does so vary, is a mere will-o'-the-wisp; and there is no non-moral quality which has anything like the claim of either rightness or goodness (except, perhaps, self-realisation, which, however, is unable, as we have seen, to bear the weight it is asked to carry). But the difficulty is to discover a theory which is more defensible than those we have already rejected, but which, like them, asserts a fundamental connection for the ordinary moral consciousness between rightness on the one hand and goodness on the other.

At the outset, it can be taken as a fact that it is acts that are right; but the matter is not so simple in the case of goodness. The theories we have already rejected were not unanimous on this point, for one found the relevant goodness in results, and the other two in motives or the will. Now in principle there are three things to which the relevant goodness might belong, the motive, the act, and the consequences. The third possibility must be put aside because it involves a view of acts as events in a causal sequence, which is not the view presupposed by certain findings of the moral consciousness. The suggestion that the relevant goodness is to be found in the motives of acts, although it is free from this radical criticism to which utilitarianism is vulnerable, is none the less untenable for other reasons. We are left, then, with the possibility that the goodness with which rightness is connected is the goodness of acts; and yet it is commonly held that the goodness of acts *is* the goodness of their motives and that acts can be good in no other way. If this is true it implies that there is no direction in which a connection between rightness and goodness may be made out. It would seem, therefore, that if the connection between rightness and goodness is to be maintained, the rightness of acts must be connected with some goodness of acts other than the moral goodness of their motives; and, consequently, our problem is to discover in what way acts may be good quite apart from the fact that they may be done from motives which are morally good.

Now this appears to be precisely one of the main problems which H. W. B. Joseph set himself in his book *Some Problems in Ethics*, which appeared about the same time as Sir David Ross's *The Right and the Good*. Thus, according to Joseph, "we do often mean by calling an act right, that we ought to do it; and if we mean this, its rightness cannot be the *ground* of our obligation; it *is* our obligation. But do we not also use the word to mean some character in the act, because of which we ought to do it? If, as I think, we do, this character must be a sort of goodness. The difficulty here is to show what common form of goodness belongs to all right acts. For moral acts, we could state what this is, viz. that they are done from a sense of duty; but this cannot be the rightness in virtue of which it is our duty to do the acts." [3] And, of course, if morality is rational, there must be some ground of rightness in actions, whether or not we use the word "rightness" (in another sense) to denote this ground. "It is perfectly correct to say, with Professor Prichard, that there is something in the nature of every right action on account of which we ought, or think we ought, to do it; for if not—if it were merely for its being an action, and not an action of some definite sort rather than another—it would be our duty to do anything that was an action, and life should be unbroken restlessness." [4] Moreover, as we have seen more than once, unless it is a single ground common to all right actions, or unless the different possible grounds are themselves related to some single principle (other than obligatoriness, *prima facie* or actual), we have on our hands the problem of a conflict of duties and are bereft of the means to solve it. With this too it seems that Joseph would have been in agreement. In one passage he refers to the problem "Whether in the actions which we ought, or think we ought, to do there is any common character for the sake of which we ought, or think we ought, to do them ", [5] and then, having given instances of philosophers who have

---

[3] *Some Problems in Ethics*, p. 59.   [4] *Ibid.*, p. 81.
[5] *Ibid.*, p. 67, cf. p. 102.

answered this question in an affirmative fashion, he says that "if they are all wrong, and there is no such character, our obligations will be an unconnected heap. . . . That conclusion", he adds, "is disconcerting to philosophy, which attempts to bring a diversity of facts under some unity of principle. And we might be tempted to say that if there is no one reason for the one fact about all these various actions, that we ought to do them, there is no reason. And then the conviction that we ought to do them might be in danger of seeming irrational." Such is Joseph's statement of the case, and it is in harmony with our own earlier findings—except in so far as Joseph tends to recognise an initial presumption in philosophy in favour of a unity of principle.

Later on we find the problem restated with admirable clarity. "Where actions have an instrumental goodness," says Joseph, "one need not look beyond their results and them. The instrumental view fails when the acting to secure something is judged good or better, but what is to be secured is not. So in the case where I debate whether to retain or give to another that, the possession of which by either seems to me equally good, say the means for a much-needed holiday, if I think I ought to give it to another, that must be because my giving it him and not just his having the holiday has a goodness absent from my taking a holiday; the having the holiday by either is equally good. And the difficulty is to see why I should judge my giving it to him better than my taking it for myself, when I judge my having it as good as his having it. *Ex hypothesi*, I am asking which I ought to do, and shall act upon that judgment, so that, whichever I do, I shall have been moved by the thought of the rightness of, i.e. a certain goodness in, the action. Where is this to be found in giving him the holiday more than in taking it? We must not confuse the question with the question whether, looking back, afterwards, I should rather approve myself for having, from a sense of obligation, or it might be from affection, let another enjoy a holiday to my loss, than for having taken it to his loss because I desired it. In that judgment the alternatives compared include differing motives supposed to have determined the alternative courses. But in the judgment which I have to make before action, when I ask which course is right, which do I owe to do, it is assumed that the same motive will have determined me in the adoption of either course; and the determining difference must be a goodness in one course that is not in the other, and which I call its rightness. It is this which is sometimes so difficult to find, even where I judge that I owe to take the one course, and not the other. It would seem then as if there are some actions which we think we owe to do, or the thought of which obliges us, but in which we apprehend no goodness to make them right, so long as we look only to them; nor can we find it by looking to their effects." [6]

Before, however, we attempt to follow Joseph in his solution to this problem which he has posed, we must notice one aspect of his complete ethical theory which, whatever be the solution which he adopts, is out of harmony with conclusions at which we have already arrived. For, it is clear from the last quotation, that in his final theory there is a place for utilitarianism, the doctrine, namely, that an act may be right because it is instrumentally good, and that whatever connection may be found between rightness and a form of goodness other than the goodness of motives or results must appear supplementary, and not alternative to the element of utilitarianism. In the passage already quoted, Joseph speaks as if the former theory accounts for those duties which, unlike other duties, are not adequately covered by the latter. But, it would appear, there are duties which the latter theory does adequately cover. Indeed, Joseph gives us in plain terms a statement which is clearly utilitarian in its outlook. "That it may be a man's duty," he says, "to bring into being, when he has the power to do so, what does not now exist, but would be recognized, if it did exist, to be good, few would be prepared to dispute. But we may well doubt whether, whenever we judge that we ought to do an action, we think that we shall thereby bring into being some good which is not the goodness of our acting, but one for the sake of which we act." [7] And he adds that there are two main kinds of example which "inspire this doubt". Thus Joseph's final and complete account of the matter really contains two theories side by side. Moreover, we do not object to this that these two theories are entirely disparate, for, on the contrary, they can be held together by a general formula asserting a connection between rightness and goodness. On Joseph's view this connection appears in two different ways. In the first place, it is present where the right act produces something good which would have been equally good if it had come about "without man's agency"; [8] while, in the

[6] *Some Problems in Ethics*, pp. 96–7.   [7] *Ibid.*, p. 92.
[8] *Ibid.*, p. 92.

second place, the rightness is connected with the goodness of the actual bringing about by human agency, that is, with the goodness of the acting. In both cases there is a connection between rightness and goodness; and the difference arises only with regard to those things wherein the relevant goodness inheres, in the one case in results, and in the other in the acting itself.

Now if the conclusions to which we have already come are to be upheld, this utilitarianism must be rejected. In the first place, it fails to do justice to what we have called the intrusive character of morality. Secondly, it presupposes what we have thought to be a false view of acts, that is, of the bearers of the predicates "right" and "wrong"; and consequently it is possible that not only do Joseph's two theories find goodness in different places but they also find rightness in different places. Thirdly, utilitarianism conflicts with the ordinary moral consciousness, for that consciousness does not believe that the rightness of an act can ever depend upon what the act actually happens to produce. An act is not made right or wrong in a moral sense by its subsequent results whether they be good, bad or indifferent. This fact is hidden in Joseph's statement of the case by the phrase "when he has the power to do so", for, as Prichard has pointed out, we never can tell that this condition is fulfilled.

At this stage, however, we need not embark upon a detailed critical examination of utilitarianism. We have already found it, even in its best form, fundamentally inadequate; and, in the present connection, we need only bear in mind that Joseph's theory does have a utilitarian side, while we proceed to examine its non-utilitarian aspect.

How then can acts be good apart from the moral goodness of their motives and the goodness of their results? To this question Joseph has a quite definite answer. He realises that the goodness which is the ground of rightness cannot be, or (he might rather say) need not be, the moral goodness of the action itself. He sees, therefore, the necessity of viewing the action in a context of one sort or another. But, he insists, this "context is not composed of the effects, nearer or more remote, of the particular right action; else we should be simply reverting to the instrumental view of rightness, which has broken down. We must look beyond the particular action not to its effects but to the rule of action of which it is a manifestation. This, however, is not enough. We must look to the whole form of life in some community, to

which all the actions manifesting this rule would belong, and
ask whether it, or some other form of life, is better, which would
be lived by the community instead, if this rule were not helping
to determine it. If we judge that it is better, then the particular
action is right, for the sake of the better system to which it
belongs ". [9] Thus if act A belongs to a certain form of life, X, and
act B belongs to another form of life, Y, and if X is better than
Y, then we ought morally to choose act A along "with the form
of life to which it belongs, and do it not so much for its own sake
as for the sake of a goodness in that form of life which the rule
requiring this action would determine, if this rule had expression
in the lives of others also who make up the community that
lives this form of life ". [10] In this way the rightness of an act is
grounded upon goodness, not the moral goodness of the action
itself, not always the goodness of its effects, but often the goodness of that form of life to which, being this kind of act rather
than another, the act belongs.

Before we consider this position critically it will be well to
inquire what precise answer it allows to the question how on this
new principle an apparent conflict of duties is met. In theory
there are two ways in which, on Joseph's principles, a solution
may be offered. In the first place, it may be held that where
there is an apparent conflict of duties that act is really a duty
which belongs to a form of life better than that to which the
other act belongs; and there is evidence in Joseph's frequent use
of the comparative of "good" that sometimes he looks upon the
matter in this light. There is, however, a second way in which it
is possible to deal with this question; and there are passages in
which Joseph appears to adopt it. It is that where there is an
apparent conflict of duties, that is, where there is a real conflict
between two different rules of duty, that rule holds good which
in the given circumstances most completely expresses the
essential principle of the form of life to which both rules belong.
"The various rules which men invoke," says Joseph, "to justify
different actions, such as the rules of the Decalogue, are not an
aggregate any more than the goodness of a life animated by
them is an aggregate. How, if they were, and stood co-ordinate,
each obliging unconditionally, should we act in a situation to
which two or more applied conflictingly? Hence, as the problem
of a particular action drives us to compare the life which would
be lived through the working of its rule therein with the life

animated by another, so the problem of a rule drives us on to consider the life that would be lived, if a more comprehensive form than this rule yields were at work therein, realizing itself sometimes through actions covered by the rule, and sometimes not. It would be the consciousness, however inadequately realized, of this all-embracing form of life, rather than of some single rule, that must really lie at the base of our unmediated judgments about the rightness of particular acts."[11] In the one case, it will be seen, the required characteristic which varies in degree and yields a solution in cases of conflict is the goodness of different forms of life, while, in the other, it is the adequacy of different rules in expressing the essential principle of the one form of life which is good. Moreover, both appear to have some place in Joseph's ethical thinking, and it is not clear which, if either, he would finally adopt.

Such, then, is the theory we are to consider as a solution to the ethical problem of rightness or obligatoriness; and although in some respects it seems to meet the needs of the situation, we shall find that other aspects require amendment.

(1) For one thing, as we have seen, that part of Joseph's theory, which is utilitarian in its outlook, must be rejected. It would be tedious to repeat a critical discussion of utilitarianism at this stage, but it is clear that in this respect the theory cannot be accepted without a drastic revision of conclusions already reached.

(2) In the second place, it is doubtful whether the theory can deal with an apparent conflict between two duties which are covered, the one by the utilitarian side of the theory, the other by its non-utilitarian side. Let us suppose, for example, that in a given situation act A is so far morally justified by the fact that its immediate effects are good, while act B is similarly justified to some extent by the fact that the form of life to which it belongs is good. That being so, the question is whether acts A and B are comparable in respect of the goodness of the two very different things to which respectively they are related, namely, an entire form of life on the one hand and an immediate, limited and determinate result on the other. It seems clear that they are not comparable in this way. For, it is to be noticed, the suggested comparison is not between the goodnesses of two different results of two different actions. If it were, a comparison *might* be possible, for it can be asked

[11] *Some Problems in Ethics*, pp. 102-3.

with some show of reason, Ought I to produce this effect or that effect? and whichever I elect to produce I shall at any rate be producing *some* effect. But Joseph is quite clear that "a form of life is not related to the rules or principles of action that work in it as a consequence to its cause".[12] The importance of this point is that it *might* be held that form of life, X, is better than determinate effect, Y, and then, *if* both were effects of their respective actions, it might be said with some show of reason that it was therefore the agent's duty to perform act A which would have X as its result rather than act B which would have Y. But the show of reason depends very largely upon the assumption that both X and Y are effects. As we have seen, however, this assumption is false so far as X is concerned. When we take account of the form of life to which an act belongs we are *not* regarding the act as an event or series of events in a causal sequence, whereas when we think of its effects we are. Thus it is impossible to make the comparison required by Joseph's theory. We might come nearer to making the comparison if we were to think of act A as the *part*-cause of form of life, X (although, it is to be noticed, this is not what is meant by the relation between an act and the form of life to which it belongs), but even here a comparison is still impossible between acts A and B. For any comparison would require to take account, not of one criterion, but of two, namely, the goodnesses of the respective effects, on the one hand, and, on the other hand, the extents to which the acts in question approximate to being the total causes required by the existing situation to realise their corresponding effects. This, of course, is the old difficulty with which John Stuart Mill's hedonistic calculus was beset. It may be that P is better than Q, and it may also be that Q is bigger than P, but it is impossible to make a single choice between P and Q on the basis of bigness and goodness taken together, unless we can say that a certain degree of bigness has the same weight as a given degree of goodness. And it is necessary only to pose that problem in order to see that it is insoluble.[13]

(3) So far our critical examination of Joseph's theory has been concerned either with its utilitarian side taken by itself or with the utilitarian and non-utilitarian sides taken as standing

---

[12] *Some Problems in Ethics*, p. 98.
[13] Gallie likewise objects to the duality in Joseph's system; cf. " Oxford Moralists ", *Philosophy*, July 1932, p. 285.

together within a single theory. It now remains to examine the non-utilitarian side considered by itself. Now this theory has much indeed to commend it. It is in harmony with what seems the inalienable conviction of the moral consciousness that there is a connection between rightness and goodness. It also provides a single criterion of rightness, however difficult it may be to apply, and the difficulty in application is hardly an objection to the theory, for, in practice, to know what is right and dutiful is not always easy. Further, the theory makes allowance for the intrusive character of morality's claim, since there will be many choices to which the ideal form of life is irrelevant. The last point, but not the least, is that justice is done to that view of acts which we found to be presupposed by certain of our ordinary moral insights. But it is to be noted that the second and fourth and, perhaps, the third of these benefits accrue only if the theory is deprived of its utilitarian partner and is compelled to stand by itself. Even so, however, and in spite of these very considerable merits, the theory requires some clarification, especially in respect of the precise formal character of the criterion, that is, of the ideal form of life.

This matter may be considered along two different lines of thought.

(a) At one stage in his argument Joseph refers to Moore's principle regarding the goodness of organic wholes. This is the principle that the value of such a whole need not be equal to, but may be more or less than, the sum of the values of its parts taken in isolation one from another. Now Joseph takes Moore to task on the score of this principle, but his objection is not to the assertion that the value of the whole is not a mathematical function of the values of the isolated parts. His objection is rather to the implication that the isolated parts have values in their isolation. "Though I think Professor Moore is right in his account of the principle of 'organic wholes' when he says that the value of the whole 'need not be the same as the sum of the values of its parts', he appears to hold, and if so, I would urge, mistakenly, that the parts may have some value as mere parts."[14] It follows then that if the parts are themselves wholes of parts the principle holds good without qualification of such complex wholes, although not without qualification of their complex parts.[15]

[14] *Some Problems in Ethics*, p. 84.
[15] The principle of organic wholes rules out theories such as Gallie's, according to which that the goodness of which renders an act right is a limited whole like

If, however, the principle of organic wholes is sound, and it does seem to be sound, there is an implication which is fatal to ideal utilitarianism, and which requires of Joseph's idealism a more precise formulation. For, since every whole is itself a part of a larger whole until we come to think of the final all-embracing whole, it follows that nothing is unconditionally good except the absolutely all-inclusive whole which is not itself the part of a larger whole. And, as we have said, this truth carries with it important consequences both for ideal utilitarianism and for Joseph's idealism.

It will be remembered that the former theory proceeds on the assumption that the more distant consequences of acts will not upset the moral estimate of them which is based upon their nearer and predictable results. It now appears that another assumption is required, namely, that the entire system of events contemporaneous with the relevant results will not upset the estimate based solely upon these results. Moreover, this is a much more questionable assumption, and less can be said in its defence. Indeed, so far as the principles of utilitarianism are relevant to the point they work against it through the incidence of the principle of organic wholes. It would therefore be more accurate to say, not that this assumption is required by utilitarianism, but that utilitarianism makes the error of abstraction. And abstraction can be a moral error.[16] In this respect utilitarianism is a doctrine of moral opportunism.

The consequence for Joseph's ethical theory is not so serious. It is that it must constantly be borne in mind that the form of life which morally justifies, or fails to justify, an act is an all-embracing and completely comprehensive form of life. And of this Joseph is aware, for he refers with apparent approval to "the thought at the bottom of Plato's doctrine, that even justice is not known to be good until it is seen as an element required for the good of the one all-including real".[17] "It would be the consciousness," he later declares, "however inadequately realized, of this all-embracing form of life, rather

---

that which consists of the fulfilment of a promise in relation to the expectation that it would be fulfilled (cf. "Oxford Moralists", *Philosophy*, July 1932, pp. 284–5). Certainly, such theories do justice to the fact that when we think it our duty to break a promise we think that a good is being sacrificed; but the position towards which we are arguing also does justice to this fact, provided that it is realised that what is sacrificed is a conditional "good".

[16] To act as "if you were the only girl in the world and I were the only boy" is almost of necessity to act wrongly in one way or another.

[17] *Some Problems in Ethics*, p. 87.

than of some single rule, that must really lie at the base of our unmediated judgments about the rightness of particular acts."[18] It is not enough to say that certain acts are right because they belong to a form of life which is good but narrow in its scope, and that on occasion such duties may have to yield to others which are duties because they belong to a form of life which is also good but more comprehensive. Thus it is not enough to say that certain acts are right because they belong to a form of family-life which is good, but that these may have to give way before other acts which are right because they belong to a form of national life which is also good. To express the matter in that way is to recreate the old difficulty, rather the impossibility, of applying two different criteria at one and the same time, in this case the criteria of goodness and comprehensiveness. We must rather say that both kinds of duty, more generally, that all kinds of duty, are demanded by an all-embracing form of life which is good.

In our entire discussion we have been concerned with the problem of goodness, not for its own sake, but only so far as it impinged upon the problem of rightness; and therefore we may be allowed to assume what is perhaps generally admitted, that for anything to be good it must involve consciousness, some form of spiritual activity or life. That being so, the present point is that the only things that are unconditionally good in a full ethical sense are all-inclusive forms of life.[19] Certainly, we do often judge that less comprehensive wholes are good, but in doing so we mean, or, when we think about it, we see that we ought to mean, only that these wholes are conditionally good, good, that is to say, under the condition that all other things are indifferent, in the sense, not only that they are neither good nor bad, but also that they do not contribute, along with the things we have judged good themselves, to constitute a whole which is either good or bad.

We conclude then that only all-inclusive forms of life are unconditionally good. There remains the question whether

---

[18] *Some Problems in Ethics*, p. 103.

[19] A possible exception to this may be found in any action done from a sense of duty, for, it may be held, respect for the ideal can *never* be out of place in the ideal form of life. But this, if it is the case, does not affect our argument, for the moral goodness of the motive can *never* be the reason for which the act is done. Further, it may be held that it *is not* the case, and on two grounds, for (i) a distinction may be drawn between the sense of duty as an insight and the sense of duty as a motive; and (ii) a distinction may be drawn between the sense of duty as it is in us and the sense of duty as it is ideally, that is, as a sense, not just of this duty, but of all duty, of the essential principle of duty.

there is only one form of life which is good or several; and this brings the argument to the second part of the critical consideration of this non-utilitarian theory.

(b) The point at issue here is whether there are degrees of goodness, whether, for example, it can be said strictly that A is better than B. In opposition to this formulation of the question, it might of course be held that although there is a plurality of all-embracing goods they are all equally good. Yet what can be meant by the phrase "equally good" unless it be "good to the same extent", that is, "good to the same degree of goodness". To say that there is a plurality of all-embracing goods necessarily implies that goodness is a matter of degree, unless indeed it is held that while A and B are both all-embracing goods, they are both good simply, that is, in such a way that A is not better than B, B is not better than A, and A and B are not, strictly speaking, equally good—a position which avoids logical inconsistency at the cost of moral absurdity. For if morality is rational its claim is one claim and not two conflicting claims. Therefore, either goodness varies in degree or else there is only one all-embracing, and consequently unconditional, good.

Now we have already found some considerable difficulty in the idea that one motive may be morally better than another. Who can say, for example, that a sense of duty is in itself and as a motive better than benevolence? There is surely room for both in the ideal human character. No doubt the one is more likely than the other to suggest the right act, but that, if it involves any kind of goodness, involves an instrumental goodness with which we have here no concern. So long as we confine our attention to simple motives it seems impossible to say that one is better than another, although it may be possible to say that one is good and the other is bad. When we turn to more complex motives the case is altered. Here we can and do speak of one motive as better than another; and, more than that, there is a perfectly good sense in which we may do so. For if we are comparing a simple motive, A, which is good, with a mixed motive, B, which is composed of both good and bad, we may say that A is better than B, and may mean thereby that it is purer. Actually, it may be replied, it is not purer but pure, and the other is mixed, so that still there is no scale of degrees to account for our use of the comparative of "good". Yet the pure motive does stand at the top of a scale of mixed

motives which may be said to be better (or worse) in the sense
that their good elements have as against their bad elements a
greater (or less) weight than in the case of others. The weight
which a motive-element carries within the total motive may
certainly vary in degree; and, it would seem, it is a scale of such
variations that the so-called scale of moral goodness really
represents. In harmony with this it might be said that even in
the case of unmixed motives we might say that A is better than
B and mean that A is stronger than B. But if that were our
intention we should probably be content to say that A is
stronger than B, while if on the contrary we employed the
word "better" we should probably be employing it with an
instrumental significance. In a word, it seems impossible to
avoid the conclusion that whereas the weight or strength of
motives may vary in degree, whereas their likeliness to produce
a given effect may also vary in degree, and whereas in mixed
motives the preponderance of the good part over the bad or of
the bad over the good, that is, the "weight-ratio" of good to
bad within the one motive, may likewise vary in degree, the
goodness of the motives cannot.

With this contention not all moralists would agree, and in
particular Sir David Ross has something to say on the opposite
side. In his discussion of the matter he keeps separate his
treatment of mixed motives from that of unmixed, and, while
dealing with the latter, declares that "it seems plain that the
desire to bring into being something good is a better desire
than the desire to bring into being a pleasure for another. This
is plainly seen in the fact that we should think concern for the
character of one's children or friends a better moral state than
concern for their pleasure. Similarly, it seems clear that the
desire to bring something bad into being is worse than the
desire to produce pain for another; just as concern for the character of another is better than concern for his pleasure, the
desire to corrupt someone's character would seem to be more
villainous than the desire to inflict pain on him".[20] But is this
really true? Is the desire to bring into being something good
better than the desire to give someone else pleasure? That is to
say, is the one in itself better than the other in itself? Or is it
not rather the case that both are good and there is room for
both in the ideal human character and life? Surely when we
consider the two motives over against one another but in

[20] *The Right and the Good*, pp. 165–6.

...e makes that con-
...e contention has meaning
...ves are not considered in complete
isolation from everything else. The abstraction is superficial and
imperfect, and the assertion that A is better than B has meaning
because a context is implicitly understood.[21] This context
appears to consist of a situation or situations, possible or actual,
into which either motive may enter; and when it is said that
motive A is better than motive B, it seems to be meant that if
A enters the situation will be better than if B had entered. It
remains, of course, to be seen whether this contention in turn
involves the recognition of degrees of goodness; but it seems
true that at least there are no degrees of *moral* goodness. Or,
against the background provided by the understood context, it
may be meant that acting from motive A would be better than
acting from motive B; but once again the precise meaning
does not appear on the surface and what is intended is probably
that while A and B are both good, the act to which A would
give rise in this situation or in most situations in which A and
B are in conflict is *right* and that to which B would give rise is
wrong.

Does the denial, however, of degrees of goodness hold of
non-moral, as well as of moral, goodness? To suggest that
knowledge is better than pleasure is to make a judgment to
which, idly, we might well give our assent, but to which, on
examination, we should find it hard to attach a meaning; and
the reason is that in speaking of knowledge and pleasure in
general we have made an abstraction from all possible
contexts, and apart from these the idea of the better is without
significance. But let us take a more concrete example. If anything is better than something else it would probably be agreed
that the state in which some seriously injured or needy person
is greatly relieved is better than that in which a healthy and
self-sufficient person has his expectation satisfied by the fulfilment of a trifling promise which had been made to him. Is
the actual state of the one person, however, really better than
the actual state of the other, when abstraction is made from

---

[21] We should probably express our meaning more accurately if we said that
on the whole A is better than B; but the phrase in italics means " in the majority
of situations ".

else, it is impossib
e is better than t
when he me

...se stat...
contrary, both are good
in isolation is better than the
thinking of some context and the processe... ...at
text these states may be achieved. By saying that state A is better
than state B we really mean that in the imagined context or in
most contexts both A and B would be good, but the act of bringing about A would be *right* while that of bringing about B would
be *wrong*. Thus, in the case of non-moral goodness as well as in
that of moral goodness, when we employ the comparative of
"good" we frequently mean that two things (motives or
states) are good, but that the act connected with the one is
right while that connected with the other is wrong. This, indeed,
may be the truth contained in Mr. Carritt's point that "the
word 'good' . . . when applied to states or events, unless it
mean useful, always means either 'satisfying desire' or 'the
sort of state or event which we should think it our duty in
normal circumstances to bring about were it in our power'."[22]
On his own confession it is with some misgiving that Mr.
Carritt puts forward this view, and it is difficult to believe that
in the end it can be upheld. But something like it seems to afford
the explanation of a large number of our judgments, not that
A is good, but that A is better than B. This is the explanation
that in such cases we really mean that A and B are both good
but that of the acts connected with them, of the acts to which
they lead or from which they result, that connected with A is
normally right and that connected with B is normally wrong.
Thus the idea of right or duty is introduced into a discussion
of "good", in order to explain, not the idea of good as Mr.
Carritt suggests, but the idea of better. And, moreover, this
does seem to be a large part of the explanation of our normal
employment of the comparative of "good"; for, when we
consider this matter, we cannot say that A is better than B
without presupposing, not only a *comparison* of A and B, but
also a *choice* between A and B, and a choice involves a situation
into which either A or B may enter.

As we have seen, however, there is another part of the
explanation according to which A is thought to be better than
B, not because although both are good the act connected with
the one is right and that connected with the other is wrong,

[22] *Theory of Morals*, p. 73.

but because although both are good a situation or system which includes A is better than one which has B in place of A. It remains, therefore, to investigate this possibility.

Now this explanation consists of four judgments: (i) that we do often judge that A is better than B; (ii) that when we consider A and B in complete abstraction from everything else we find ourselves unable to give any meaning to this judgment; (iii) that, consequently, when we do make the judgment significantly we are silently assuming a context, a system or a situation, into which A or B may enter; and (iv) that if we do not mean that A is good and B is bad, and if we do not mean that while A and B are both good the *act* connected with the one is right and that connected with the other wrong, we can only mean that the system with A in it is better than that with B instead of A. It is clear, however, that if we use the symbol A' to denote the system with A in it, and the symbol B' to denote the system with B instead of A, a similar argument holds, with A' taking the place of A and B' taking the place of B, until the system with some A or B in it is itself the all-inclusive, completely comprehensive, system.

The outcome of the argument, so far as it has gone, is then that there are no degrees of conditional goodness, and that, unless there are degrees of unconditional goodness, that is, of the goodness of the whole, goodness never does vary in degree. Does, then, unconditional goodness vary in degree?

The complete answer to this question does not stand out at a glance, but certain points seem to be beyond doubt. In the first place, *if* we find that apparently significant judgments are made which employ a comparative of unconditional goodness, that apparent significance cannot be explained in either of the two main ways in which we have already explained the apparent significance of judgments which employ a comparative of conditional goodness. On the one hand, there is no "larger" system to which the comparative of goodness can be passed on in the case of unconditional goodness as there was in the case of conditional goodness; and, on the other hand, the explanation cannot proceed by reducing "better" to "good" plus the assertion that some act is right and another is wrong, for on the present hypothesis such an explanation would involve a circular argument. In the second place, and on the other side, it is clear that it cannot be said with even a semblance of significance that one all-inclusive whole is better than another, for outwith *the* all-inclusive whole there is nothing with which can be made a comparison in point of goodness, or, for that matter, in point of anything else. If there were, the "all-inclusive" whole would not after all be all-inclusive.

This difficulty would be avoided if it could be said that the all-inclusive whole might be better than it is. Yet, if a judgment were made to that effect, what could it mean? The intention would appear to be this, that while in certain respects the given whole is good, in certain other respects it is deficient in goodness, falls short of goodness and is bad. In other words, in judging that the whole might be better than it is we are already dividing it up into parts, are mentally subtracting some parts and adding others, and are consequently really concerned, not with unconditional goodness, but with conditional goodness. Just as in our search for a "betterness" in things we were passed on from parts to ever-increasing parts until we came to the all-inclusive whole without reaching any certainty in our search, so now in looking for a "less goodness" of the whole we seem to find instead a badness of parts. Moreover, not only does this seem an account which may well be true sometimes when it is judged that the whole might be better than it is, but on examination it does not appear that we can ever mean anything else by such a judgment.

It may be argued that this is due to the fact, not that genuine degrees of unconditional goodness are inconceivable, but that the all-inclusive whole itself, as a whole, defies *our finite* conception. This argument, however, even at its best, is essentially an appeal to a possibility which is such that, if nothing can be said against it, nothing can be said in its favour. Further, there is this to be said against it, that on examination goodness reveals itself, not as a quality capable of extension *ad infinitum*, but as a norm, a standard, so that things conforming to it are judged good, and things departing from it are judged bad. Thus, we find Aristotle defining the Chief Good, "that which all things aim at", [23] the good of the whole (or an important part of the Chief Good) as Virtue, and Virtue, in turn, as "a middle state between two faulty ones, in the way of excess on one side, and of defect on the other", and, finally, declaring that "just as of perfected self-mastery and courage there is no excess and defect, because the mean is in one point of view the highest possible state, so neither of those faulty states can you have a mean

[23] *Nicomachean Ethics*, 1094a.

state, excess, or defect, but howsoever done they are wrong: you cannot, in short, have of excess and defect a mean state, nor of a mean state excess and defect ". [24] In Christian literature we find other statements which harmonise with the general tenor of this one, as when St. Paul declares that "there is no difference; for all have sinned, and come short of the glory of God ". [25]

Nevertheless, there is one question which does call for some further consideration, and it is a question which may be suggested, not perhaps by Aristotle's treatment of virtue in general, but by his treatment of particular virtues. The question is whether, allowing that unconditional goodness belongs only to the whole, and also that it is not a quality capable of extension *ad infinitum*, but a norm or a standard, it cannot still be said that one may be near to, or far from, the standard, that is, that one's approach to the norm may be subject to variations of degree. Aristotle, for instance, denotes courage a virtue, a mean state between rashness and cowardice; but on either side may there not be infinite gradations between the extreme positions and courage itself? Again, we may say that in rifle-practice, for example, short of hitting the mark, men may miss it by much or little, and that, in what appears to be a perfectly legitimate sense, it may be said that they have fired well or ill, and some better than others. In the same way, the suggestion is, it can be said that a certain state of the whole is good, without being *the* good, and that some states of the whole are better than others. In this fashion, it might be held, degrees of goodness are reintroduced.

This, then, is the possibility we are to consider; and the first comment is that this defence of degrees of goodness may well have overleaped itself, for the goodness to which it points is not only variable in degree, but also relative. This is clear in the example of rifle-practice, in respect of good marksmanship, for the goodness here is plainly relative and is based upon the general attainment in the matter of hitting the mark. What passes for good marksmanship in one community may well be bad in another. Similarly, when we talk of good and better in an apparently moral sense, our reference is to a relative standard based largely upon current attainment; and when we do not realise this our failure is due to a confusion between the

---

[24] *Nicomachean Ethics*, 1107a.
[25] *Epistle to the Romans*, iii, 22, 23.

relative standard and the absolute standard which is denominated *the* good. *The* good, as Aristotle saw, is just *the* good,
and is not subject to variations in degree; and when we seem to
use the term "good" both in a moral and in a comparative sense,
we are using it in a sense which is moral but not completely so,
which contains a reference to *the* good but is based upon the
current achievement in that direction. Used in this sense, it can
with little change be transferred to the field of rifle-marksman-
ship, for there the comparative element and the reference to
current attainment still remain, although the target is no longer
a moral one. But without the reference to current attainment
the comparative finds no place for itself; a thing is either good
or bad, a hit or a miss, just as a judgment is either true or
false.

Here, however, we must take account of a curious complication in the argument which arises at this point, for, although
it may be admitted that the comparative use of "good" is a
relative use (since what is good in one place may be bad elsewhere), and, when moral, is also a derivative and not completely
ethical use, it may none the less be argued that, however "good"
may vary in application from place to place, the judgment that
A is *better* than B is, if true at all, true universally. A shot twelve
inches from the bull may be good in one community, bad in
another, but in all it is better than one eighteen inches from the
bull, and worse than one six inches from the bull. The
point is that, though the starting-point of this relative goodness may vary, the relation between any two points on the
scale is invariable. Consequently, if a fixed starting-point could
be found there would arise degrees of absolute goodness; and,
the argument might hold, there is no reason why such a
starting-point should not be found in the good itself. The
assumption is, however, that the good varies only in degree from
approximations to it; whereas the difference is not a difference
in degree but a difference in kind. When a rifleman hits the
mark for the first time he has done something new, and not just
something which he had done before to a lower degree; he has
hit, whereas before he had always missed.

It will be noticed that there is a curious coincidence between
our conclusions regarding goodness and our conclusions
regarding rightness, for we have been driven to suppose, not
only that neither goodness nor rightness can vary in degree,
but also that in both cases there is a derivative concept, which

When, however, we seek to deal with the content of this demand and to set it down in a single formula, we find that in our finite hands the single self-consistent claim of morality has become many. Just as in our hands, the ideal itself becomes many, a list of conditional goods, a list of virtues or a list of both, so the claim also becomes many, a demand that we tell the truth, that we keep our promises, and so on. Moreover, it is clear that there is no mechanical rule by which a conflict of these may be resolved. When we are confronted by a conflict of duties we can deal with the problem on moral grounds only by an appeal to the good and to the claim which it exercises upon us, and by a consideration of the question, in that light, which of several "rules" best or most adequately expresses in the circumstances the essential principle of the ideal. If we cannot give a detailed account of the ideal itself, we cannot describe in detail the working out of this method of solution in any particular case;[27] but that it is the method appears to follow from the argument which has gone before, both in the elimination of alternative accounts, and in the adumbration of more positive considerations which point in this direction.

To which, then, of the three main types of ethical theory does this account of the matter belong? The answer is that it belongs to none of them. It does not find the ground of rightness in the moral goodness of motives, nor does it find it exactly in the character of the acts themselves, nor, again, in the goodness of the consequences of acts. It finds it, rather, in an all-inclusive form of life, a comprehensive system of personal relationships, which is *the* good, the ideal. Indeed, the moral goodness of motives and the goodness of consequences are found to point beyond themselves to this more fundamental conception, that of the good; while the various rules of right action reveal themselves as echoes of a more comprehensive demand, the single self-consistent claim which the Good Life makes upon the attention of men, who are essentially fallible beings.

[27] Field has laid down an excellent test of the adequacy of any moral theory. "We must look", he says ("Kant's First Moral Principle", *Mind*, January 1932, p. 31), "for something other than actions, which is always and absolutely good. And its relation to actions must be such that it is possible to see why certain types of action are generally right but in exceptional circumstances may be wrong." This has been done, it is claimed, *in so far as the subject-matter will allow*, and a reason has been given why a more complete fulfilment of the test is not possible, namely, that it is possible to *see*, but not to *say* (except in very general and formal terms), why normally right acts are in exceptional circumstances wrong.

INDEX

Act and action, 155f.
  and consequences, 215–18
  and intention, 50, 67–9, 207–12, 214–15, 220–7
  and motive, 67–9, 124, 155–8, 162–4, 189–90, 194, 219–38
  and will, 212, 214–15, 229
Actions, nature of, 158–64, 194–5, 205–15, 220–5, 271
Ambrose, St., 26
Aquinas, St. Thomas, 27–8
Aristotle, 22, 23, 24, 27, 134, 324–5, 326
Asceticism, 127, 128, 129, 293–4
Augustine, St., 26

Baillie, J., 19, 22
Balguy, J., 62–5
Benevolence, 40–53 (passim), 55–6, 64–5, 66, 120
Bentham, J., 82–6, 87, 88, 89, 92, 93–4
Berkeley, Bishop, 257
Bosanquet, B., 297
Bradley, F. H., 125, 128–32, 133, 287–8, 303–4, 328n.
Broad, C. D., 169
Brown, J., 79, 81
Buber, M., 256–7
Burgh, W. G. de, 179, 286, 289–91, 293–4, 295
Butler, Bishop, 50–3, 63, 134, 189

Calculus, agathistic, 101–2, 266–7, 315, 318
  hedonistic, 83–5, 87–8, 93–4
Carritt, E. F., 133–47, 173, 192, 283, 322
Casuistry, 27, 126
Catholicism, morality in, 26–9
Claims and rights, 253–5, 297–9
Clarke, S., 59–62, 170, 183–4
Conflict of duties, 131, 143–4, 145–7, 278–84, 285–329 (passim)
Conscience, nature of, 53–4, 62–3, 65–6, 126
Cudworth, R., 57–9

Desire and will, 107–10, 212
Divine law, 28
Doubt, 209–11, 212–15
Duns Scotus, 28–9
Duties, conflict of, 131, 143–4, 145–7, 278–84, 285–329 (passim)
  to oneself, 252

Dutiful will, 72–4
  will, and good will, 72–3
Duty, 141, 167–73, 190, 197–205, 229–30

Elliot, H., 89n.
Ethical and moral judgments, 187–8
Ethics and metaphysics, 58–9, 180–1
  and physical science, 21–2, 89–93, 180
  method of, 20–2
  science or philosophy? 18–20
  subject-matter, 17–18, 181–2

Gallie, I., 315n., 316n.
Gay, J., 79, 81
Good, meaning of, 97–8, 110–11, 113–14, 118–19, 123, 135–6, 140, 173–5, 322
Good will, the, 72–4, 118–23, 124–5, 128–9, 260, 287–8
Goodness, degrees of, 319, 321–7
Grace, morality of, 199, 295, 296–302
Green, T. H., 104–25, 129–30, 134, 194
Guyau, 92n.

Hartley, D., 93
Hartmann, N., 306
Hastings, A. W., 81n.
Hebrew thought, 26
Hegel, G. W. F., 104
Herrmann, W., 29
Hobbes, T., 35–9, 40, 42, 43, 45, 46, 49, 50, 57
Holland, T. E., 254
Holy will, 73
Hutcheson, F., 43–8, 49, 50, 51, 52, 54, 55, 56, 79

I-It relationship, 256–7
I-Thou relationship, 256–7
Idealism, ethics of, 104–32, 179, 191–2, 194, 307–8
Intention and act, 50, 67–9, 207–12, 214–15, 220–7
  and motive, 47–8, 55–6, 220–4, 262–3
  and will, 229
Intuitionism, 57–70, 133–54, 155–75, 192–3, 231–8, 255–6, 272–5, 278–83

Jessop, T. E., 295–302
Joseph, H. W. B., 134, 179, 309–18